D0916059

THE JEWISH
TRAVEL GUIDE

BETSY SHELDON

HUNTER

Hunter Publishing, Inc.
130 Campus Drive
Edison, NJ 08818-7816
☎ 732-225-1900 / 800-255 0343 / Fax 732-417-1744
Web site: www.hunterpublishing.com
E-mail: hunterp@bellsouth.net

IN CANADA
Ulysses Travel Publications
4176 Saint-Denis
Montreal, Québec H2W 2M5 Canada
☎ 514-843-9882, Ext. 2232 / Fax 514-843-9448

IN THE UK
Windsor Books International
The Boundary, Wheatley Road
Garsington, Oxford OX44 9EJ England
☎ 01865-361122 / Fax 01865-361133

ISBN 1-55650-879-4
© 2001 Betsy Sheldon

Cover photo:
Detail of stained glass window in the
Gumenick Chapel, Temple Israel of Greater Miami
Courtesy of Kenneth Treister

Indexing by Nancy Wolff

4   3   2   1

DEDICATION

*To my sons Aaron and Ben: May all your life's journeys
bring you home again, in gladness and in peace.*

ACKNOWLEDGMENTS

Of *course* I didn't visit all the places covered in this book. I
frequently relied on the ears, eyes, and experiences of other
experts – long-time residents, archivists, librarians, volun-
teers, rabbis, teachers, historians, tour guides, authors, re-
porters, administrative staff, and others who shared with
me the sights, attractions, events, and stories that make
each place included in this book special.

Much appreciation to Kim André at Hunter Publishing,
who gave me the opportunity to write this book, and to Lissa
K. Dailey, also with Hunter Publishing, who patiently shep-
herded the project through. Special thanks to M. Kathryn
Dailey, who served as proofreader, not to mention analyst
and walking companion when deadline pressures mounted.
Also thanks to Ben Sheldon, my faithful part-time research
assistant who spent many an afternoon chasing down phone
leads and venturing on fact-finding missions instead of do-
ing his homework.

BALTIMORE
Bruce Mendelsohn, Baltimore Hebrew University
Herbert Habel, Jewish Information Service
Linda Skolnik and Virginia North, Jewish Museum of Maryland
Phyllis Hirsch, Jewish Community Center
Jeanine Disviscour, Maryland Historical Society
Barbara Pash and Amanda Krotki, *Baltimore Jewish Times*
Jesse Harris, Temple Oheb Shalom
Sylvan Feit, Baltimore Hebrew Congregation
Brian & Eva Schwartz
Marvin Solomon, Marvin Solomon Tours

BOSTON
Dr. Murray Tuchman and Roselyn Farren, Hebrew College
Ellen Smith and Laura Peimer, American Jewish Historical Soci-
 ety Museum
Patrick Leehey, Paul Revere House
Margie Weber, Shalom Boston

Michael Ross, Boston Walks Jewish Friendship Trail
Miriam Behar, Four Seasons Kosher B&B
Deborah Bogin Cohen, Vilna Center for Jewish Heritage, Inc.
Stephen Dickerman, Friends of the New England
  Holocaust Memorial
Shawn Noelle, Boston University
Nathan Erlich, Hebrew College

CHICAGO
Marilyn Guest, Spertus Institute of Jewish Studies
Leah Axelrod, My Kind of Town Tours
Lynn Foreman, volunteer at K.A.M. Isaiah Israel
Nina Perlmutter, Spertus Institute of Jewish Studies
Wendy Strode, Mayer Kaplan JCC
Cheryl Banks, North Suburban Beth El

CLEVELAND
Deborah Mayers, Jewish Cleveland Federation.
Jane Avner, The Western Reserve Historical Society
Judah Rubinstein, historian, archivist, and tour guide
Helen Wolf, Jewish Education Center of Cleveland
Carol Kranitz, Mayfield JCC
Scott Hersch, Shticks at Cleveland Hillel
Dorothy Aufuldish, Wickllliffe Area Chamber of Commerce
Suzanne Tishkoff, Cleveland College of Jewish Studies
Rosalie Gussow, Cleveland native and Hoosier transplant

DENVER
Elizabeth Bono, Elizabeth Kelsen, and Joanne Marks Kauver, Jew-
  ish Community Center of Denver
Rosemary Fetter, Golda Meir House
Bob Rubin, Synagogue Council of Greater Denver
Dr. Jeanne Abrams, Rocky Mountain Jewish Historical Society
Phil Goodstein, author, *Exploring Jewish Colorado*

LOS ANGELES
Sherri Kadovitz, Zimmer Discovery Children's Museum
Jerry Freedman Habush, Freedman Habush Associates Tours
Nancy Herz and Carmen Tellez, Jewish Federation Council

MIAMI
Nancy Zombek and Lynn Hirsch, Jewish Information and Refer-
  ral Service
Remko Jansonius and Annette Fromm, Sanford L. Ziff Jewish
  Museum of Florida
Milton Heller, JTEN Tours
Kenneth Treister, Temple Israel of Greater Miami

MONTREAL
David Liss, Saidye Bronfman Centre for the Arts
Ron Finegold, Jewish Public Library
Allan Raymond, Montreal Jewish Historical Society
Pearl Robin, Shaar HaShomayim Congregation
Barbara Harman, Montreal Jewish Directory
Ellen Samuel, Temple Emanu-El
Rabbi David Merling, Hillel Jewish Student Center
Carole Saifer Worsoff, Beth Zion Congregation
Susan Alper and Christine Burt, Montreal Jewish Film Festival

NEW YORK CITY
Jane Abraham, UJA Resouce Line
Reuven Steinberg, Center for Jewish History
Bonni-Dara Michaels, Yeshiva University Museum
Katherine Snider, Benjamin Trimmer, Lower East Side Tenement
 Museum
Mark Altman, Folksbiene Yiddish Theatre
Andi Rosenthal, Museum of Jewish Heritage

PHILADELPHIA
Harry D. Boonin, author, *The Jewish Quarter of Philadelphia, A
 History and Guide*
Rabbi Robert Layman, United Synagogue of Conservative Judaism
Rabbi Gabbai, Congregation Mikveh Israel
Rabbi Sanford H. Hahn, Board of Rabbis.
Phoebe Resnick and Sarah Ausprich, Resnick Communications,
 Inc., for the National Museum of American Jewish History.
Lillian Youman, Jewish Information and Referral Service
Carol Perloff, Rodeph Shalom
Lisa Eisen, The Gershman Y
Michael Elkin, *Jewish Exponent*
Dr. Hayim Sheynin, Gratz College

SAN FRANCISCO
Gale Green and Judy Musante, Jewish Community Information
 & Referral
Patti Moskovitz, author and San Francisco resident
Paula Friedman, Judah L. Magnes Museum
Lyla Max, Haas-Lilienthal House
Felix Warburg, Jewish Landmark Tours
Nancy Levenberg, Hagafen Cellars
Larissa Siegel, Congregation Emanu-El

ST. LOUIS
Bob Cohn, editor and publisher, *Jewish Light*
Linda Meckfessel, St. Louis Jewish Legacy Tours
Dorothy and Pauline, Jewish Information Services

Rudy Oppenheim, Ohave Shalom Cemetery
Leanie Mendelsohn, Holocaust Museum and Learning Center
Emily Troxell, Missouri Historical Society
Steven Zucker, Jewish Community Center
Jennifer L. Baer, Jewish Federation of St. Louis
Kathleen F. Sitzer, New Jewish Theatre

TORONTO
Joel Verbin, Jewish Information Services
Katya Rudzik, My Jewish Discovery Place
Rabbi Spero, Anshei Minsk
David Hart, Holy Blossom Temple
Dr. Stephen Speisman, Jewish Federation of Greater Toronto

WASHINGTON DC
Laura Apelbaum, Jewish Historical Society of Greater Washington
Leo Crane, Smithsonian National Museum of American History
Richard Feldman and Amanda Chorowski, DC JCC
Sandy Cohen, National Museum of American Jewish Military
   History
Phillip Ratner, Dennis and Phillip RatnerMuseum

AND...
Andrew Muchin, *Jewish Heartland*
Rabbi Arnold Mark Belzer, Mickve Israel, Savannah
Rabbi Stanley Savage of Beth Hamedrash Hagadol, Pittsburgh
Diane Rodgers, Jewish Historical Society in Vancouver
Tom Hanley, Golda Meir Elementary School, Milwaukee.
David Gradwohl and Jody Hramits, Iowa Jewish Historical Society
Sandy Tucker, Mississippi Department of Economic and
   Community Development
Dr. Stanley Hordes, University of New Mexico
Eleanor Cuthbertson, Clay County Historical Museum, Missouri

Contents

About The Author

Betsy Sheldon has been writing about travel for more than 20 years. In the 1970s she lived in Israel and studied there. She has written several books, including *City Smart Indianapolis*, and has more than 200 published travel pieces to her credit. She is currently editor in chief for *Journey*, a monthly travel magazine.

In the Jewish community, Betsy has been active as a religious school teacher, as well as a board member of the Indianapolis JCC and her synagogue.

Betsy is the mother of two sons, Aaron and Ben. Although she's lived abroad and on both coasts (California and New Jersey), she always seems to return to Indianapolis, where she now lives.

INTRODUCTION

We didn't lack for sights to see. Colonial Williamsburg, historic Jamestown, and the battlefields of the Revolutionary War enticed us from one direction – the bustling boardwalk of Virginia Beach lured us from the other. A short drive away, the Eastern Shore and salt-sprayed Chincoteague Island tempted. And nearby the roller coasters and amusement rides of Busch Gardens promised thrills.

So why, instead, did we wander downtown Norfolk, lost for 45 minutes in search of a modest structure nearly camouflaged by construction? Why did we wait outside for another half-hour for the site to open? And why did we endure a tedious tour led by poorly costumed guides? After all, finer, grander, easier-to-find historical homes advertised throughout the area. Why was this site different from all others?

Because – we'd read – this particular home was built and owned by a prominent *Jewish* family. The Federal architecture and collections of art and period furnishings were indeed intriguing – but we marveled, instead, at traces of Jewishness. We studied the Shabbat candles, and lingered over the tarnished silver spice box. We searched for clues of observance of kashrut (dietary law) in the dark kitchen. And we imagined how the family of Moses Myers – the first Jewish family in Norfolk – must have struggled to gain acceptance from the community and maintain their Jewish connections.

To be sure, we visited Williamsburg, Jamestown, and Virginia Beach on our summer trip to southeastern Virginia. But, as we often do when we travel, we added unique sights of Jewish interest to our itinerary, as well.

THE "JEWISH CONNECTION"

This tendency to look for the "Jewish connection" is typical of Jewish travelers – for a variety of reasons: Some of us want to expose our children to their heritage, others strive to retrace the steps of Jewish history and culture. A growing number of us proactively search for the threads of genealogy that tie us to our ancestors. And many of us traveling for business seek the solace of familiar rituals when we find ourselves in a strange place. Observant Jews may want to connect religiously to a community, and seek out synagogues, kosher restaurants, even private homes that may welcome Jewish out-of-towners. When visiting for *simchas* such as weddings or bar/bat mitzvahs, we may want to enhance the meaning of the event by taking in some Jewish sightseeing. Whatever the impetus, ultimately the goal is the same – *to connect*.

Although level of affiliation varies among individuals, overall, most of us seek to connect in some way to the greater Jewish world. We may belong to a synagogue, we may join a JCC or YMHA, we may volunteer time or contribute to Jewish causes, we may affiliate with Jewish organizations such as Hadassah, ORT, and B'nai B'rith.

In short, although we are a diverse group in terms of religious perspective and cultural connection, most of us identify ourselves as Jews in some way. And that identification extends to our travels. Whether on vacation or traveling for work or family business, we remain on the lookout for Jewish connections when we're on the road.

Traveling within North America, it's unlikely that many of us will dedicate a trip to a "Jewish" itinerary; we'll head to Boston to see the Freedom Trail just like other vacationers. We'll plan a beach retreat in New England. We'll visit the Rocky Mountains to ski. And we'll travel to Santa Fe for Southwestern culture and art. But while we're there... wouldn't it be nice to know about the lovingly restored immigrant shul just a walk from a historic landmark? Or to tour the oldest synagogue in North America? Or to visit the Golda

Meir home? Or to learn about crypto-Jewish communities in the Southwest?

THE BEST IN
JEWISH SIGHTSEEING

For the Jewish traveler – or for anyone interested in Jewish history, culture, and contributions in the United States and Canada – *The Jewish Travel Guide* is a valuable resource. This book is more than a mere yellow pages of Jewish sights, synagogues, centers, and resources. In fact, it is a concise, easy-to-use handbook for those who want to experience the *best* in Jewish sightseeing and travel.

The Jewish Travel Guide serves readers in two ways: it provides a directory of resources – synagogues, JCCs, kosher restaurants, Judaica shops, lodgings, and Jewish establishments; and it also reveals a treasury of Jewish sights. Hundreds of listings highlight museums, notable homes, one-of-a-kind communities, historic synagogues, and sites of Jewishly significant events. It includes the most celebrated landmarks – such as the Holocaust Museum in Washington DC and the Lower East Side in Manhattan – as well as best-kept secrets, surprises, and just-for-fun stops, such as:

❖ A *build-it-and-they-will-come* Orthodox community in the middle of Iowa cornfields. (This one isn't centered around baseball, but rather a kosher meat-packing business.)

❖ A plantation tour of Mississippi, highlighting historic synagogues, antebellum mansions once owned by prominent Jews, and the role played by Jews in Southern history.

❖ A Jewish retreat – complete with meditation and mystics – in upstate New York.

❖ Jewish cowboys? You *betcha*! Weathered ghost towns were once home to Jewish settlers from Kansas to California.

❖ A Jewish winery in the heart of California wine country.

Complete contact information for individual listings is enhanced with colorful descriptions and little-known facts. A mix of major metropolitan areas and small communities throughout the United States and Canada is featured.

HOW TO USE THIS GUIDE

The first part of the book features 15 major North American cities, selected because of the number and quality of Jewish sights and attractions, population size, and existence of a solid Jewish infrastructure (synagogues, kosher dining, JCCs, etc.). Each chapter begins with a brief description of the city's Jewish character. Then, a standard structure of listings follows.

SIGHTSEEING HIGHLIGHTS

Museums, historic synagogues, homes or birthplaces of notable Jews, religious colleges, or sites of Jewish significance are just some of the attractions that may be featured in this section. In addition, unique neighborhoods, cemeteries, sculpture, or public areas may be included. Often, a general-interest attraction, say, the Levi Strauss museum in San Francisco, will be mentioned because of its unique Jewish connections.

Each listing includes contact information – a street address or directions to the site, a phone number, and, when available, a Web site address. A description of the attraction identifies highlights and list hours and admission fees, if any.

SYNAGOGUES

A synagogue, for the Jewish traveler, offers much more than a place to attend a religious service. For example, a visitor may call a synagogue for information on anything from good restaurants (kosher and otherwise), long-lost friends or relatives who might be part of the community, hotel recommendations, or an invitation to a Sabbath meal.

We list just a *few* synagogues for each city profile, merely to offer the reader a starting point. The number of synagogues in a given community varies greatly based on the population – the metropolitan area of New York City has enough to fill a small telephone book!

We've included synagogues representing each of the three major movements – Reform, Conservative, and Orthodox. We attempt to limit the selections to well-established congregations that offer the most services of value to the visitor – for example, regular Shabbat services at a permanent location, daily minyan for the traveler wishing to say Kaddish, special services catering to the visitor, such as Shabbat meals and home hospitality, and accessibility from areas where the traveler will most likely be staying.

Selection or exclusion of any given synagogue should not be interpreted as a rating of that particular congregation. Whenever possible, we provide a central phone number that will offer more information about other synagogues in the community.

Kosher Dining

Jews observe religious dietary laws (kashrut) to varying degrees – or not at all. While those who observe kashrut most strictly will only eat at or buy food from establishments with the most stringent supervision, others are comfortable with dining at any restaurant, while being selective in what they order.

Included in this section are only restaurants that are certified kosher. Not included are kosher-*style* restaurants or establishments that are vegetarian, vegan, or otherwise acceptable to many who keep kosher. We also limit our listings to restaurants that offer sit-down dining. There may be, in addition, carry-out delicatessens and bakeries where certified kosher food is available.

Whenever possible, particularly in cities that have few kosher restaurant options, we list student centers and other resources where it might be possible to find home hospitality or kosher meals.

Each listing includes a brief description of the type of food featured, as well as general hours of operation. It's important to call ahead, though, to determine exact hours of operation. Unless otherwise noted, all restaurants are closed for Shabbat, but the hours may vary during the year.

Because kashrut certification is subject to change, whenever possible the phone number for the governing organization is included so that readers may call for updates and changes.

JEWISH COMMUNITY CENTERS

Most JCCs offer reciprocity for members from other cities. The JCCs also present opportunities to find out more about the Jewish community in general. In addition to offering recreational facilities for members, most JCCs are hotbeds of community activity and cultural events – art shows, musical performances, theater productions, lectures, and special celebrations. Many offer cafés or delis, gift shops, and on-site galleries and museums.

Often, a JCC may have more than one location in a given community. The listings in this book will include any site that offers services of interest to the *visitor*. In other words, if a particular satellite facility offers only day-care, it will not be included; if it offers an indoor pool, fitness center, or gift shop, it will.

SHOPPING

In addition to synagogue gift shops, many communities support stores that carry Judaica. These will be listed in the *Shopping* section. Only bookstores and gift shops that sell *primarily* Jewish-related products will be included. A national-chain bookstore, although it may feature a large Jewish studies section, will *not* be listed. Likewise, an art gallery or boutique that showcases an occasional *mezuzah* or jewelry featuring the star of David, will not make the list. In most cases, unless the offerings are particularly unusual, the listings will not include a description of stock featured.

LODGING

Only when a hotel, bed-and-breakfast, or accommodation offers something uniquely Jewish, will this category be included in a city profile. For example, a bed-and-breakfast might offer a special Jewish ambiance or kosher meals. A large chain hotel may be within walking distance of an Orthodox synagogue or Jewish neighborhood. Or a historic inn may once have been a home built or owned by a prominent Jewish family.

EVENTS

Book fairs, music and film festivals, Israel fests, holiday celebrations, and other community-wide events are listed in this section. Only significant community events are included – a synagogue's Chanuka bazaar, for example, will not be listed – with descriptions of activities, length of the festivities, and cost information.

HERITAGE TOURS

Some cities profiled in this book have the good fortune of harboring an active Jewish historical society. In many cases, knowledgeable members are able to offer fascinating "insider" tours of the community. In addition, a few cities have Jewish-oriented tours or companies that offer custom tours of Jewish-related sights and attractions.

Often, such tours are designed for larger groups – some will accept a minimum of 20 or so individuals – or must be scheduled far in advance. But it may be worthwhile for individuals and families to contact these sources, even if they won't be visiting with a group, if just to gather information about the community's best-kept Jewish secrets and sights.

Because many of these tours and services are operated by individuals from their homes, often the listing will only include a phone number or Web site address rather than a street address.

RESOURCES

This section is the place to go for contact information that may not be covered in the other listings. Whenever possible or applicable, listings for the following sources will be included.

- ❖ Jewish Federations offices
- ❖ Jewish historical societies
- ❖ Jewish genealogical societies
- ❖ Jewish publications
- ❖ Other Jewish media (radio or TV)
- ❖ Jewish Web sites

❖ Kashrut supervisory agencies

❖ Convention and visitors bureaus

TRIVIA

Sprinkled throughout the city profile, you'll discover tidbits of information, lore, and trivia related to the city's Jewish community or history. Typically featured will be celebrity connections and colorful historic events.

ADDITIONAL SIGHTS

If we limited the book to Jewish sights and attractions found only in the 15 cities profiled, we'd be missing some vital and colorful contributions to Jewish life in North America. Some of the most unusual and surprising sites are found in the rural corners of the country, or in communities where the Jewish neighborhoods have moved away.

The second part of the book, then, offers a state-by-state roundup of Jewish sights that may exist in the absence of a community, as well as listings of smaller Jewish communities and their outstanding attractions. This section is formatted as a series of site listings and city write-ups. For example, under the state subhead *Mississippi,* listings include *The Museum of Southern Jewish History* in Jackson; *Natchez,* a city with many Jewish historic sites; and *Mississippi Jews & Blues Alley,* a bicycle tour that offers Jewish-interest trips through Mississippi.

One caveat to the reader: This guidebook is by no means a comprehensive guide to Jewish sightseeing in North America! As I began my research for this book, I discovered that even those most intimate with a particular Jewish community were often surprised when I asked about a site I'd heard about. It might have been the first they'd heard of the attraction. Often, I'd have to call two, three, four or more resources to unearth the information I needed to share with readers.

My point is, the discovery of Jewish sights is an ongoing process. We discover that a structure that has served for decades as a church or a theater was originally a synagogue. We reveal that an abandoned bungalow scheduled for demolition is in fact the one-time home of a great Jewish leader. We learn that a tangled and overgrown plot of land was once a cemetery for a Jewish community that has since moved on.

It is my hope that you'll use this guide as a stimulus, as an appetizer for further Jewish exploration in your travels. On your next trip to wherever, visit the sights listed in the book, but use the resources to discover other surprises (and I'd love to hear about your discoveries to include them in future editions).

THE WAYFARER'S PRAYER

*May it be your will, **Eternal One**, our God and the God of our Ancestors, to lead us in peace and make us reach our destination alive, happy, and in peace. May You deliver us from enemies, ambush, bandits, and evil animals along the way. May we find favor, kindness, and mercy in Your eyes and in the eyes of all we meet. Hear our prayers, for you are God Who listens to prayers. Blessed are You, **Eternal One**, Who hears prayer.*

The "T'filat Haderekh" is the Wayfarer's Prayer, traditionally recited when Jewish travelers embark upon journeys. It developed during an era when all travels were fraught with danger, and invokes protection against threats along the way and prayers that we may be delivered to our destinations – and returned to our homes – in life, gladness, and peace.

In this time and in this part of the world, travel is, thankfully, a happy and anticipated experience. But a prayer for a good journey is always fitting. And it is my prayer that all your journeys bring you enlightenment and wisdom, and that you are delivered to your destinations – and back to your homes – in life, gladness, and peace.

BALTIMORE

Sandwiched between Little Italy and Fells Point in East Baltimore, the Jewish Museum of Maryland is more than a repository of historical artifacts and papers. This complex marks the place where Baltimore's early Jewish immigrant communities settled and matured. Two synagogues – one still serving a downtown congregation – stand restored to tell the story of the community's early spiritual development.

A small but dedicated group of worshipers continues to pray at the Museum's B'nai Israel congregation. Although the Jews of Baltimore no longer live, shop, or earn a living in this area, the community remembers and celebrates its roots, which reach back to the 18th century.

An agrarian-based economy and harsh religious laws discouraged Jews from settling in Baltimore until well into the 1700s. The growing harborfront began attracting handfuls of Jewish merchants, and others followed, particularly those from Bavaria. For the most part, Jews were able to prosper, but the community continued to struggle with equality – a decades-long fight for equality resulted in a law known as the "Jew Bill," passed in 1826 to protect Jewish civil rights and give the right to hold office.

The Baltimore Hebrew Congregation – the community's first – was established in 1830 and met over a grocery store. The congregation raised funds by exacting fines – an errant congregant might have been required to pay a quarter for singing louder than the hazzan or chewing tobacco during services. Maryland's first synagogue, on Lloyd Street, was dedicated in 1845.

The community continued to swell with the waves of Eastern European immigrants hitting Baltimore's shores between 1880 and the early 1900s. In the meantime, the prosperous members of the community moved north. In the 1870s, wealthy Jews built homes in the Bolton Hill area, a neighborhood described as an American Champs Elysées, with broad boulevards and grand synagogues.

The move north continues today, with the Jewish population clustering in such suburbs as Owings Mills and Pikesville. Nearly 100,000 Jews reside in the Baltimore area, supporting more than 40 synagogues, as well as Jewish businesses, day schools, and social service organizations. Notables from the community attract attention to the city, and some, such as film director Barry Levinson, choose to celebrate the origins of the Jews in Baltimore in their art.

❖ DID YOU KNOW?

In 1859, Baltimore's Oheb Shalom welcomed its new rabbi, Benjamin Szold, who became an active player in the local and national Jewish communities. His daughter Henrietta, one of five, also developed into a Jewish leader of international prominence. The outspoken Zionist is credited for having founded Hadassah Hospital, and laying the groundwork for the charitable direction of Hadassah.

SIGHTSEEING HIGHLIGHTS

MUSEUMS & GALLERIES

The Jewish Museum of Maryland, 15 Lloyd St., ☎ 410-732-6400, www.jhsm.org. This complex in the center of the old Jewish community of East Baltimore encompasses two historic synagogues, the Jewish Historical Society of Maryland, and more than a million photos, artifacts, and historical papers. It is acknowledged to be the largest museum in the country concerned with the preservation and interpretation of regional American Jewish history. Its permanent exhibit, *The Golden Land: A Jewish Family Learning Place*, is designed to give children a hands-on opportunity to learn about their Jewish origins. Guided tours include walks through the two synagogues: the Lloyd Street synagogue, the state's first; and the B'nai Israel synagogue, the city's oldest operating synagogue. Hours: Tuesday-Thursday, Sunday, noon-4. Admission: $4 adults, $2 children.

The Norman and Sarah Brown Art Gallery, JCC, 5700 Park Heights Ave., ☎ 410-542-4900, Ext. 239. Located in the Jewish Community Center complex, the gallery offers year-round changing exhibits by Jewish artists or involving Jewish themes. Some items are for sale. Hours: Monday-Tuesday, 11-5; Wednesday-Thursday, 3-5; Friday, noon-2:30; Sunday, noon-5.

HISTORIC SITES

B'nai Israel Synagogue, on the campus of the Jewish Museum of Maryland, 14 Lloyd St., ☎ 410-732-6400. The synagogue, established in 1876, is recognized as the city's oldest operating synagogue. It was first the home of Chizuk Amuno Congregation. B'nai Israel bought the building in 1895. The structure has been restored by the Jewish Historical Society, and is the only functioning downtown synagogue. Moorish Revival architecture with intricately carved woodwork and graceful arches recalls Middle Eastern motifs. Look for gas lights around the exterior wall of the sanctuary and the lower edge of the women's gallery, the large chandelier specially designed for the building, and the intricate wooden ark. See the listing for the Jewish Museum of Maryland for hours and admission details.

Lloyd Street Synagogue, on the campus of the Jewish Museum of Maryland, 15 Lloyd St., ☎ 410-732-6400. In 1845 the Baltimore Hebrew Congregation broke ground for Maryland's first synagogue, in the heart of East Baltimore's immigrant neighborhood. Although no longer in use as a place of worship, the Greek Revival structure is the third-oldest standing synagogue building in the United States. Among its leaders was Abraham Rice, the first ordained rabbi to come to America. A large matzah oven and a mikvah are highlights of the museum. A stained-glass window is thought to be the earliest architectural use of the star of David in the United States. See the listing for the Jewish Museum of Maryland for hours and admission details.

Site of first Baltimore Hebrew Congregation, 1534 Fleet St. (at Bond and Fleet streets), ☎ 410-653-1987. The fact that the original meeting place of the city's first Jewish congregation still exists is miracle enough: The upstairs room above a grocery store at Bond and Fleet streets held the group of 13, which barely exceeded a minyan, from 1830 to 1832. The owners of the vacant building, Brian and Eva Schwartz, are renovating the structure and hope to restore the second floor to the appearance it had when it housed the congregation. Throughout the centuries, the three-story brick building served as a private home, a saloon, a market, a boarding house, an auto parts store, and most recently a glass shop.

FORMER SYNAGOGUES

Several structures are well worth a drive-by. The former site of Temple Oheb Shalom, known as the **Eutaw Place Temple,** is now the Prince Hall Grand Lodge (1307 Eutaw Place, at the corner of Lanvale). The structure is located in an uptown neighborhood, Bolton Hill, which once swelled as prosperous Jews moved out of East Baltimore in the late 1800s. Just a few blocks away, the **Berea Temple**, a Seventh-Day Adventist church, once served the Baltimore Hebrew Congregation from the early 1890s to mid-20th century. It was known as the **Madison Avenue Temple**. Farther north at the end of Eutaw Place is the **Shaarei Tfiloh** synagogue, built in 1921 and still serving a small Orthodox congregation. At the south end of Bolton Hill (2014 W. North Ave.), the former **Har Zion** is now the Mount Hebron Baptist Church.

MONUMENTS, MARKERS & MEMORIALS

Holocaust Memorial, Water, Lombard and Gay Street, ☎ 410-542-4850. Near the Inner Harbor, the Holocaust Memorial, maintained by the Baltimore Jewish Council, incorporates a dramatic sculpture and outdoor space to provide a place for reflection. The triangle-shaped urban plaza recalls the railway system used during the Holocaust to transport millions of people to the camps. Two concrete monoliths suggest rail cars. The words of Santayana are displayed prominently in the plaza: "Those who do not remember the past are destined to repeat it."

NEIGHBORHOODS

North and west of the city, a stretch of business and residential areas bound by two parallel arteries – **Reisterstown Road** and **Park Heights Avenue** – is home to a thriving Jewish enclave, with a cluster of synagogues, Jewish businesses, and Jewish neighborhoods. Within this area is the Baltimore Hebrew University campus. Along Reisterstown Road, shoppers choose from a wealth of kosher carry-outs, butchers, bakeries, and restaurants. Along Park Heights Avenue, which is more residential, all major movements of Judaism – Orthodox, Conservative, Reform, and Reconstructionist – are represented.

COLLEGES & UNIVERSITIES

Baltimore Hebrew University, 5800 Park Heights Ave., ☎ 410-578-6936 (library) or 578-6900. Located in Baltimore's "Jewish neighborhood," BHU boasts an impressive Judaic library, including a rare book room and a Jewish Heritage Video Collection. This is a great stop for travelers who want to learn more about local and national Jewish history. And it's within walking distance of several synagogues and kosher restaurants. Hours: Monday-Thursday, 9-9; Friday, 9-4; Sunday, 11-4. Call ahead for summer hours.

GENERAL-INTEREST SIGHTS WITH JEWISH CONNECTION

Maryland Historical Society, 201 W. Monument St., ☎ 410-685-3750, www.mdhs.org. Its collections and galleries feature a rich mix of fine arts and decorative arts. Included in the permanent collections are portraits, furniture, silver items, and other artifacts from two of Baltimore's leading Jewish families of the 19th century – the Cohens and the Ettings. Hours: Tuesday-Friday, 10-5; Saturday, 9-5; Sunday, 1-5. Admission: $4 adults; $3 seniors, students, and children 13-17; children 12 and under free.

BALTIMORE

SYNAGOGUES

ORTHODOX

Beth Tfiloh, 3300 Old Court Rd., ☎ 410-486-1900.

Beth Jacob, 5713 Park Heights Ave., ☎ 410-486-1900.

B'nai Israel, 14 Lloyd St., ☎ 410-732-5454. Located within the complex of the downtown Jewish Museum of Maryland, this historic structure dates to 1876 (see *Historic Sites*, page 13).

Shearith Israel, 5835 Park Heights Ave., ☎ 410-466-3060. Mikvah.

CONSERVATIVE

Beth El, 8101 Park Heights Ave., ☎ 410-484-0411. Gift shop.

Beth Israel, 3706 Crondall Ln., Owings Mills, ☎ 410-654-0800. Mikvah.

Chizuk Amuno, 8100 Stevenson Rd., ☎ 410-486-6400. Historic congregation. The synagogue's museum contains an interesting collection of mezuzot, as well as other ritual objects.

REFORM

Baltimore Hebrew Congregation, 7401 Park Heights Ave., ☎ 410-764-1587. Historic congregation.

Har Sinai, 6300 Park Heights Ave., ☎ 410-764-2882. Historic congregation.

Oheb Shalom, 7310 Park Heights Ave., ☎ 410-358-0105, www.templeohebshalom.org. Historic congregation. Designed by Walter Gropius and built in 1960, the structure attracts architectural students who are frequently seen exploring, drawing, and photographing it.

❖ **DID YOU KNOW?**

Baltimore boasts the distinction of having employed the first ordained rabbi in the United States. Abraham Rice arrived in Baltimore in 1840 – he was from Bavaria – to lead Rosh Hashana services for the Baltimore Hebrew Congregation.

KOSHER DINING

❖ For up-to-date listings of restaurants with kashrut certification, call the **Vaad Hakashrus,** Star K Kosher Certification, ☎ 410-484-4110.

The Brasserie, 1700 Reisterstown Rd., ☎ 410-484-0476. The deli-style menu offers selections from meat to fish to vegetarian. Open for lunch and dinner; dine in or carry out.

Chapp's at Pomona, 1700 Reisterstown Rd., ☎ 410-653-3199. Go for Chinese or a traditional menu for lunch or dinner. Dine in or carry out. Serves lunch and dinner, open Saturday after sundown (except during summer).

I Can't Believe It's Yogurt, 1430 Reisterstown Rd., ☎ 410-484-4411. There's yogurt, of course, but the dairy menu also features bagels and lox, omelettes, and muffins for breakfast; pizza, sandwiches, soups, and other dairy deli favorites. Open for breakfast, lunch, and dinner, and Saturday after sundown.

Knish Shop, 508 Reisterstown Rd., ☎ 410-484-5850. This quick-stop mostly caters to carry-out clientele, but there are a few tables for eat-in service. Open for breakfast, lunch, and dinner.

Kosher Bite, 6309 Reisterstown Rd., ☎ 410-358-6349. Light bites and fast-food features are fried chicken, hamburgers, and health salads. Dine in or carry out. Open for lunch and dinner, and Saturday after sundown.

> ### ❖ DID YOU KNOW?
>
> Baltimore's Jewish "who's who" list is a lengthy one. In addition to historic figures such as Henrietta Szold, community notables include actor Josh Charles (of TV's *Sports Night* and the film *Dead Poet's Society*); author Leon Uris; songwriting duo Leiber and Stoller ("Hound Dog" and "Poison Ivy"); and Adam Duritz, lead singer for Counting Crows.

Mama Leah's Gourmet Kosher Pizza, 607-A Reisterstown Rd., ☎ 410-653-7600. Mostly carry-out, but a few tables are set up for diners. Open for lunch, dinner, and Saturday after sundown.

Milk and Honey Bistro, Commerce Center, 1777 Reisterstown Rd., ☎ 410-486-4344. Dine in or carry out. Open for breakfast, lunch, and dinner.

Royal Restaurant, Colonial Village, 7006 Reisterstown Rd., ☎ 410-484-3544. This full menu features Israeli specialties. Also offers carry-out. Open for lunch and dinner.

Tov Pizza, 6313 Reisterstown Rd., ☎ 410-358-5238. A full dairy menu offers eat-in or carry-out favorites. Open for lunch, dinner, and Saturday after sundown.

JEWISH COMMUNITY CENTERS

Jewish Community Center, 5700 Park Heights Ave., ☎ 410-542-4900. Major renovations have resulted in a vastly expanded menu of services. A full-service fitness center with indoor pool is available; a café is in the works. Also on site is the Norman and Sarah Brown Art Gallery, with year-round changing exhibits.

Jewish Community Center, 3506 Gwynnbrook Ave., Owings Mills, ☎ 410-356-5200, www.gordoncenter.com. This site features the Gordon Center for Performing Arts with theater, concerts, and other events. Located on a larger tract of land than the Park Heights facility, the Owings Mills location will experience expansion and continued improvements for several years. Members enjoy an indoor and outdoor pool, and full-service fitness and recreational amenities. A restaurant is also slated.

SHOPPING

Central Hebrew Book Store, 228 Reisterstown Rd., Pikesville, ☎ 410-653-0550.

Jacob's Ladder, Club Centre, 1500 Reisterstown Rd., ☎ 410-602-2363.

Jewish Museum of Maryland Museum Shop, 15 Lloyd St., ☎ 410-732-6400

Pern's Hebrew Book and Gift Shop, 7012 Reisterstown Rd., ☎ 410-653-2450.

Shabsi's Judaica Center, 6830-A Reisterstown Rd., ☎ 410-358-2200.

EVENTS

Jewish Book Festival, Jewish Community Center, 3506 Gwynnbrook Ave., Owings Mills, ☎ 410-356-5200, Ext. 324. The 10-day event features programming, author appearances, and plenty of books for sale. The festival is always scheduled during November, Jewish Book Month. Most events will take place at the Owings Mills JCC.

Jewish Film Festival, Jewish Community Center, 3506 Gwynnbrook Ave., Owings Mills, ☎ 410-542-4900, Ext. 239, www.gordoncenter.com. The focus is on Jewish-themed film during the three-week period in April, when the Gordon Center for Performing Arts presents premiere showings to the Baltimore community. Special programming – lectures with writers and actors, for example – supplement the film schedule. Tickets may be purchased in advance or at the door.

HERITAGE TOURS

Jewish Historical Society of Maryland, 15 Lloyd St., ☎ 410-732-6400. There are no regularly scheduled tours of Jewish Baltimore, but the Jewish Historical Society frequently conducts group tours.

The Society, housed on the campus of the Jewish Museum of Maryland, encourages those interested to call as far in advance as possible, particularly for visits planned for the summer months.

Marvin Solomon Tours, ☎ 410-484-0427. When Baltimore Hebrew University's Elderhostel program gets a request for a tour of Jewish Baltimore, they turn to Marvin Solomon. The Baltimore native owned a business in the Harbour area for decades, and in recent years has served as an information guide for the city. Although Solomon offers a standard tour, which features the Jewish Museum and East Baltimore area and the new Jewish neighborhoods, he's willing to customize his tours to personal interests. He recommends making arrangements at least two months in advance.

RESOURCES

The Associated: Jewish Community Federation of Baltimore, 101 W. Mt. Royal Ave., ☎ 410-727-4828.

Jewish Information Service, 5750 Park Heights Ave., ☎ 410-466-4636, www.jfs.org.

Jewish Historical Society of Maryland, 15 Lloyd St., ☎ 410-732-6400. Contact the archivist to schedule genealogical research.

❖ DID YOU KNOW?

Before becoming a "Mama," Baltimore native Cass Elliott served as an intern at the *Baltimore Jewish Times*. She discovered, however, that singing was her preferred mode of creative expression, and went on to perform with the Mamas and the Papas in the 1960s.

Baltimore Jewish Times, 2104 N. Charles St., ☎ 410-752-3504, www.jewishtimes.com. This weekly newspaper keeps residents and visitors apprised of happenings in the Jewish community. Also available through the offices is a guidebook to Jewish Baltimore. It's available in area bookstores around town. The Web site is a great place to track down information about other local agencies, organizations, and activities.

The Making of an American Jewish Community, by Isaac M. Fein, Jewish Historical Society of America, 1985. This book offers detailed history of the Baltimore Jewish community from 1773 to 1920.

Baltimore Convention and Visitors Association, 300 W. Pratt St., ☎ 800-282-6632.

❖ DID YOU KNOW?

Hollywood movie director Barry Levinson frequently returns home to film. His movies, including *Diner, Avalon,* and *Liberty Heights,* are often autobiographical and showcase Baltimore scenes and landmarks – as well as uniquely Jewish experiences.

BOSTON

Follow Boston's famed Freedom Trail, and you'll walk in the shadows of some of the most vibrant Jewish immigrant neighborhoods in the Northeast – but you won't know it. Sadly, little remains to mark the time when Eastern European Jews swelled North End neighborhoods between 1880 and 1920, creating something as close to a "Lower East Side" as Boston ever experienced. Other immigrant-era conclaves existed in the West End as well as sections of the South End – but most of the synagogues, schools, homes, and sights of significance were razed or rebuilt in urban renewal efforts. What few sights remain, however, are outstanding and do a lot to bring the history of Jews in Boston to life.

The city's founding fathers may have considered themselves "Christian Israelites," but they offered a less-than-friendly welcome to Jews during the Puritan beginnings. The stern New Englanders turned to their Old Testament for guidance and taught Hebrew at Harvard from its earliest days. But they remained wary of the few Jewish merchants and peddlers in the 1600s and through the Revolutionary period. Public records indicate a concern that Jewish newcomers might become public charges.

A handful of Jews played important roles during the Revolution. But the slow stream of shopkeepers and peddlers didn't build to a significant population until the late 1840s. At that time, the first congregation, Ohabei Shalom, was organized.

By the mid-1850s, a German Jewish community was firmly rooted in the South End, and grew as the Civil War brought an industrial boom to New England. But it wasn't until the wave of immigration from Eastern Europe (1870-1920) swept the East Coast

Boston's Jewish numbers spiked. The population flooded the North End, then the West End.

Today, nearly 214,000 Jews live in Greater Boston, most of the population concentrated in suburbs of Brookline, Brighton, and Newton. Despite the loss of many historical structures that testified to Boston's historic Jewish presence, fascinating examples remain. Additionally, a rich academic legacy leaves wonderful archives, museums, and collections of Jewish interest. Galleries, monuments, and even architectural attractions round out a healthy sightseeing agenda.

It may take some effort to track down the sights listed in this profile – Boston's confusing street patterns (or lack thereof) pose challenges to getting around. Guided tours are recommended (some resources are mentioned), and additional detail has been given when possible along with addresses. It is always advisable to call specific sights ahead to verify hours and get directions.

SIGHTSEEING HIGHLIGHTS

MUSEUMS & GALLERIES

American Jewish Historical Society Museum, Two Thornton Rd., Waltham, accessible only through Brandeis University, ☎ 781-891-8110. Its holdings – 15 million archival documents and tens of thousands of paintings, photos, artifacts, and museum objects – are the largest in the world relating to the Jewish experience in America. Although its library and many of its collections have now moved to the new Center for Jewish History in Manhattan (see page 135), its two small exhibition galleries are must-sees. A permanent exhibition showcases portraits, miniatures, objects, and documents of early American Jewry. There are also a number of changing temporary exhibitions. Hours: Monday-Friday, 9-4:30. Call in advance for special Sunday programs. No admission charged.

Starr Gallery, Leventhal-Sidman JCC, 333 Nahanton St., Newton, ☎ 617-558-6485. Jewish history and culture are showcased in historic and contemporary rotating exhibits, at the largest dedicated Jewish exhibition site in the Northeast. There's also a schedule of workshops and lectures. Hours are Monday-Thursday,

10-4; Friday, 10-2; Sunday, 11-4; Tuesday and Wednesday evenings, 6-9.

HISTORIC SITES

Plenty of tour companies offer historic walks through Boston proper, and some will point out plaques, buildings, or other attractions connected to Boston's Jewish legacy. Specifically, Boston Walks, Jewish Friendship Trail spotlights Jewish sites that may go unnoticed – tucked at the end of an alley, buried by new construction, unmarked by plaque or marker.

❖ DID YOU KNOW?

In the West End at Otis Place stand the homes once occupied by two prominent Boston Jews – **Justice Louis D. Brandeis**, the first Jewish Supreme Court Justice, and **Edward A. Filene**, department store patriarch. The homes are privately owned and not open for touring, but worthwhile to see from the outside.

Vilna Center for Jewish Heritage, Inc. 14-18 Phillips St., near north slope of Boston's Beacon Hill and Freedom Trail, ☎ 617-523-2324. Web site: shamash.org/places/boston. This National Historic Landmark is a museum and cultural center in the making. The structure served as the Vilna Shul from 1920 – when many of the Lithuanian immigrant congregants pitched in to build it – until the early 1980s. The modest structure, typical of a small, working-class shul, is a rare find – it's the only immigrant-era synagogue that survives in Boston. Currently, the center is open irregularly and visitors should call ahead for hours or to schedule a tour. In the works are plans for special events, concerts, lectures, and permanent and visiting exhibits.

Columbus Avenue A. M. E. Zion Church, 600 Columbus Ave., South End, ☎ 617-266-2758. In the stained-glass windows that face Northampton Street, passersby can distinguish the stars of David, indicating the building's origins as a synagogue – Temple Israel. A highlight of the well-preserved structure is the striking great rose window that faces Columbus Avenue. This steepled building, erected in 1885, provided an architectural model for two generations of synagogues in Boston, although it has served as a church for nearly 100 years. Hours: Wednesday, 11-2; Saturday, 11-3.

Two other South End sights are worth at least a walk-by. Both the **Greek Orthodox Church,** 11 Union Park St., and the **Charles Street Playhouse,** 784 Warrenton St., were once home to the Temple Ohabei Shalom congregation. The second location is acknowledged as the oldest building (1839) still standing that was once a synagogue in Boston.

Museum of Afro American History, 8 Smith Court (off Joy Street on north side of Beacon Hill, West End), ☎ 617-739-1200. This museum marks the site of the first free Black Baptist church in the New England area. Built in 1805, the African Meeting House is just one component of the museum site and the Black Heritage Trail. So what's the Jewish connection? From 1899 until the early 1970s, the historic structure served congregation Anshe Libawitz. The building, a National Historic Landmark, has been beautifully restored, and of special note is a lovely circular staircase – it once led to the women's section of the Orthodox synagogue. Hours: Daily, 10-4; closed weekends from Labor Day to Memorial Day. No admission charged; donations appreciated.

SUBURBAN SYNAGOGUES

Two synagogues in Roxbury and one in Chelsea are worth a drive-by. **Adath Jeshuran,** 397 Blue Hill Ave., Roxbury, is today the First Haitian Baptist Church of Boston. The immigrant-era synagogue has recently been declared a National Historic Landmark. At the corner of Elm Hill Avenue and Seaver Street is **Mishkan Tefila.** Ellen Smith, curator of the American Jewish Historical Society, calls it the "Crown Jewel" of Boston synagogues. This magnificent 1925 structure, which suffered from neglect until recently, has been restored as a church.

In nearby Chelsea, **Agudas Sholom,** also known as the Walnut Street Shul, still serves a dwindling congregation. A highlight is the cloud-painted ceiling, says David Kaufman, synagogue expert and co-author of *The Jews of Boston.*

MONUMENTS, MARKERS & MEMORIALS

The **Edward A. Filene Memorial** is a plaque at the corner of Boylston St. and Carver, near the entrance to Boston Common. The patriarch of the department store dynasty is honored as one of the founders of the credit union movement.

The New England Holocaust Memorial, Carmen Park, on Congress Street near Faneuil Hall and Freedom Trail, ☎ 617-457-0755. At night the six glass towers pick up the lights of the city and cast a greenish glow, reminding passersby of a menorah – or death camp chimneys. The towers are etched with six million numbers in memory of the Jews who died in the Holocaust. Blending into the heart of Boston, near the Freedom Trail and Faneuil Hall, the solemn monument provokes reflection on freedom and human rights. Visitors often leave stones and flowers on the surfaces of the memorial.

NEIGHBORHOODS

Coolidge Corner, Harvard Street in Brookline. If you're looking for the "Jewish neighborhood," travel to the suburb of Brookline. Here you'll find an ethnically diverse area, with plenty of kosher restaurants, Judaica shops, and Jewish soul. From the 1960s, this area has served as the heart of Jewish Boston.

COLLEGES & UNIVERSITIES

Brandeis University, 415 South Street, Waltham, ☎ 781-736-2000. Named for famed Boston resident Louis D. Brandeis, the first nonsectarian Jewish-founded university in the Western Hemisphere has attracted students to its inviting campus overlooking the Charles River since 1948. There are too many worthwhile sights to list, but highlights include the **Three Chapels** area, with Jewish, Catholic, and Protestant houses of worship, grouped around a heart-shaped pool. The **Holocaust Monument**, a bronze statue of Job by Nathan Rappaport, is modeled after the original, which stands at Yad Vashem in Jerusalem. Pieces from the **Tumen Collection of Judaica** are always on display in the Goldfarb Farber Libraries.

Hebrew College, 43 Hawes St., Brookline, ☎ 617-232-8710. Just a few blocks from the Coolidge Corner area, Hebrew College offers the visitor a number of treasures in a jewel-box setting. The centerpiece of the campus is a turn-of-the-century Beaux Arts mansion, containing an extensive library of rare books. As you walk through the halls, you'll enjoy Judaic artwork, including sculpture, paintings, and wall hangings. The museum in **the Benjamin A. and Julia M. Trustman Hall** holds a small collection of ritual objects from 19th- and 20th-century Eastern and Central Europe. Museum and library hours: Monday-Thursday, 9-9; Friday, 9-noon; Sunday, 9-3. No admission charged.

❖ DID YOU KNOW?

Arthur Fiedler was the father of the much-loved Boston Pops Concerts that have entertained outdoor summer crowds since 1930. An appropriate honor, then, to name a bridge after a man who connected people to an art form many considered beyond their reach. The **Arthur Fiedler Bridge** connects Beacon St. with the park along the Charles River where Hatch Memorial Shell is located.

GENERAL-INTEREST SIGHTS WITH JEWISH CONNECTION

Boston Public Library, 700 Boylston St., ☎ 617-536-5400. In the John Singer Sargent Gallery, the wall painting, *The Synagogue,* once attracted controversy; many found its depiction of the synagogue as a haggard old woman to be anti-Semitic. The painting is dark and in need of restoration. Perhaps of greater interest today is Sargent's *Frieze of the Prophets,* depicting Moses with the tablets and prophets, their names labeled in Hebrew.

Boston University, Mugar Memorial Library, 771 Commonwealth Ave. ☎ 617-353-2000. The Samuel Weisberg Memorial Collection of Jewish Ritual Silver contains menorahs, Torah ornaments, seder plates, besamim, and other ritual objects, and is located on the first floor of the Mugar Memorial Library. Library hours: Monday-Thursday, 8am-midnight; Friday-Saturday, 8-11; Sunday, 10am-midnight. Call for summer hours.

Paul Revere House, 19 North Square, ☎ 617-523-2338. No, Paul Revere wasn't Jewish. But this stop on the Freedom Trail does have some Jewish connection. A tour of the two homes, the Paul Revere House and the Pierce/Hichborn House next door, incudes commentary about the ethnic populations that once lived in the North End. And evidence indicates that around the turn of the century, a Jewish-owned grocery store operated from the Paul Revere House. Hours: Daily, mid-April through October 31, 9:30-5:15; November 1-April 14, 9:30-4:15. Admission: $2.50; $2 seniors and students; $1 children ages five-17.

SYNAGOGUES

Most of Greater Boston's synagogues will be found in the outlying suburbs of Newton, Brighton, and Brookline, with a few exceptions. Call the Synagogue Council of Massachusetts (☎ 617-244-6506) for more listings and more information.

ORTHODOX

The Boston Synagogue, 55 Martha Rd., ☎ 617-723-2863. Identified as Orthodox in the Synagogue Council directory; however, the congregation defines itself as Traditional, with separate and mixed seating for men and women. It is one of the few synagogues in Boston proper.

Congregation Agudas Achim-Anshe Sfard, 168 Adams St., Newton, ☎ 617-730-4183. This synagogue, also referred to as the Adams Street Shul, is the oldest congregation in Newton (1912), and one of the oldest in the Boston area. It's listed on the National Registry of Historic Buildings.

Congregation Beth El-Atereth Israel, 561 Ward St., Newton, ☎ 617-244-7233.

Congregation Beth Pinchas, 1710 Beacon St., Brookline, ☎ 617-734-5100. The Bostoner Rebbe's congregation.

Congregation Kadimah-Toras Moshe, 113 Washington St., Brighton, ☎ 617-254-1333. Next door is the Daughters of Israel mikvah.

Congregation Shaarei Tefillah, 35 Morseland Ave., Newton, ☎ 617-527-7637.

Young Israel of Brookline, 62 Green St., Brookline, ☎ 617-734-0276.

CONSERVATIVE

Temple Emanuel, 385 Ward St., Newton, ☎ 617-558-8510.

Temple Emeth, 194 Grove St., Newton, ☎ 617-469-9400.

Congregation Kehillath Israel, 384 Harvard St., Brookline, ☎ 617-277-9155.

Temple Mishkan Tefila, 300 Hammond Pond Pkwy., Newton, ☎ 617-332-7770. Contains a small museum with an interesting collection of ritual objects.

Temple Reyim, 1860 Washington St., Newton, ☎ 617-527-2410.

REFORM

Temple Beth Avodah, 45 Puddingstone Ln., Newton, ☎ 617-527-0045, Web site: 222.shamash.org/reform/uahc/congs/ma/ma007.

Temple Israel, Longwood Ave. and Plymouth St., ☎ 617-731-1557, e-mail tisrael@shore.net. Of special note is a 20-foot sculpture, *Covenant, Covenant,* by renowned sculptress Louise Nevelson, and a memorial garden with Biblical flowers and plants.

Temple Ohabei Shalom, 1187 Beacon St., Brookline, ☎ 617-277-6610. The second-largest Byzantine-like structure in the United States, the synagogue stands like a beacon in Coolidge Corner, its dramatic dome a neighborhood landmark.

Temple Shalom, 175 Temple St., Newton, ☎ 617-332-9550.

Temple Sinai, 50 Sewall Ave., Brookline, ☎ 617-277-5842.

KOSHER DINING

Café Aviv, 14A Pleasant St., Brookline, ☎ 617-731-9780. A meat restaurant, with Middle Eastern and Moroccan flavors. Eat in or carry out. Open for lunch and dinner, Saturday after sundown.

Casa Mia, 9 Babcock St., Brookline, ☎ 617-739-1515. An Italian meat menu offers other Mediterranean dishes as well. Eat in or carry out. Open for lunch and dinner, Saturday after sundown.

Café Shiraz, 1030 Commonwealth Ave., Brookline, ☎ 617-566-8888. The focus is on Persian and Middle Eastern, with both meat and vegetarian items on the menu. Open for dinner only, and Saturday after sundown.

Galilee Restaurant, 406 Harvard St., Brookline, ☎ 617-731-1818. For an upscale ambiance, diners seek out dairy, fish, and vegetarian entrées, as well as pizza and ice cream. The restaurant also offers carry-out.

Milk Street Café, Post Office Square, 50 Milk Street, Boston, ☎ 617-542-3663. This dairy establishment offers soups, salads, pizza, and sandwiches cafeteria-style for breakfast and lunch. Open for breakfast and lunch; and Sunday brunch during summer.

Milk Street Café, The Park at Post Office Square, corner of Congress and Franklin Streets, ☎ 617-350-7275. The deli side of the establishment specializes in hot dogs and chili dogs. Open for breakfast and lunch.

Rami's, 324 Harvard St., Brookline, ☎ 617-738-3577. A taste of Israel with a meat menu that includes felafel, shwarma, and other Middle Eastern favorites. Open for lunch.

Rubin's Kosher Delicatessen & Restaurant, 500 Harvard St., Brookline, ☎ 617-731-8787. Eat in or carry out from this meat deli. Open for breakfast, lunch, and dinner.

Ruth's Kitchen, 401 Harvard St., Brookline, ☎ 617-734-9810. In addition to a full Chinese menu, Jewish and American meat and vegetarian entrées are available. Eat in or carry out. Open for lunch and dinner.

BOSTON

Shalom Hunan Restaurant, 92 Harvard St., Brookline, ☎ 617-731-9760. A meat menu presents Chinese favorites. Open for lunch and dinner, Saturday after sundown.

Vittorio's Pizza, 1398 Beacon St., Brookline, ☎ 617-730-9903, www1.usa1.com/leibco/vittorios/. Dairy favorites include pizza, felafel, and ice cream. Eat in or carry out. Open for lunch and dinner, Saturday after sundown.

Zaatar's Oven, 242 Harvard St., Brookline, ☎ 617-731-6836. Mediterranean dishes, baked-onsite flatbreads, and pizza highlight this dairy menu. Eat in or carry out. Open for breakfast, lunch and dinner, Saturday after sundown.

JEWISH COMMUNITY CENTERS

Leventhal-Sidman JCC, 333 Nahanton St., Newton, ☎ 617-558-6522. www.lsjcc.org. The Newton location includes the Starr Gallery, fitness facilities, pool, and theater. Beautifully restored 19th-century structures share the campus with modern facilities, and hint at the area's history, originally as a Jesuit seminary, and later as an orphanage.

Striar JCC, 445 Central St., Stoughton, ☎ 781-341-2016. The full-service facility offers fitness and amenities for out-of-town members seeking reciprocal privileges. A central courtyard is worth a visit – its walls are built from Jerusalem stone.

SHOPPING

Israel Book Shop, 410 Harvard St., Brookline, ☎ 617-566-7113.

Kolbo Gifts, 435 Harvard St., Brookline, ☎ 617-731-8743.

LODGING

Four Seasons Kosher B&B, 15 Madoc St., Newton Centre, ☎ 617-928-1128. Joe and Miriam Behar welcome guests into their modern home with the look of a charming country cottage. They serve kosher breakfasts, provide a *Shomer Shabbat* atmosphere, and offer a homey base within walking distance of three Orthodox synagogues and two Conservative congregations. The B&B is within easy commute to Boston. Miriam's full breakfasts are highlighted by her homemade breads, and occasional frittata. Miriam will prepare Shabbat meals for an extra charge, if arranged in advance. Two rooms are available. No children under 12. The rates are quite modest, well under $100 for two.

EVENTS

Boston Jewish Film Festival, Waltham, ☎ 617-244-9899. A series of films, classics and currents, is scheduled during November.

Jewish Chamber Orchestra, Leventhal-Sidman JCC, 333 Nahanton St., Newton, ☎ 617-965-5226. The orchestra performs twice a year, and features notable musicians as well as undiscovered geniuses of the Jewish music world. Call for dates of performances.

The Jewish Theatre of New England, Leventhal-Sidman JCC, 333 Nahanton St., Newton, ☎ 617-965-5226. Its season runs from October to May, and features contemporary and classical performances within the context of the Jewish experience – everything from Klezmer concerts to Jewish soloists to theatrical works, as well as some children's programs. Box office hours: Tuesday-Thursday, noon-5.

HERITAGE TOURS

Boston Walks, Jewish Friendship Trail, 50 Grove St., Belmont, ☎ 617-489-5020. Native Bostonian Michael Ross regales participants with tales of Boston's Jewish past, as he points out synagogues, historic businesses, and other points of interest in the West End, North End, South End, and Cambridge. Many of the city's most intriguing sites are well-hidden. Ross offers walks as well as bicycle tours. Scheduled tours are more frequent in warm weather, generally on Sunday afternoons. But given enough notice, he will arrange private tours as well. The tours typically last from one to 2½ hours and cost $20 or less.

RESOURCES

Combined Jewish Philanthropies of Greater Boston, Inc., 126 High St., ☎ 617-457-8500, www.cjp.org.

❖ DID YOU KNOW?

Since the TV series *Star Trek* soared into the entertainment universe in the 1960s, Jews have wondered about parallels between Captain Kirk's Federation and Jewish institutions similarly named. Key character Spock frequently flashed the sign of the Kohane (creating a "V" shape by splitting the fingers), inciting further speculation. The fact that actor Leonard Nimoy (who portrayed Spock) is Jewish creates even more. Nimoy is the son of a Boston barber.

The Synagogue Council of Massachusetts, 1320 Centre St., Newton Centre, ☎ 617-244-6506.

This body, a joint venture of state UAHC (Reform), USCJ (Conservative), Orthodox, and Reconstructionist congregations, publishes a directory of synagogues and may be a helpful source for visitors seeking information about specific congregations in the Greater Boston area.

Jewish Advocate, 15 School St., Boston, ☎ 617-367-9100, Ext. 20, www.neponset.com/jewish_advocate. The Jewish community's weekly newspaper. Its Web site is a great place to find listings of local organizations, as well as editorial and news.

www.jewishboston.org has the lowdown on all things Jewish in the Greater Boston area, from synagogue listings, to kosher dining, to a calendar of community events.

Alef Cable Network, Bureau of Jewish Education, 333 Nahanton St., Newton, ☎ 617-965-7350. Presents Jewish public affairs programming, with both local and international content. Call for a listing of channels in the Boston area.

The Jewish Genealogical Society of Greater Boston, PO Box 610366, Newton Highlands, MA 02161-0366, ☎ 617-283-8003, www.jewishgen.org/boston/jgsgb.html.

The Jews of Boston, edited by Jonathan D. Sarna and Ellen Smith (Combined Jewish Philanthropies of Greater Boston, 1995).

CHICAGO

Chicago is a city of architecture and neighborhoods. And the traveler with a Jewish focus will likewise look for dramatic structures – particularly in synagogues, which span the design spectrum from traditional to ultra-modern – and neighborhoods past and present. In addition, there are some top-rated museums and collections – not the least of which is the Spertus Institute.

With some 260,000-plus Jews living in and around Chicago, the area boasts the largest Jewish population in the Midwest. As in other major metropolitan centers, evidence of Jewish life and history in Chicago is prevalent. Some of the city's most familiar institutions and monuments are the gifts of Jewish philanthropists – the Adler Planetarium, gift of Max Adler; the Museum of Contemporary Art, founded by Joseph Shapiro; and the Museum of Science and Industry, whose benefactor was Julius Rosenwald.

Jews have been part of the Chicago landscape since its earliest days. As in other parts of the Midwest, Jewish merchants, mostly from Germany, settled in small numbers until the Civil War spurred growth. Despite the infamous Chicago fire in 1871, the population increased steadily as the Eastern European immigrations gained momentum in the late 1800s.

By 1900, Jews were well-established on the city's near west side. No area was as reminiscent of an old-world community as Maxwell Street. Here, pushcart peddlers hawked everything from produce fresh from the countryside, to shoes and clothing, to pots and pans, to live chickens. This was the heart of the Jewish community, often compared to New York City's Orchard Street on the

Lower East Side. Located here were marriage brokers, mohels, immigrant aid agencies, Yiddish theater, and some 32 synagogues. Today, the Maxwell Street market has been relocated on Canal Street, but a Jewish presence has vanished.

❖ DID YOU KNOW?

Maxwell Street produced bandleader Benny Goodman, actor Paul Muni, Supreme Court Justice Arthur Goldberg, and CBS founder William Paley.

New Jewish neighborhoods emerged throughout the first half of the 20th century: At its heyday in the 1930s and 40s Lawndale boasted some 40 synagogues, and shopping, social life, and cultural agencies. The area, with broad streets and shady parks, was once called the "Jerusalem of Chicago." Other enclaves of Jewish life were Albany Park, Humboldt Park, Hyde Park, Lake View, Rogers Park, and others that have waxed and waned over time.

The Jewish community has fanned out in many directions, with large populations in northern suburbs such as Skokie, Evanston, Glencoe, Highland Park, and Winnetka. In all of these places, you'll find Jewish commerce, but also an occasional art collection, Holocaust memorial, historic synagogue, or museum. Chicago is definitely not a place where all Jewish life is concentrated in one neighborhood, so be prepared to travel in order to take it all in.

SIGHTSEEING HIGHLIGHTS

MUSEUMS & GALLERIES

Spertus Institute of Jewish Studies, 618 S. Michigan Ave., ☎ 312-922-9012, www.spertus.edu. Within the Institute are a number of museums and collections of note, not to mention its accredited graduate degree programs, and year-round schedule of special events, lectures, workshops, and family programs. Following are some Spertus attractions that are particularly appealing to the visitor.

❖ **Spertus Museum of Judaica**, 618 South Michigan Ave., ☎ 312-322-1747, www.spertus.edu. It's the largest Jewish museum in the Midwest, featuring traveling exhibits, workshops, permanent displays, and a hands-on children's museum. The seed collection for the museum, from Maurice Spertus in 1968, contains ritual objects, textiles, costumes, coins, and a contemporary, Bezalel-designed Torah ark. Archival materials are also displayed. The Julian and Daris Wineberg Sculpture Garden contains a number of works, including the *Flame of Hope* by Leonardo Nierman. Hours: Sunday-Thursday, 10-5; Friday, 10-3. (In winter, Thursday hours are 10-8.) Admission: $5 adults; $3 seniors and students; $10 family.

❖ **Zell Holocaust Memorial,** 618 S. Michigan Ave., ☎ 312-322-1747, www.spertus.edu. Visitors who wander through the two exhibit areas of this Holocaust museum often leave stones atop a sculpture that resembles a gravestone. Displays feature the remnants of the horror – a canister of Zyklon-B gas, instruments for extracting gold teeth, a uniform, a leg brace with a shoe. Hours: same as above. Admission: same as above; all museums included in one fee.

❖ **Rosenbaum ARTiFACT Center,** 618 S. Michigan Ave., ☎ 312-322-1754, www.spertus.edu. Kids and adults enjoy participating in simulated digs at this permanent family exhibit on archaeology of the Middle East. The Marketplace contains stalls where visitors can examine objects from ancient Israel – with hands-on activities including scribal arts, pottery, and music. For younger children the Israelite House introduces the sounds, colors, and textures of ancient Israel, with costumes, farm animals, and workshops. Hours: Sunday-Thursday, 1-4:30 (mornings are reserved for group tours). Admission: same as above; all museums included in one fee.

Holocaust Memorial Foundation of Illinois, Holocaust Museum and Resource Center, 4255 W. Main St., Skokie, ☎ 847-677-4640. Much of this large collection is made up of memorabilia donated by Skokie's community of survivors. The museum also contains paintings, sculptures, and woodcuts on Holocaust themes, as well as a Wall of Remembrance. Serving as docents are many survivors. Check the schedule for programs and events. Hours: Monday-

CHICAGO

Thursday, 9-4:30; Friday, 9-3; Sunday, noon-4. No admission charged; donations appreciated.

Hebrew Theological College, 7135 North Carpenter Rd., Skokie, ☎ 847-674-7750. A small collection of ritual objects, including chanukiot and Torah pointers, is part of the reading room display. The yeshiva also boasts a large collection of Holocaust and Yizkor books, and rare publications, some that date to the 1600s. Several memorial plaques from synagogues that no longer exist are also on display. Hours: Monday-Thursday, 9-5; Friday, 9-1:30; Sunday, 9:15-12:15. No admission charged.

Frank Rosenthal Memorial Collection, Temple Anshe Sholom, 20820 Western Ave., Olympia Fields, ☎ 708-748-6010. Temple Anshe Sholom displays the extensive private collection of Judaica in numerous cases lining the school wing. The objects and books were gathered by Rabbi Frank F. Rosenthal during his worldwide travels. Congregants continue to donate artifacts, which range from ancient Middle Eastern tools to medieval ritual objects to religious items that survived the Holocaust. Hours: Monday-Friday, 9-4; Sunday mornings, hours vary. No admission charged.

HISTORIC SITES

In Chicago, architecture *is* history. The city that was virtually destroyed by a fire in 1871 reinvented itself, constructing a gleaming skyline that attracts international attention and has identified Chicago as the birthplace of tradition-breaking design. Not surprisingly, many synagogues also reflect this innovation. Thus, some of the structures listed here may not be sightworthy so much because of their history, but because of their architectural interest.

Chicago Loop Synagogue, 16 S. Clark St., ☎ 312-346-7370. It's not that the building is so old (it was constructed about 40 years ago), but the art and architecture is so intriguing that it draws groups from the Art Institute on a regular basis. They come to see the stained-glass windows created by artist Abraham Rattner. Within the jewel-like wall of glass are dazzling themes, including the weblike Tree of Life, the Twelve Tribes of Israel, and the menorah. Outside, the "Hands of Peace" sculpture depicts the priestly blessing and seems to welcome visitors into the synagogue. The Chicago Loop Synagogue has been a downtown fixture since 1929. It still draws a daily minyan. Call in advance if you're interested in a tour. All are welcome for services.

K.A.M. Isaiah Israel, 1100 East Hyde Park Blvd., ☎ 773-924-1234. The oldest congregation in the state (established in 1847) still worships in a landmark structure built in 1924. The synagogue was designed to resemble a Byzantine-period, octagonal-shaped synagogue in Ravenna, Italy. The massive arched ceiling is the focal point of the large sanctuary. A small Judaica museum contains a collection of Iranian artifacts and rare manuscripts. Of special note are some unusual illuminated ketubot and a letter from Sir Moses Montefiore dated 1883. Call in advance to tour this southside synagogue or visit the museum.

Pilgrim Baptist Church, 3301 S. Indiana, ☎ 312-842-5830. Innovative Chicago School architects Dankmar Adler and Louis Sullivan built this former K. A. M. structure in 1891. Adler had a particular connection to the congregation – his father served as its first rabbi. Adler and Sullivan shocked traditionalists at the time with their daring use of materials and styles. The structure evokes a fortress-like feel with its heavy stonework and deep, narrow windows. A soaring arched ceiling draws the eye upward in the sanctuary.

North Shore Congregation Israel, 1185 Sheridan Rd., Glencoe, ☎ 847-835-0724, www.uahc.org/congs/il/il002/. Designed by Minoru Yamasaki in 1963, this modern structure combines a variety of styles to result in a gentle, harmonious form. From certain perspectives, the sanctuary appears to be sheltered by giant petals, unfolding to reveal the bimah and Ark. Hints of Moorish influences are found in the curving arched windows, and glass patterns suggest Art Nouveau motifs.

Public School, 3448 W. Douglas Blvd., no telephone. The structure was once the home of the Jewish Theological Seminary during the 1920s, when the Lawndale neighborhood was often referred to as the "Jerusalem of Chicago." The building is designated as a National Historic Landmark.

CHICAGO

Chicago's Jewish neighborhoods have produced a number of well-known names. From Lawndale, young Bernie Schwartz began his acting career, destined to entertain the world as Tony Curtis; and it was Lawndale where author Leo Rosten taught English to immigrants. Comedian Shelley Berman and Admiral Hyman Rickover also hail from Lawndale.

Lawndale Community Academy, 3500 W. Douglas Blvd., ☎ 773-534-1635. In the 1920s, the Jewish People's Institute, the predecessor to the Jewish Community Center, served as the heart of the community, providing assistance to immigrants and offering a place for people to gather and socialize. Today, the structure is home to a public school, and is listed on the National Register of Historic Landmarks.

St Basil's Greek Orthodox, 733 South Ashland, ☎ 312-243-3738. The Anshe Sholom congregation worshiped in this Classical structure, built by Alexander Levy in 1910. The Eastern European congregation suffered a rift in the late 1920s and split into two congregations as they followed the movement of the congregants west and south. Today, one Orthodox branch worships at Melrose Avenue.

North Suburban Beth El, 1175 Sheridan Rd., Highland Park, ☎ 847-432-8900, www.nssbethel.org. The mansion dates to the turn of the century (built from 1900 to 1914 in phases), and has been enveloped by a modern structure designed by noted architect Percival Goodman, built in the 1960s. The synagogue overlooks Lake Michigan.

MONUMENTS, MARKERS & MEMORIALS

Federal Center, Clark St. between Adams and Jackson boulevards. No marker indicates where Chicago's first minyan worshiped in 1845, in an upstairs haberdashery at the corner of Lake and Wells. But nearby, at the Federal Building on Clark, a plaque identifies the site of the first synagogue. At this spot, worshipers of the Kehilath Anshe Maariv (K.A.M.) congregation first gathered in

1851. The plaque was originally affixed in 1918, but saved to put on the new Federal building when the synagogue was torn down.

Hebrew Benevolent Society Cemetery, 3900 block of N. Clark St., ☎ 847-279-8115. Those who've enjoyed a weekend picnic or a run through Chicago's Lincoln Park may be surprised to learn that in the place was once a Jewish burial ground. The cemetery was moved in 1854 after the Hebrew Benevolent Society purchased nearby land for a burial ground. Known as the Jewish Graceland Cemetery, this burial ground is next to the nationally known Graceland Cemetery, and remains the oldest extant Jewish cemetery in the city. Look for the grave of Colonel Marcus Spiegel, a Civil War hero buried in 1864. His tombstone features a likeness of his face. Spiegel is connected to the Spiegel catalog family. Other notables include the grandparents of novelist Edna Ferber.

Chagall Wall, First National Bank Plaza on Dearborn St., between Monroe and Madison streets. Chagall's 70-foot freestanding mosaic wall, *The Four Seasons,* delights passersby at this bank plaza.

Agam Column, northwest corner of Michigan Ave. and Randolph. The colorful monolith is easily recognized as the work of noted Israeli artist Agam. The geometric patterns seeming to move like a kaleidoscope as walkers approach and pass by the work.

Henry Horner Memorial Monument, Horner Park, Montrose and California streets. Henry Horner was the first Jew to be elected governor of the state of Illinois. Horner, born in Chicago in 1878, was elected to two terms, the first in 1932.

Haym Salomon Monument, Heald Square and Wacker and Wabash. Dedicated in 1941, on the 150th anniversary of the ratification of Bill of Rights, this monument honors Salomon, a hero of the Revolutionary War, as well as George Washington and Robert Morris. Carved into the base are words from Washington's letter to the Touro Synagogue, promoting tolerance of religious differences. The monument has Chicago landmark status.

NEIGHBORHOODS

With the largest Jewish population of any Midwestern metropolis, Chicago boasts several neighborhoods where Jewish business and culture thrives – in the city as well as in outlying suburbs. Two neighborhoods where you'll find vibrant life:

CHICAGO

West Rogers Park. Get yourself to Devon Street near the intersection of California, and you'll have no doubt that you've found one of Chicago's most "Jewish" neighborhoods. Here, the street signs sport names such as "Torah V'Chesed" and the donuts from a national fast-food franchise are kosher. Bordering on the southern edge of Evanston, West Rogers Park is experiencing something of a rebirth, as Orthodox families and Russian Jews continue to swell the population. Several Jewish agencies, including the Bernard Horwich JCC, the Ark, and the Chicago Community Kollel are located here. This is also where you'll find most of the city's kosher restaurants – everything from carry-out pizza and Chinese to upscale gourmet dining.

Skokie. Skokie's Jewish community is perhaps the most well-known of Chicago's northern suburbs. Skokie came to national attention in 1978, when a Nazi group gained permission to march through neighborhoods where Holocaust survivors lived. While the streets feel a little scruffy, there is plenty of Jewish life here, particularly on Dempster Street, with strip malls packed with Jewish businesses and kosher restaurants. Here the Kaplan JCC, a Holocaust Memorial, and Hebrew Theological College are found, not to mention a dozen or so synagogues.

❖ DID YOU KNOW?

Many speculate that writer Saul Bellow's *Humboldt's Gift* is a tribute to his old neighborhood. Bellow grew up in Chicago's Humboldt Park.

GENERAL-INTEREST SIGHTS WITH JEWISH CONNECTION

University of Chicago, Visitor Center, 1212 E. 59th St., ☎ 312-702-1234. The university is located near Hyde Park, once a thriving Jewish neighborhood. A number of buildings on campus are named for and built by Jews, including the Nathan Goldblatt Memorial Hospital, Epstein Archive – a collection that includes paintings and art, Albert Pick Hall for International Studies, Pritzker School of Medicine, Joseph Regenstein Library, and Rosenwald Hall, occupied by the School of Business. Call ☎ 312-702-8374 to schedule a tour of the campus.

Art Institute of Chicago, Michigan Avenue at Adams St., ☎ 312-443-3600. In the Chagall Gallery are two works, *The Praying Jew* and another of a crucifixion, that have caused some controversy. There are also Chagall's *America Windows*. The Art Institute also holds works by other Jewish artists too numerous to list. Hours: Monday, Wednesday, Friday, 10:30-4:30; Tuesday, 10:30-8; Saturday, 10-5; Sunday, noon-5. Admission: $8 adults; $5 seniors, students, and children.

Newberry Library, 60 W. Walton St. (between N. Dearborn and N. Clark streets), ☎ 312-943-9090, www.newberry.org. This private library is one of the finest resources for genealogical searches in the country. In its collection are some of the music manuscripts of Felix Mendelssohn, and the Louis H. Silver collection of rare books. The building itself is sightworthy, constructed in 1892 in Romanesque Revival style. Hours: Monday, Friday, Saturday, 9-5; Tuesday-Thursday, 9-7:30. No admission charged; donations appreciated.

SYNAGOGUES

ORTHODOX

Anshe Sholom B'nai Israel Congregation, 540 W. Melrose, ☎ 773-248-9200, www.asbi.org. Congregants welcome visitors into their homes for Shabbat. Call for home hospitality arrangements.

Congregation Anshe Mizrach, 534 W. Stratford Pl., ☎ 312-525-4034.

Congregation Or Torah, 3800 W. Dempster, Skokie, ☎ 847-679-3645, www.ortorah.org. Largest Orthodox congregation in Skokie.

Young Israel of West Rogers Park, 2716 West Touhy Ave., ☎ 773-743-9400.

Young Israel of Skokie, 3708 W. Dempster, Skokie, ☎ 847-329-0990, www.skokieyoungisrael.jewishchicago.com.

CONSERVATIVE

Chicago's Central Congregation, Chicago Sinai Congregation Building, 15 W. Delaware Pl., ☎ 312-787-0450, www.central.jew-ishchicago.com. Convenient to travelers staying downtown. Shabbat services only; lunch is served after service.

Anshe Emet Synagogue, 3760 N. Pine Grove, ☎ 773-281-1423, www.ansheemet.org. Large congregation, with large gift shop, Destination Judaica.

Congregation Ezra-Habonim, the Rogers Park Conservative Synagogue, 2800 W. Sherwin Ave., ☎ 773-743-0154.

Congregation Shaare Tikvah, 5800 N. Kimball Ave., ☎ 773-539-2202.

Congregation B'nai Emunah, 9131 Niles Center Rd., Skokie, ☎ 847-674-9292, www.members.tripod.com/Egalitarian.

North Suburban Synagogue Beth El, 1175 Sheridan Rd., Highland Park, ☎ 847-432-8900, www.nssbethel.org.

REFORM

Chicago Sinai Congregation, 15 W. Delaware Pl., ☎ 312-867-7000.

Congregation Kol Ami, 845 N. Michigan Ave., Ste. 913E (Water Tower Place), ☎ 312-664-4775.

Temple Sholom of Chicago, 3480 N. Lake Shore Dr., ☎ 773-525-4707.

Beth Emet The Free Synagogue, 1224 W. Dempster, Evanston, ☎ 847-869-4230, www.bethemet.org.

Temple Judea Mizpah, 8610 Niles Center Rd., Skokie, ☎ 847-676-1566, www.mcs.net.

Lakeside Congregation for Reform Judaism, 1221 County Line Rd., Highland Park, ☎ 847-432-7950, shamash.org/reform/uahc/congs/il/i1003/.

TRADITIONAL

Chicago Loop Synagogue, 16 S. Clark St., ☎ 312-346-7370.

A. G. Beth Israel, 3635 W. Devon, ☎ 773-539-9060.

KOSHER DINING

❖ Most of Chicago's kosher eat-in dining opportunities are clustered in Skokie on Dempster, or on Devon Street in the north Chicago neighborhood of West Rogers Park. The establishments offer variety, with a plethora of pizza and felafel spots, as well as gourmet cuisine and ethnic choices from Chinese to Mexican to Thai. Several of the restaurants open up after Shabbat on Saturday evenings. For the most current listing of certified kosher restaurants, contact the **Chicago Rabbinical Council,** ☎ 773-588-2141.

Good Morgan Fish, 2948 W. Devon Ave., ☎ 773-764-8115. Mostly take-out, but limited table service allows for on-site enjoyment of grilled or fried fish, pastas, salads, and homemade gefilte fish.

Great Chicago Food & Beverage Co., 3149 W. Devon Ave., ☎ 773-465-9030. Traditional American diner ambiance enhances a menu of hot dogs, hamburgers, and fried and barbecued chicken. Open for lunch and dinner.

Hava Nagila, 2748 W. Devon Ave., ☎ 773-743-6893. Middle Eastern and Israeli specialties are the draw at this meat restaurant. Open for lunch and dinner, and after Shabbat.

Jerusalem Kosher Restaurant, 3014 W. Devon Ave., ☎ 773-262-0515. Israeli and American vegetarian, fish, and dairy items are featured. Desserts are tempting. The place is open for lunch and dinner, and is open after Shabbat.

Kirshner's Cuisine, 2839 W. Touhy Ave., ☎ 773-465-6247. An all-you-can-eat buffet is available at this establishment Tuesdays and Thursdays from 5-8; and during the winter after Shabbat on Saturday evenings. The menu, almost always meat, changes from day to day.

CHICAGO

Mi-Tsu-Yun, 3010 W. Devon St., ☎ 773-262-4630. Choose from Chinese favorites and American classics from a dine-in or carryout menu. Open for lunch and dinner.

Shallots, 2324 N. Clark St., ☎ 773-755-5205. Who knew venison was kosher? Sample it at this upscale CRC-supervised establishment with a small bar and valet parking. If deer meat is not your cup of tea, choose from a menu of Mediterranean specialties. Open for dinner only.

Tel Aviv Kosher Pizza, 6349 N. California Ave., ☎ 773-764-3776. This sit-down establishment with counter service specializes in pizza – *plus*. Try pasta, felafel, Israeli, Mexican, or a vegetarian entrée for lunch or dinner. The restaurant also opens after Shabbat Saturday evening.

Bagel Country, 9306 N. Skokie Blvd., Skokie, ☎ 847-673-3030. Dairy soups, salads, sandwiches, and a bagel bakery draw the hungry for breakfast, lunch, and dinner. All bread products are parve. Bagel Country opens Saturday evening.

Bugsy's, 3353 W. Dempster St., Skokie, ☎ 847-675-2847. This lively 1920s-style steak place offers six different steak choices, as well as chicken, shish kebab, and plenty of sides. Open for dinner only.

Da'Nali's, 4032 W. Oakton St., Skokie, ☎ 847-677-2782. The specialty is brick-oven style pizza and dairy-based pasta entrées, available for lunch or dinner.

Felafel King Israeli Restaurant, 4507 W. Oakton St., Skokie, ☎ 847-677-6020. Choose from American or Middle Eastern dishes, or selections such as Italian beef, for lunch or dinner.

Hy Life Bistro, 4120-26 W. Dempster, Skokie, ☎ 847-674-2021. A fine-dining menu features international cuisine and choices such as duck, veal, fish, steak, and pasta. Bar service is available. The restaurant is open for dinner.

Jerusalem Kosher Restaurant, 3014 W. Devon, ☎ 773-262-1028. Dairy and vegetarian choices are available for lunch or dinner. Pizza, soups, and desserts are popular. The restaurant opens after Shabbat for Saturday evening.

Ken's Diner, 3353 W. Dempster St., Skokie, ☎ 847-679-2850. Step back into the 1950s at this nostalgic Jewish-American fast-food establishment. The menu features meat favorites for lunch and dinner.

Now We're Cook'n Grill, 710 Central St., Highland Park, ☎ 847-432-7310. You'll be challenged to choose from this extensive menu of meat choices, ranging from Texas beef ribs, to herb chicken to a selection of pastas. Most dinners come with filling sides. The restaurant is open for lunch and dinner.

Slice of Life, 4120-26 W. Dempster St., Skokie, ☎ 847-674-2021. A healthy variety tempts diners with wholesome vegetarian and dairy dishes. Italian specialties, as well as fish dishes and soups, salads, and desserts, are available for lunch and dinner. The restaurant operates a full-service bar. It is also open for breakfast, and after Shabbat on Saturday evening.

Tu Do Restaurant, 3320 W. Dempster St., Skokie, ☎ 847-675-8836. Thai favorites feature chicken, beef, and vegetarian selections, as well as noodles, soups, and salads, for lunch and dinner.

JEWISH COMMUNITY CENTERS

More than a half-dozen JCCs and satellites in the Chicago area serve the community, from providing day care to senior services. But the three listed here offer expanded fitness services, which is what most traveling members are seeking.

Bernard Horwich JCC, 3003 W. Touhy Ave., ☎ 773-761-9100, www.jccofchicago.org. This JCC offers a full-service fitness facility with fully equipped workout areas, exercise classes, indoor pool, personal trainers, and a basketball gym. Kids will love the climbing wall. Follow your workout with a relaxing sauna and a meal in the Council Café, offering cafeteria-style breakfast and lunch.

Mayer Kaplan JCC, 5050 W. Church St., Skokie, ☎ 847-675-2200, www.jccofchicago.org. Another family-oriented fitness center, with kids' locker rooms and indoor swimming pool. The workout and strength training rooms offer state-of-the-art cardiovascular and weight training equipment, personal training, and instruction. Sauna, steam, and whirlpools are available in the adult locker room. The Kaplan center also houses a theater and a full-service library.

Bernard Weinger JCC, 300 Revere Dr., Northbrook, ☎ 847-205-9480, www.jccofchicago.org. Full fitness facilities and an aquatic center are available at this JCC in the northern suburb of Northbrook. There's also a schedule of aerobics, yoga, and other mind-body classes – some are structured for walk-ins.

SHOPPING

Bariff Gift Shop, Spertus Institute, 618 S. Michigan Ave., ☎ 312-322-1740. Original artwork by Jewish artists or with a Judaic theme, as well as ceremonial objects, books, and music.

Chicago Hebrew Bookstore, 2942 W. Devon, ☎ 773-973-6465.

Destination Judaica Gift Gallery, at Anshe Emet, 3760 N. Pine Grove, ☎ 773-868-5132, www.ansheemet.org. Everything from Purim costumes to beauty products from the Dead Sea, as well as the traditional ceremonial objects and life-cycle events gifts.

Hamakor Gallery Ltd., 4150 W. Dempster St., Skokie, ☎ 847-677-4150, www.jewishsource.com. You get the catalog; here's the source of all that great stuff: Judaic fine art, jewelry, ceremonial objects, books, and more.

Juke Box, 2957 W. Devon Ave., ☎ 773-274-1269. An all-Jewish music store with thousands of CDs, cassettes, videos, and music books. State-of-the-art listening units make your selection process easier.

Marcus Studio, 1900 Beverly Pl., ☎ 847-432-8425.

Maya Polsky Galleries, 311 W. Superior St., ☎ 312-440-0055.

Menshenables Judaica, 1173 McHenry Rd., Buffalo Grove, ☎ 847-478-8282.

Richard Bitterman, 1701 W. Chase Ave., ☎ 773-743-1511.

Rosenblum's World of Judaica, 2906 W. Devon, ☎ 773-262-1700.

Terri Miller Galleries, 4263 Teri-Lyn Lane, Northbrook, ☎ 847-564-4023. A co-op of Jewish artists, working in painting, sculpture, fabrics, ceramics, and graphics.

LODGING

Anshe Sholom B'nai Israel Congregation, 540 W. Melrose St., ☎ 773-248-9200. Anshe Sholom, in Lake View, offers home hospitality and meals.

EVENTS

Greater Chicago Jewish Folk Arts Festival, 8939 Karlov Ave., Skokie, ☎ 847-675-1998, www.pocet.org. This biennial festival of Jewish music, art, dance, and food has been drawing crowds since 1980 to a celebration of Jewish culture and art. The next event is scheduled for June 16, 2002. The Festival is one of the largest and longest-running Jewish festivals in the United States, and the largest Jewish event in the Chicago area. The outdoor showcase includes seven hours of continuous music and dance on four stages, a hands-on activity area, an art fair, a craft fair, and an ethnic food fair.

> ### ❖ DID YOU KNOW?
>
> Actor and Yiddish song revivalist Mandy Patinkin first entertained crowds at a neighborhood youth center in Hyde Park.

Jewish Film Project, Film Center of the School of the Art Institute of Chicago, Columbus Dr. and Jackson Blvd. entrance, ☎ 312-322-1769, www.spertus.edu. The year-round film series is sponsored by Spertus and the Film Center to bring films of Jewish and Israeli focus to viewers. The screenings are scheduled two to three times a month at the Film Center. Call Spertus to order tickets and get the schedule.

Asher Library Book Fair, Spertus Institute, 618 S. Michigan Ave., ☎ 312-922-9012, www.spertus.edu. A one-day celebration of Jewish books is slated for late November, with the focus on adult topics. Authors speak and sign books throughout the day. At least one children's author is also scheduled.

CHICAGO

Something Else!, Spertus Institute, 618 S. Michigan Ave., ☎ 312-922-9012, www.spertus.edu. Except when December 25th falls on Shabbat, Spertus Institute is the place to be for Jewish families. A day packed with entertainment, music, projects, games, and fun is a great alternative to a movie and Chinese restaurant. No admission charged.

HERITAGE TOURS

Chicago Jewish Historical Society & Tours, Chicago Jewish Historical Society, 618 S. Michigan Ave., ☎ 312-663-5634. Walking tours of the downtown area and various neighborhoods can be scheduled and customized for various interests. Additionally, the Historical Society offers a summer schedule of tours to nearby sights; in 1999, they visited Jewish resort areas in Michigan as well as the historic community of Ligonier, Indiana.

My Kind of Town Tours, 2100 Linden Ave., Highland Park, ☎ 847-432-7003. Leah Axelrod has been leading tours of Chicago, both with a general orientation and a Jewish focus, since 1975. She typically offers a full-day group tour with a lunch stop and transportation included, for $50 per person. Group size is anywhere from 15 to 55. All of Axelrod's tours are customized to the particular interests of the group.

RESOURCES

Jewish United Fund/Jewish Federation of Metropolitan Chicago, 1 S. Franklin St., ☎ 312-346-6700, www.juf.org.

Chicago Jewish Historical Society, 618 S. Michigan, ☎ 312-663-5634.

Virtual Jewish Chicago, www.vjc.org.

The Jewish Chicago Community on the Internet, www.jewish-chicago.com.

Jewish Genealogical Society of Illinois, ☎ 312-666-0100 or ☎ 847-679-3268, www.jewishgen.org.

Newberry Library, 60 W. Walton St., ☎ 312-943-9090. Largest collection of pre-1800 Hebraica in US. A family-history section with important Jewish resources.

Chicago Jewish Star, ☎ 847-674-7827. A twice-monthly newspaper, free. Chicago and suburbs.

Chicago Jewish News, 2501 W. Peterson Ave., ☎ 773-728-3636, www.chijewishnews.com. Weekly newspaper, sold primarily by subscription.

Jewish Image, 6132 N. Monticello St., ☎ 312-583-4001. Monthly magazine; free distribution.

JUF News, 1. S. Franklin St., Ste. 701G, ☎ 312-357-4848. A monthly news magazine, published by the Jewish United Fund, which also publishes an annual directory, a guide to Jewish Chicago.

The Jews of Chicago: From Shtetl to Suburb, by Irving Cutler, 1996, University of Illinois Press.

Chicago Convention and Tourism Bureau, ☎ 312-567-8500, www.chicago.il.org.

❖ **DID YOU KNOW?**

Max Adler's hobby was astrology. He was a fiend for planetariums and visited them when he traveled. A principal in Sears Roebuck & Co., he built the 1930 Adler Planetarium and Astronomical Museum on the Chicago lakefront – the first in the Western Hemisphere.

CHICAGO

CLEVELAND

If you're lucky enough to explore Jewish Cleveland with Judah Rubinstein, you're likely to start at a spot overlooking Jacobs Field. Not that the new baseball stadium has much to do with Jewish history, but – as Rubinstein, a long-time resident and local historian, will tell you – this is where the earliest roots of the Jewish community in Cleveland took hold. Here, 19 immigrants from Bavaria settled in 1839, after following fellow townsman Simpson Thormon, who established his fur trading business in the wilds of Ohio.

Sadly, much of a tour of Jewish Cleveland involves visiting spots such as Jacobs Field – and learning about what is no longer there. Many of the original institutions have been demolished or abandoned. However, some landmark sites remain. In addition to a first-rate Judaica museum situated in a National Landmark synagogue, Cleveland offers some wonderful examples of 20th-century synagogue architecture, a historic cemetery, and former synagogues-turned-churches. Most of the sightseeing, however, should involve a vehicle *and* a knowledgeable tour guide.

Rubinstein rattles off names of now-nonexistent Jewish institutions or shops, wracking his memory for an exact address here, a precise date there, as he recounts the story of the German settlers who scratched out livelihoods as peddlers, cigar rollers, tailors, and proprietors of dry goods stores, butcher shops, and bakeries.

Between 1880 and the 1920s, Cleveland's Jewish population grew from 3,500 to 90,000 with the influx of immigrants from Eastern Europe – and over time the community abandoned the central city. Jews moved ever eastward, from Woodland to the 105th

Street area to Glenville to Cleveland Heights. What eventually emerged was a ring of communities where Jews settled, which includes Cleveland Heights, South Euclid, University Heights, and Shaker Heights. Today landmark Jewish institutions and agencies remain as evidence of the neighborhoods' once-vibrant communities. For example, Mt. Sinai Hospital, nearly a century old now, serves the entire community at 105th Street.

❖ DID YOU KNOW?

Cleveland's Jewish community has produced a number of proactive rabbis who've gained international renown. **Rabbi Abba Hillel Silver** (of The Temple-Tifereth Israel) is recognized for his role in Zionism and the promotion of Israel's statehood. **Rabbi Barnett Brickner** was a nationally known leader of the Fairmount Temple (known during his leadership as the Brickner Temple). And **Rabbi Lelyveld,** also of the Fairmount Temple, marched with many Civil Rights leaders in the 1960s.

The eastern migration continues today, as Jews settle in suburbs such as Beachwood, Pepper Pike, Solon, and Chagrin Falls. But the Taylor Road area remains a hub of Jewish life, including a vibrant Orthodox community. Clustered in the neighborhood are synagogues, restaurants, and Judaica shops. Several Jewish agencies committed to staying in the older neighborhoods in order to stabilize them, beginning in the 1960s when the Federation built its new offices at 18th and Euclid.

Now numbering approximately 80,000, the Cleveland Jewish community has faced struggles with a diminishing population in the past decades. But the visitor to Cleveland will find welcoming congregations, and hospitable residents such as historian Judah Rubinstein, only too happy to share their history and pride in the Jewish community with those who express interest.

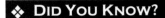

> **❖ DID YOU KNOW?**
>
> Comedian Adam Sandler reminds us that Paul Newman is "half-Jewish." But what his Chanuka anthem failed to mention is that Newman hailed from Shaker Heights. His family still owns Newman Stern Sporting Goods in Cleveland.

SIGHTSEEING HIGHLIGHTS

MUSEUMS & GALLERIES

The Temple Museum of Religious Art, University Circle at Silver Park, ☎ 216-831-3233, www.ttti.org. Founded in 1950, this is the fourth-oldest Judaica museum in the United States. Housed in the National Landmark synagogue of The Temple-Tifereth Israel (see page 58), the museum holds a collection of ceremonial and ritual Judaica objects, Torah scrolls saved from the Holocaust, Torah ornaments – dating to 17th-century Europe – and bibles, historic documents, sculpture, and paintings by famous Jewish artists. The museum has a satellite gallery in Beachwood, at 26000 Shaker Blvd. (same phone number). The museum is open by appointment only. Hours: Monday-Friday, 9-4.

Olyn and Joseph B. Horwitz Collection, Anshe Chesed – Fairmount Temple, 23737 Fairmount Blvd., ☎ 216-464-1330. The synagogue has completed a major renovation and the art collection is now displayed in its own gallery. In addition to the Horwitz collection of ceremonial objects and Judaica, the Fairmount Temple is generously scattered with sculpture, tapestries, and ritual objects of note – almost all of it abstract or modern, to complement the building's architecture. The entrance is guarded by two mosaic pillars designed by Abraham Rattner, whose tapestries and textile art decorate the interior.

HISTORIC SITES

Park Synagogue, 3300 Mayfield Rd., ☎ 216-371-2244. The modern, gold-domed synagogue is a Cleveland Heights landmark. It was designed by prominent architect Erich Mendelsohn in 1951,

CLEVELAND

and described by local historian Judah Rubinstein as "a gem." Inside is a collection of Jewish art and sculpture.

The Temple-Tifereth Israel, University Circle at Silver Park, ☎ 216-831-3233, www.ttti.org. The National Landmark synagogue was designed by renowned Boston architect Charles Greco and dedicated in 1924. It's Byzantine, with three domes. The synagogue also houses The Temple Museum of Religious Art (see page 57). But the artistic details of the building itself are worth of admiration. See the stained-glass windows designed by artist Arthur Szyk.

Liberty Hill Baptist Church, 8206 Euclid Ave., ☎ 216-791-5841. The former site of the Anshe Chesed synagogue, or Euclid Avenue Temple, is a designated historic landmark. The congregation, organized in 1846, built the synagogue in 1912. The structure is now used by a local church. Distinctively Jewish symbols are still clearly visible in the brick and mortar of the exterior, and the Tiffany stained-glass windows are striking.

Cory United Methodist Congregation, 1117 East 105 St. (between Grantwood and Drexel), ☎ 216-451-9704. Built in 1922, the former Cleveland Jewish Center is now a church. But large Roman columns hint at its Judaic origins. Inscribed in Hebrew on the columns are the name of great Jewish thinkers and leaders, including Rashi and Rambam. What's most interesting, though, is the indoor pool. The congregation leaders, hoping to make it a center of community life, built the pool, thus earning the synagogue the nickname, "the shul with the pool."

The Civic, 3130 Mayfield Rd., ☎ 216-371-3498. The Moorish-Byzantine structure continues to attract attention. The former site of Congregation B'nai Jeshuran, built in 1926, was designed by noted architect Charles Greco (he built The Temple Tifereth's current structure). The Civic houses several organizations, but residents comment on the fact that the building is still remembered as a synagogue.

Friendship Baptist Church, Willson Ave. and East 55th St., no telephone. There's little to indicate this stately structure was once a synagogue. But the regal edifice was built for congregation Tifereth Israel in 1894 – making it Cleveland's oldest standing building that was originally constructed as a synagogue.

The **Shiloh Baptist Church,** East 55th and Scoville, ☎ 216-881-7337. In 1906 Congregation B'nai Jeshuran built a grand, golden-domed structure that dominated the neighborhood skyline for decades. Today the building serves as a church, and the golden dome was removed quite some time ago. Worth a drive-by.

❖ DID YOU KNOW?

To care for children orphaned by the Civil War, Cleveland's B'nai Brith established the Jewish Orphan Asylum. (One of its wards was Maurice Saltzman, philanthropist and founder of Bobbie Brooks women's wear.) The institution is now called Bellefaire and is known nationwide as an excellent residential treatment facility for troubled adolescents.

MONUMENTS, MARKERS & MEMORIALS

Hebrew Cultural Gardens, north of Superior Rd. on East Blvd., no telephone. In the early 1920s, the community began developing a series of cultural gardens – German, Hungarian, Japanese, Shakespearean. One of the first planted was the Hebrew Cultural Garden in the 105th Street area. No Jewish community remains in the neighborhood, but the garden is maintained, although a little wilted from its former glory. Much of the flora, based around a pond, was biblical in theme, including cedars, myrtle, and willow trees. Zionist leaders planted trees here in the early 1930s.

Willett Street Cemetery, 2254 Fulton Rd., ☎ 216-321-1733. One of the few Jewish sites on the west side of the city, the cemetery is the oldest Jewish burial site in the region. A stroll through the cemetery will reveal the headstones of the first German settlers who came from Bavaria in the late 1830s. The cemetery is no longer active, but is still maintained by congregations Tifereth Israel and Anshe Chesed.

NEIGHBORHOODS

Taylor Road. Older, tree-shaded single-family homes and lowrise apartment complexes fill the neighborhoods in the Taylor Road area, bounded by Cedar and Mayfield roads. The business stretches feature local institutions such as Ungers Kosher Foods

CLEVELAND

and Shimon's Fish and Chicken. Several Orthodox shuls, a Hebrew day school, and Jewish agencies – not to mention the city's only Jewish funeral home (actually an amalgamation of five separate funeral directors) – are scattered throughout. Although the Cleveland Jewish population, including the Orthodox community, continues to migrate to eastern suburbs, Taylor Road, firmly entrenched even in the 1930s, still emanates a strong Jewish feel. From I-271 on the East Side, Take the Cedar Road exit and go west to Taylor Road. From downtown, take Euclid Avenue and turn right onto Mayfield Road.

COLLEGES & UNIVERSITIES

Cleveland College of Jewish Studies, 26500 Shaker Blvd., Beachwood, ☎ 216-464-4050. The accredited institution of higher Jewish learning offers degree programs at the undergraduate and graduate level, a day high school, as well as continuing education courses for adults. But of greater interest to the visitor are its ongoing educational exhibits on Jewish culture. The facility houses part of the Olyn and Joseph B. Horwitz Judaica Collection – other artifacts of this large collection are maintained at the Fairmount Temple (see page 57) and the Klutznik Museum in Washington DC. Hours: Monday-Thursday, 8:30-5; Friday, 8:30-4.

Telshe Rabbinical College – Tanenbaum Campus, Euclid Ave. and East 284th St., Wickliffe, ☎ 440-943-5300. There's really nothing of sightseeing note on this lovely campus housing a rabbinical institution. But the history of both the college and the estate it now occupies is interesting. Organized in Lithuania in 1875, the yeshiva faced annihilation during World War II. Some students and teachers escaped first to Shanghai, and eventually founded this campus on a former estate outside of Cleveland.

❖ DID YOU KNOW?

What? Superman's from Cleveland? Sort of. Jerry Siegel and Joe Shuster, two imaginative Cleveland teenagers, created the powerful comic-book superhero in the 1930s.

SYNAGOGUES

The Greater Cleveland area offers 30-some synagogues. For a complete list, call the Jewish Information Service, ☎ 216-691-4636.

ORTHODOX

Green Road Synagogue, 2437 Green Rd., Beachwood, ☎ 216-381-4757.

Nearby is the **Green Road Mikvah**, 2479 S. Green Rd., ☎ 216-381-3170.

Taylor Road Synagogue, 1970 South Taylor Rd., Cleveland Heights, ☎ 216-321-4875.

Telshe Yeshiva, 28400 Euclid Ave., Wickliffe, ☎ 216-943-5300. Offers kosher meals for travelers. Mikvah.

Warrensville Center Synagogue, 1508 Warrensville Center Rd., Cleveland Heights, ☎ 216-382-6566.

Beachwood Kehilla, 25400 Fairmount Blvd., ☎ 216-595-1299.

CONSERVATIVE

B'nai Jeshuran – Temple on the Heights, 27501 Fairmount Blvd., ☎ 216-831-6555.

Congregation Shaarey Tikvah, 26811 Fairmount Blvd., Beachwood. ☎ 216-765-8300.

The Park Synagogue, 3300 Mayfield Rd., ☎ 216-371-2244.

The Park Synagogue East, 27575 Shaker Blvd., Pepper Pike, ☎ 216-831-5363.

Congregation Bethaynu, 27900 Gates Mill Blvd., ☎ 216-292-2931.

Beth Israel – The West Temple, 14308 Triskett Rd., ☎ 216-941-8882.

REFORM

Anshe Chesed – Fairmount Temple, 23737 Fairmount Blvd., ☎ 216-464-1330.

The Suburban Temple, 22401 Chagrin Blvd., ☎ 216-991-0700.

Temple Emanu El, 2200 South Green Rd., ☎ 216-381-6600.

The Temple Tifereth Israel, University Circle at Silver Park, ☎ 216-791-7755.

The Temple East, 26000 Shaker Blvd., ☎ 216-831-3233.

KOSHER DINING

❖ For more detail on hashgachah, contact the **Vaad HaKashruth of Cleveland,** ☎ 216-514-1424. For questions or information about home hospitality in the Orthodox community, call **Orthodox Hospitality,** ☎ 216-321-3845.

Abba's in Cedar Center, 13937 Cedar Rd., South Euclid, ☎ 216-321-5660. This casual meat restaurant features fresh-baked pita, Israeli specialties, as well as Chinese and grill items. The place is open for breakfast, lunch, and dinner.

Contempo Cuisine, 13898 Cedar Rd., ☎ 216-3997-3520. Finer dining and a varied menu of American, Italian, Chinese, and Middle Eastern entrées draws crowds for dinners only.

Empire Kosher Chicken Restaurant, 2234 Warrensville Center Rd., ☎ 216-691-0006. Family favorites range from chicken, turkey, steaks, and sandwiches. Open for lunch and dinner.

Ruchama's, Mandel JCC, 26001 South Woodland Rd., ☎ 216-831-0700. Eat-in or carry-out Israeli and American meat items are available for breakfast or lunch. Ruchama, who also runs an upscale Asian restaurant, is reputed to make the best strudel and bourekas around. Open for lunch.

Ruchama's Singapore, 2172 Warrensville Center Road, University Heights, ☎ 216-321-1100. This upscale establishment bills itself as "Where the Far East meets the Middle East." On the meat menu are Asian specialties, Israeli favorites, and American classics. It's also the only kosher restaurant in Cleveland with a full bar. Open for dinner and lunch, and after Shabbat in the winter.

Kinneret Kosher Restaurant, 1869 South Taylor Rd., ☎ 216-321-1404. The highlight is the pizza, deemed by locals as "the best." But the casual restaurant offers plenty of Israeli and American dishes for lunch and dinner.

Shticks, Cleveland Hillel on CWRU campus, 11291 Euclid Ave., ☎ 216-231-0922. Located in the campus Hillel House, Shticks is open to the general public for lunch and dinner Monday through Thursday, and lunch on Friday. The dairy à la carte menu features made-from-scratch soups, felafel, wraps, and melts. All at student-friendly prices.

Yacov's Restaurant, 13969 Cedar Rd., ☎ 216-932-8848. Yacov's serves up Israeli and Italian dairy and vegetarian favorites, as well as pizza, popular for lunch and dinner.

JEWISH COMMUNITY CENTERS

Mandel JCC, 26001 South Woodland Rd., Beachwood, ☎ 216-831-0700. The Mandel JCC has a family recreation park with an outdoor pool, baseball fields, tennis and basketball courts, and picnic areas. The Mt. Sinai/Annie May Myers Wellness Center is also located at the Mandel JCC. Just opened in the fall of 1999, the Café at the J is a full-service coffee shop with inviting couches, a library of newspapers – and a menu of coffees and desserts.

Mayfield JCC, 3505 Mayfield Rd., Cleveland Heights, ☎ 216-382-4000. Fitness facilities are available for men and women at specific times (call ahead) and include lots of cardio equipment, as well as an indoor swimming pool (also scheduled for mixed and gender-separate swimming), and health club pluses such as steam room, sauna, and whirlpool. The Blanche R. Halle Theatre is located at the Mayfield JCC.

CLEVELAND

Shopping

Treasures Gift Shop, Cleveland College of Jewish Studies, 26500 Shaker Blvd., ☎ 216-464-4050. Authentic Israeli sterling silver, gold jewelry, ritual objects, handicrafts, books.

Frank's Hebrew Book Store, 14425 Cedar Rd., ☎ 216-291-9847. Books, as well as Israeli-made gift ware, music, jewelry, sterling silver kiddush cups, religious supplies.

Jacob's Judaic Book & Gift Center, 13896 Cedar Rd., ☎ 216-321-7200. Books, gifts, music, computer software, art, and religious objects.

JCC Gift Shop, 26001 South Woodland Rd., ☎ 216-831-0700.

Merkaz Judaica, 27629 Chagrin Blvd., ☎ 216-595-0707.

Traditions Art Judaica, 27500 Cedar Rd., Ste. 307, ☎ 216-292-2648. Representing artists who do Judaica. Commission work.

Lodging

Holiday Inn, 28500 Euclid Ave., Wickliffe, ☎ 216-585-2750. The hotel is within walking distance of Telshe Yeshiva, which offers to arrange kosher meals for Jewish travelers. 216-943-4300.

Events

Jewish Book Fair, Mandel JCC, 26001 S. Woodland Rd., Beachwood, ☎ 216-831-0700. Contests for kids, as well as author signings, workshops, and lectures fill a week of activity during the November festivities.

Eugene S. & Blanche R. Halle Theatre, 3505 Mayfield Rd., Cleveland Heights, ☎ 216-382-4000. Plays, performances, and musical entertainment, with a focus on Jewish content from Klezmer to contemporary humor – the JCC's theater presents a variety of entertainment year-round. Some events are held at the Stonehill auditorium at the Mandel JCC.

❖ DID YOU KNOW?

Cleveland's Jewish community seems to breed writers, sculptors, and baseball heroes. Hailing from the city are: authors **Herbert Gold** and **Alix Kates Shulman**; 20th-century sculptors **Max Kalish** and **William Zorach**; and Hall of Famer **Al Rosen**. Also among the Jewish "who's who" are actress **Debra Winger** and former US Senator **Howard Metzenbaum**.

HERITAGE TOURS

Jewish Community Federation of Cleveland, 1750 Euclid Ave., ☎ 216-566-9200, www.jewishcleveland.org. There is no official tour operator that specializes in city explorations with a Jewish focus. But those interested should contact the Federation – there are a few citizens who informally do tours and, depending on their schedules, are frequently happy to oblige a group or family.

RESOURCES

Jewish Community Federation of Cleveland, 1750 Euclid Ave., ☎ 216-566-9200, www.jewishcleveland.org. Their Web site is outstanding; it's well organized and offers complete information.

Jewish Information Services, Mayfield JCC, 3505 Mayfield Rd., ☎ 216-691-4636.

Jewish Genealogy Society of Cleveland, 996 Eastlawn Drive 44143, ☎ 440-449-2326. The JGS helps out-of-town researchers locate "lost" family in Cleveland. It maintains burial lists for six Cleveland Jewish cemeteries. Another good source of genealogical information is the **Western Reserve Historical Society** (☎ 216-721-5722), which houses one of the largest genealogical archives in the country. The two organizations often work together in genealogical or archival pursuits.

Cleveland Jewish News, 3645 Warrensville Center Rd., Ste. 230, ☎ 216-991-8300. This weekly newspaper, published on Fridays, features local, national, and world news of Jewish interest. It's a good source for upcoming community events, and happenings in Cleveland.

The Jewish Scene, Mayfield JCC, 3505 Mayfield Rd., ☎ 216-382-4000. A locally produced radio magazine featuring news, entertainment, people, events, Torah commentary, and more. Music. WERE AM 1300 (6:30 am); WUJC FM 88.7 (7 am); WRRO AM 1440 (9 am); and WCLV FM 95.5 (6:05 pm) on Sundays.

History of the Jews of Cleveland, by Lloyd Gartner, and *Merging Traditions,* by Sydney Vincent and Judah Rubinstein. These two books, written by Cleveland natives, chronicle in depth the growth and maturation of the Cleveland Jewish community.

Convention and Visitors Bureau of Greater Cleveland, ☎ 216-621-4110.

DENVER

G old fever and the itch to go west infected Jewish adventurers who sought their fortunes in Colorado. Today, visitors can trace their history in graveyards that date back to the 1880s, in sturdy old buildings, and in some of the city's most visited museums.

The history of Jews in Denver began in the 1850s, when prairie schooners started delivering Jewish settlers to the rough-and-tumble mining camps that dotted the area. The first Jew known to have been in Colorado was Solomon Nunes Carvalho, artist and photographer with Colonel John C. Fremont's 1853-1854 expedition.

One such new arrival was Fred Salomon, who in short order built a store (the area's first brick building), dug the first water supply ditch, helped organize the first bank, was key in bringing the railroad, and opened the first brewery in Denver.

Others joined him. By Rosh Hashana in 1859, there were enough Jews for a minyan. They held the first Jewish services in Colorado on the banks of the Cherry Creek River. By 1866, 100 Jews lived in Denver, and a mohel was brought in. During the 1860s and 70s, Jews established stores, banks, theaters, stagecoach lines, freight companies, and saloons.

Denver's Jews enjoyed positions of respect and prominence from the earliest days. The Jewish population boomed between 1870 and 1890. The community was strongly secular, largely made up of Germans. Eastern Europeans followed toward the end of the 19th century.

DENVER

❖ DID YOU KNOW?

Fans of the Guggenheim Museum have the Colorado mining country to thank for the wealth in treasures exhibited there. The Guggenheim fortune began in Leadville, just a couple of hours from Denver, where the family's $5,000 interest in one of the mines exploded into $15 million in just a few years.

Besides gold fever, the "white plague," tuberculosis, did a lot to stimulate the healthy growth of the Jewish population in Denver. During the early years of the 20th century, TB wracked the tenement populations of the East Coast and Midwest, and many took their cure in the rejuvenating mountain air of the Rockies. The AMC Cancer Research Center, then known as the Jewish Consumptives' Relief Society, and the National Jewish Center for Immunology and Respiratory Medicine are institutions of Jewish origins that attracted many Jews, including the sister of Golda Meir.

Modern Denver holds major sights of Jewish interest – including a nationally acclaimed Jewish museum, a Holocaust memorial, and a restored home once lived in by Golda Meir – not to mention a spectacular resource in the Center for Jewish Studies under the auspices of the University of Denver. The **Ira M. Beck Memorial Archives** houses more than a million documents, 5,000 photos, 400 oral histories, and a manuscript collection.

Although an Orthodox community remains in the West Colfax neighborhood, 35% of the more than 95,000 Jews in Denver live in the Hilltop area, and the rest are scattered throughout the metropolitan area. For the traveling Jew seeking a Jewish environment, Denver offers plenty of synagogues of all movements, a thriving Jewish Community Center, a few kosher restaurants, and a calendar of events and activities.

SIGHTSEEING HIGHLIGHTS

MUSEUMS & GALLERIES

Mizel Museum of Judaica, 560 South Monaco Pkwy., ☎ 303-333-4156, www.jewishmuseums.com/mizelmus.htm, e-mail mizelmus@dnvr.uswest.net. The museum is tiny, but mighty. Permanent and changing exhibits give a fascinating perspective of Jewish art and culture, and a wealth of programming offers adults and children hands-on involvement and interactive experiences. For example, accompanying an exhibit on Cuban Jewish art, visitors might create brightly colored tiles and mosaics of their own, make musical instruments, or watch a film about Cuba's Jewish immigrants. Such programs generally cost $2 to $5. Seven major exhibits are mounted each year with a schedule of complimentary lectures, dances, poetry readings, films, and music performances. The museum's permanent collections feature four themes – Torah, Beautifying Rituals, Pioneering Jews of Colorado, and The Legacy of Bezalel: The Israel Arts and Crafts Movement. Hours: Monday-Friday, 10-4; Sunday, noon-4; Closed Saturday and holidays. No admission charged.

Singer Art Gallery, JCC, 350 South Dahlia St., ☎ 303-399-2660, www.mizelarts.com. Opened in 1995, the gallery is housed in the new wing of the Mizel Family Cultural Arts Center. Six changing exhibits are featured each year, featuring Jewish art, Jewish themes, and Jewish artists. The exhibits are enhanced by public programs, lectures, panel discussions, talks, films, and performances. One past exhibit, "Red Scare/Black List," explored the impact of McCarthyism on the arts. Hours: Monday-Friday, 9-4; Sunday 1-4; Closed Saturday and holidays. No admission charged.

> ### ❖ DID YOU KNOW?
>
> Who knew Barbie was Jewish? Ruth Handler, creator of Mattel's most famous 12-inch supermodel, is originally from Denver.

Emanuel Gallery, 10th and Lawrence, Auraria Higher Education Center, ☎ 303-556-8337. Atop the stone building, the star of David and Hebrew lettering attest to the fact that this historical

DENVER

structure was once a synagogue. The edifice, originally built as a church in 1877, was purchased by Shearith Israel in 1903, and the small but active congregation thrived there until 1958, when it moved to a new building. The structure, also known as the Tenth Street Shul, was named a historic landmark in 1976. Today it serves as a student information center and art gallery. Nothing remains inside to remind visitors of its former days as a synagogue. The memorial tablets that once hung inside are now at Congregation Rodef Shalom, 450 S. Kearney.

HISTORIC SITES

Golda Meir House, 1146 Ninth St., Auraria Campus, ☎ 303-556-3291. In 1913, 15-year-old Goldie Mabovitch ran away from her parents' home in Milwaukee to live with her sister, who came to Denver for the TB cure. She attended high school, worked, met Morris Meyerson, the man she would marry, and, of course, left Denver for Palestine where she Hebraicized her name to Golda Meir and became one of Israel's greatest leaders. Her Denver home, a modest brick duplex, has been moved, restored, and opened as a museum. Its journey, perhaps not as momentous as Golda's, has been fraught with struggle all the same, confronting financial threats, vandalism, and near-demolition. The living room and bedroom hold exhibits and original artifacts, including a mezuzah, a tzedakah box, and a notice admonishing the residents to "bury your dead chickens and stop throwing them out in the alley." The home is currently open by appointment only. The staff appreciates 24-hour notice, but can often accommodate same-day appointments. Admission is free.

Isaac Solomon Synagogue, AMC Cancer Research Center, 1600 Pierce St., Lakewood, ☎ 303-233-6501. On the grounds of the center stands the synagogue, a reminder of the complex's origins as the Jewish Consumptives' Relief Society treatment center for tuberculosis in 1904. The synagogue, built in 1925, as well as the entire campus reflect the look and feel of the original center. A small cottage replicates the patient accommodations. The site is on the National Register of Historic Places.

Anfenger House, 2900 Champa St., Curtis Park. No telephone. The stately, Italianate mansion was built in 1884, as the Curtis Park area attracted Denver's wealthy. Louis Anfenger, a prominent Jew and active founder of Temple Emanuel, lived in the home until his death in 1900. The neighborhood has gone through a period of neglect, and the house itself has some sordid stories attached to it. During the early 1970s, it was known as the "House of Nightmares," when a self-avowed voodoo priest lived in it. It was purchased in 1976 by Historic Denver and declared a historic landmark. Currently, it is privately owned and not open for tours.

Pearl Street Temple Center, 16th and Pearl St., ☎ 303-860-9400. "Synagogues in Denver don't look like this anymore," observes one member of the Jewish community. Indeed, the dramatic Moorish structure might seem more fitting in Spain or Morocco. The building served the Temple Emanuel congregation from 1899 until the late 1950s, then as the home for two churches. In the 1980s, the building was saved from demolition and restored as the Pearl Street Temple Center. The publicly owned center is dedicated to preserving and restoring the building, and attracting artistic and cultural events. Its distinctive stained-glass windows and elegant ambiance enhance a festive mood, whatever special event is held here.

MONUMENTS, MARKERS & MEMORIALS

Babi Yar Park, Havana and Yale roads, ☎ 303-759-1827. Two stone tablets stand in haunting tribute to the 200,000 Jews and Ukraines murdered at Babi Yar in 1941. The scruffy, sparse landscaping is designed to recreate the desolate terrain of Babi Yar, near Kiev in the Ukraine. The site, in addition to acres of open space that invite reflection, includes an amphitheater, a special audio program, a grove of trees, and a walled bridge traversing a gulley. Babi Yar Park is listed by the Smithsonian Institute as one of Denver's most noted statues and memorials. The park is open from dawn till dusk.

Golden Hill Cemetery, 12000 West Colfax, Golden, ☎ 303-237-0573. The cemetery was established in 1920, but grave sites date back to the 1890s. Originally, the burial grounds were established as a charity cemetery, and much of the graveyard is divided into areas where the wealthy are buried and others of mostly paupers' graves. The grave of David Edelstadt, 19th-century Yiddish poet, is here. His epitaph, in Yiddish, is from one of his poems.

DENVER

NEIGHBORHOODS

West Colfax Area. Once the heart of Jewish Denver, the West Colfax area harbored synagogues, kosher delis, butchers, bakeries, mikvahs, Yiddish theater, and schools. Little survives of the community that, today, is overtaken by the Colfax viaduct. Some buildings that still stand are the former **Solf Building,** 2644 West Colfax, the current home of Brooklyn's, a sports bar. Through the first half of the 20th century, the site was the Schachet Mercantile Company, a major, Jewish-owned department store with delicatessen. **Rude Park,** at 13th and Decatur and named for the philanthropist Isadore Rude who built it, was once a popular family gathering spot. An Orthodox community still lives in the area, supporting a yeshiva, a school for girls, two Orthodox synagogues, and a mikvah. Occasionally the **Rocky Mountain Jewish Historical Society** (☎ 303-871-3016) runs tours of the neighborhood. It's advisable to go with someone who knows the area – the half-dozen or more drive-by sights are difficult to discern if you don't know they're there.

❖ DID YOU KNOW?

Bugsy Siegel may have spent his most notorious hours in Las Vegas, but when he was in Denver, he frequented the deli at the Schachet Mercantile Company, where Brooklyn's, a sports bar, stands today.

GENERAL-INTEREST SIGHTS
WITH JEWISH CONNECTION

Colorado Railroad Museum, 17555 W. 44th Ave (State Highway 58) in Golden, ☎ 303-279-4591. Jewish pioneer Otto Mears played a major role in the building of the Silverton (1887) railroads, and also marked trails that evolved into roads. His toll roads and rail routes are used today. While there's not much detail specifically about Mears, train lovers will be fascinated. Hours: Daily 9-5. Admission: $4 adults; $2 children under 16; $9.50 families.

Colorado Hall of Fame, 200 E. Colfax Ave., ☎ 303-866-2604. The rotunda in the State Capitol features stained-glass window portraits of 16 outstanding Colorado pioneers. Featured are two Jews – Frances Wisebart Jacobs, known as "the mother of Charities," for her community work and donations, and pioneer Otto Mears. Hours: Monday-Saturday, 9:30-2:30. Free admission.

SYNAGOGUES

Approximately 25 congregations serve the Denver and Boulder areas; many are loosely structured havurot that don't offer full service, Shabbat, or daily minyan services. Check with the Synagogue Council of Greater Denver (☎ 303-759-8485) for details about these and other area synagogues.

ORTHODOX

B.M.K.Y. (TRI), 295 S. Locust St., ☎ 303-377-1200 or 399-8917. In addition to home hospitality, this congregation offers a weekly calendar of classes and "drop-in" sessions.

BMH-BJ Congregation, 560 South Monaco Pkwy., ☎ 303-388-4203.

CONSERVATIVE

Hebrew Educational Alliance, 3600 S. Ivanhoe, ☎ 303-758-9400.

Rodef Shalom, 450 S. Kearney, ☎ 303-399-0035.

REFORM

Congregation Emanuel, 51 Grape St., ☎ 303-388-4013.

Temple Micah, 2600 Leyden, ☎ 303-388-4239.

Temple Sinai, 3509 S. Glencoe, ☎ 303-759-1827.

RECONSTRUCTIONIST

B'nai Havurah, 6445 East Ohio Ave., ☎ 303-388-4441.

DENVER

KOSHER DINING

❖ For more information regarding updates on kashrut designation, or to find out about groceries, delis, bakeries, and caterers that offer kosher items, call the **Vaad Hakashrus of Denver,** ☎ 303-595-9349.

East Side Kosher Deli, 5475 Leetsdale Dr., ☎ 303-322-9862. Eat in or carry out from this meat deli that also offers groceries. Its mission is to provide the best Glatt kosher food available at reasonable prices.

Mediterranean Health Café, 2817 East 3rd Ave., ☎ 303-399-2940. A health-oriented menu features standard Middle Eastern dishes (felafel platters, hummus, tabouli) as well as some fusion fare – pita enchilada, linguini Southwestern, and sweet & sour tofu. All items are dairy, fish, or vegetarian. Hours: Monday-Thursday, 11-8; Friday, 11-2; Sunday, noon-8.

JEWISH COMMUNITY CENTERS

Jewish Community Center of Denver, 350 S. Dahlia St., ☎ 303-399-2660, e-mail jccdenvr@ix.netcom.com, www.jccdenver.org. The complex features a full-service Sports & Fitness Center with a schedule of classes, extensive exercise equipment, and an indoor and outdoor pool. The Mizel Family Cultural Arts Center offers films, theater productions, concerts, and the Singer Art Gallery features changing exhibits.

SHOPPING

Boutique Judaica, 5078 East Hampden Ave., ☎ 303-757-1317.

Aharon's Books, 400 South Holly St., ☎ 800-850-1770 or ☎ 303-329-0211.

EVENTS

Jewish Cultural Festival, Robert E. Loup Jewish Community Center, 350 South Dahlia St., ☎ 303-399-2660. A frenzy of food, music, dancing, crafts, and children's activities is a joyous celebration that reaches out to the entire community. The event, which includes the Denver Jewish Folk Music Festival, is scheduled each year in August or September. A highlight is the Chicken Soup Cookoff. Hours: Sunday, 11-5. No admission fee.

JCC Celebration of Books, Robert E. Loup Jewish Community Center, 350 South Dahlia St., ☎ 303-399-2660. Scheduled in late fall for Chanuka shopping convenience, the book fair is indeed a celebration – with thousands of books of Jewish interest and content, and featuring a schedule of Jewish authors, a lecture series, family activities, and a Chanuka gift shop. The schedule for the two-week event varies from day to day. Admission charged for some of the programs.

Denver Jewish Film Festival, Robert E. Loup Jewish Community Center, 350 South Dahlia St., ☎ 303-399-2660. The seven-day celebration of Jewish film is held in August and is co-sponsored by the Denver Film Society. The films are complemented by lectures and exhibits. The schedule of films varies. Tickets are $7; packages are available.

Sounds of Summer Music Under the Stars, Robert E. Loup Jewish Community Center, 350 South Dahlia St., ☎ 303-399-2660. The JCC's outdoor summer concert series always features Jewish performers and Jewish music, but themes vary from year to year. Concerts are scheduled during summer evenings, usually Thursday, at dusk. Bring blankets, buy a box dinner, sit back, and enjoy the show! Admission: $15 per performance.

HERITAGE TOURS

Rocky Mountain Jewish Historical Society, Center for Judaic Studies, University of Denver, ☎ 303-871-3016, e-mail jabrams@du.edu. Knowledgeable professors and guides from the Center for Judaic Studies lead ad hoc tours as requested. A typical tour is

DENVER

three hours and can be arranged for groups of varying sizes. Call at least a month in advance to schedule.

RESOURCES

Allied Jewish Federation of Colorado, 300 South Dahlia St., Ste. 300, ☎ 303-321-3399.

Chabad/Lubavitch of Colorado, 400 South Holly St., ☎ 303-329-0211.

Vaad Hakashrus of Denver, 1350 Vrain, ☎ 303-595-9349.

Intermountain Jewish News, 1275 Sherman Ave., Ste. 214, ☎ 303-861-2234.

Jewish Genealogy Society of Colorado, ☎ 303-755-8384 (evenings).

Rocky Mountain Jewish Historical Society, Center for Judaic Studies, University of Denver, ☎ 303-871-3016, e-mail jabrams@ du.edu.

Exploring Jewish Colorado, by Phil Goodstein (Denver Institute of Jewish Studies, 1992).

Denver Metro Convention and Visitors Bureau, 1555 California, Ste. 300, ☎ 303-892-1112.

❖ DID YOU KNOW?

The Schwayder Brothers, who settled in Denver at the turn of the century, are the founders of the luggage dynasty, Samsonite. When, in 1907, the brothers designed a suitcase strong enough to endure the brutal beatings of travel, they named their product after a favorite Biblical hero, Samson.

DETROIT

In sites as surprising as a downtown auto plant, a church, and an industrial skyline, Detroit's Jewish legacy emerges to claim its part in shaping the city landscape. Although many Jewish structures have been razed, the visitor or curious Detroiter will discover fascinating finds, not to mention a world-renowned Holocaust Center and some fine galleries and museums.

The Jewish presence in Detroit dates back to 1762 when Montreal fur trader Chapman Abraham settled here. The Jewish population grew slowly until 1880, when the city experienced an explosive influx of Eastern Europeans fleeing pogroms. Within a 20-year period, the Jewish census jumped from 1,000 to 10,000.

The community flourished in the 20th century, with Jewish leaders contributing to all facets of Detroit life – from music to business to architecture to sports. Architect Albert Kahn's pioneering designs for factories, business headquarters, and synagogues, are well-preserved throughout the city. World-famed conductor of the Detroit Symphony Orchestra (1918-1936) Ossip Gabrilowitsch, married to Mark Twain's daughter, Clara Clemens, insisted on building the acoustically perfect Orchestra Hall, recently restored and in use once again. And, of course, baseball great Hank Greenberg led the Detroit Tigers to victory after victory in the 1930s and 40s.

❖ DID YOU KNOW?

Baseball Hall of Famer **Hank Greenberg** played for the **Detroit Tigers** from 1933 to 1946. During the 1934 pennant race, his refusal to play on Yom Kippur created controversy among baseball fans throughout the country. One Detroit native argued that the Jewish holidays occurred each year, but Detroit hadn't won a pennant in 25 years. Greenberg attended services at Congregation Shaarey Zedek that Yom Kippur day – and the Tigers lost.

Jews were represented in the city's crime community as well, with one of the country's most remembered crime organizations, the Purple Gang, based in the city's Oakland area. Detroit natives prefer to forget this, as well as other ugly chapters of the city's history. During the 1920s and 30s the virulent Father Coughlin and his flock stirred anti-Semitic passions nationwide. Today there is little evidence of these times – the reign of the Purple Gang fizzled out generations ago. The church in Royal Oak from which Father Coughlin preached still stands, but the congregation now hosts interdenominational Holocaust memorials – dismantling the anti-Semitic image that once tarnished the city.

Detroit's Jewish population has moved to the suburbs – and indeed the infrastructure of modern Jewish life is found there. Today, an estimated 96,000 Jews live in the tri-county area – more than two-thirds living within southern Oakland County. The largest Jewish neighborhoods are Southfield, West Bloomfield, Farmington Hills, and Oak Park.

Visitors will find a friendly Jewish community, and with nearly 50 congregations, a Jewish Community Center undergoing massive expansion, a world of cultural activities, shops, kosher restaurants, and a calendar of community events, plenty of chances to interact with Detroiters.

SIGHTSEEING HIGHLIGHTS

MUSEUMS & GALLERIES

Holocaust Memorial Center, 6602 West Maple Rd., West Bloomfield, ☎ 248-661-0840, www.holocaustcenter.org, e-mail infor@ holocaustcenter.org. Dedicated in the mid-1980s, Detroit's Holocaust Memorial Center is America's first Holocaust center. The story of persecution is told through dioramas such as the eerily lit Nazi book-burning and the re-created gates of Auschwitz. Visitors listen to the stories of Holocaust survivors in an intimate video theater. The Center not only documents the Holocaust and the historical events leading up to it, but focuses on the thriving 2,000 years of Jewish history that were forever scarred. An extensive information database allows access to historical information about European Jewish communities and Jewish families. Hours: Sunday-Thursday, 10-3:30; Friday, 9-12:30. Closed Friday, June-August. No admission.

Janice Charach Epstein Museum Gallery, Jewish Community Center, 6600 West Maple Rd., West Bloomfield, ☎ 248-661-7641. Works by Jewish artists or of Jewish themes are showcased in this 8,000-square-foot gallery, as new traveling exhibits change every six weeks. An annual glass show, in collaboration with Detroit's world-renowned Habitat Gallery, is a draw each April. Many of the exhibits are selling shows. Docent tours are arranged upon request.

The Shapiro Museum, Temple Beth El, 7400 Telegraph Rd., Bloomfield Hills, ☎ 248-851-1100. A collection of silver Judaic ceremonial objects grew from the donation of a family collection. Elaborate and detailed, some encrusted with semi-precious stones, candlesticks, Torah pointers, an assortment of whimsical animal-shaped spice boxes, and kiddush cups – one dating to the 16th century – draw fascinating contemplation. Although 90% of the collection is made up of silver ritual pieces, of special interest is a terra cotta jug dating to 800 BCE, a gift from the collection of Moshe Dayan. No admission charged. Call ahead for hours.

HISTORIC SITES

Bonstelle Theater, 3424 Woodward Ave., on the campus of Wayne State University, ☎ 313-577-2960. This structure originally housed Temple Beth El, built by the firm of internationally renowned Detroit architect Albert Kahn in 1902 and served the congregation until 1922. Today it is a theater. While the facade has been renovated, the dramatic dome still dominates the neighborhood skyline.

> ### ❖ DID YOU KNOW?
>
> He may have been the world's greatest escape artist, but **Harry Houdini** (nee Eric Weiss) couldn't escape death in Detroit. Punched in the stomach following a Toronto performance, he performed at the **Garrick Theater** despite fever and pain, then died on Oct. 31, 1926, at Grace Hospital.

Lighthouse Cathedral Church, 8801 Woodward Ave., downtown. ☎ 313-873-4411. This church was originally a synagogue, serving the Temple Beth El congregation from 1922 until the 1970s. Of additional Jewish interest, the classical-style building with Greek columns is an Albert Kahn design (he was a member of the congregation at the time it was built). The stone engraving above the lintel still reads "Beth El." Inside are some impressive Myron Barlow frescoes. Although it is an active church now, visitors are permitted to tour the building when services are not being held.

Site of the first congregation in Detroit, at the corner of East Congress and St. Antoine, downtown. All that remains of Detroit's first official congregation is a small plaque, commemorating the spot where a modest structure housed the members of congregation Bet El, established in 1850.

MONUMENTS, MARKERS & MEMORIALS

Beth Olam Cemetery, Joseph Campau and Clay Avenues, on the site of the General Motors Detroit Hamtramck Plant. No telephone. It's not easy to find this "best-kept secret," partly because the auto plant is protective of its new car designs developed and tested at this site. The walled-in cemetery, inactive since the 1920s, is open to the public only twice a year – the Sunday before Passover and the Sunday before Rosh Hashana – or by special arrangement. Established in 1862 by the then Orthodox congregation Shaarey Zedeck, the historical site hints of the early tribulations of the Jews of Detroit, including an influenza epidemic that wiped out entire families – clusters of headstones share the same family name and indicate death dates within days of each other.

Jewish Cemetery, 1200 Elmwood Ave. A half-block north of Lafayette St. at MacDougal St. ☎ 313-567-3453. Also known as the Beth El Cemetery or Lafayette Street Cemetery, this burial ground was organized by the area's first congregation in 1851. It is now part of the Elmwood Cemetery, a state historical site that was designed by Frederick Law Olmsted, architect of New York City's Central Park. Jewish Civil War soldiers who had been buried in the Beth Olam cemetery were eventually moved to this graveyard, to rest with prominent political figures and soldiers of American wars. Cemetery fans and Jewish genealogy buffs won't want to miss three other graveyards: **Woodmere Cemetery,** 9400 West Fort St., ☎ 313-841-0188, includes a Jewish section that goes back 140 years. Two other cemeteries, both about 90 years old, are **Machpelah,** 21701 Woodward Ave., Ferndale, ☎ 248-542-1146 and **Clover Hill Park Cemetery,** 3607 West 14 Mile Rd., Royal Oak, ☎ 248-549-3411.

NEIGHBORHOODS

Boston-Edison District. Boston and Edison Streets north of Grand Blvd. and west of Woodward Ave. A number of well-known Jewish Detroiters once lived in this historic, tree-shaded neighborhood of 900 prestigious homes built between 1904 and 1922. Just a few blocks from Henry Ford's home lived S. S. Kresge (department store patriarch), Ossip Gabrilowitsch (the father of the city's first symphony), and other notables. In recent years, increased interest in restoring these magnificent mansions to their former splendor has attracted attention and resulted in some fascinating home tours. The Jewish Historical Society will assist in arranging tours with the local neighborhood association.

GENERAL-INTEREST SIGHTS WITH JEWISH CONNECTION

Detroit Historical Museum, 5401 Woodward Ave., ☎ 313-833-1805. Two permanent exhibits showcase the role of the city's Jews. "Frontiers to Factories" features historic figures who influenced Detroit's growth from 1701 to 1901. One such character is Abba Keidan, a Polish Jew who immigrated in the 1880s and opened a store in Detroit. The exhibit also highlights M. Jacob and Sons, one of the seven local businesses listed that were founded by Jews and in business for a century or more. In the "Motor City" exhibit, featuring highlights of the 20th century, there's a section on Albert Kahn, and some of the major Detroit area landmarks he designed. Hours: Wednesday-Friday, 9:30-5, Saturday-Sunday, 10-5. Admission: $3 adults, $1.50 seniors and students; children under 12 free.

The **Fisher, General Motors**, and **New Center** buildings, 3011 W. Grand Blvd., 3044 W. Grand Blvd., and 7430 Second Ave., downtown. These are among the city's most notable structures, all National Historic Landmarks, designed by world-renowned industrial architect Albert Kahn. The German-born Kahn pioneered the design of modern factories, and worked successfully with Henry Ford during the 1920s, despite anti-Semitic sentiment in Detroit. In addition to his factory and plant buildings (his work in the Soviet Union was said to have saved some buildings from Nazi destruction), he designed several Jewish institutions in Detroit, including the Temple Beth El synagogue and the Shaarey Zedeck synagogue in Southfield.

SYNAGOGUES

Nearly 50 congregations in metropolitan Detroit serve a Jewish population that is largely concentrated in three suburbs. The following are some of the largest and most well-known.

ORTHODOX

Chabad Torah Center, 5595 West Maple Rd., West Bloomfield, ☎ 248-855-6170. There is also a mikvah on site. To learn about other Chabad congregations in the Detroit area, call ☎ 248-737-7000.

Congregation Or Chadash, 14420 Sherwood, Oak Park, ☎ 248-544-2687 or 248-547-2814.

Congregation Shaarey Shomayim, 15110 West Ten Mile Rd., Oak Park, ☎ 248-542-4444 or 248-967-4030.

Young Israel of Oak Park, 15140 West Ten Mile Rd., Oak Park, ☎ 248-967-3655, e-mail yiop@speedlink.net.

CONSERVATIVE

Adat Shalom Synagogue, 29901 Middlebelt Rd., Farmington Hills, ☎ 248-851-5100, e-mail adatshalom@aol.com. Gift shop.

Congregation Beth Abraham Hillel Moses, 5075 West Maple Rd., West Bloomfield, ☎ 248-851-6880, www.cbahm.org. Egalitarian.

Congregation Beth Shalom, 14601 West Lincoln Rd., Oak Park, ☎ 248-547-7970, e-mail cbs@congbethshalom.org. Egalitarian. Gift shop.

Congregation B'nai Moshe, 6800 Drake Rd., West Bloomfield, ☎ 248-788-0600, e-mail cbminfo@bnaimoshe.org. Gift shop.

Congregation Shaarey Zedek, 27375 Bell Rd., Southfield, ☎ 248-357-5544. Marked with a plaque as a Michigan Historical Site, this is the sixth building of this congregation founded as part of the original Traditional Bet El congregation.

REFORM

Temple Beth El, 7400 Telegraph Rd., Bloomfield Hills, ☎ 248-851-1100, www.templebethel.net. Well-known rabbi and author Daniel B. Syme is one of the leaders of this historical congregation, which evolved from the first congregation in Detroit *and* Michigan.

Temple Emanu-El, 14450 West Ten Mile Rd., Oak Park, ☎ 248-967-4020, e-mail jpklein@voy.net, www.members.aol.com/akjess/emanu-el. Gift shop.

Temple Israel, 5725 Walnut Lake Rd., West Bloomfield, ☎ 248-661-5700, www.Temple-Israel.org. Mikvah. Gift shop.

Temple Kol Ami, 5085 Walnut Lake Rd., West Bloomfield, ☎ 248-661-0040, e-mail kolami@speedlink.net. Gift counter.

Temple Shir Shalom, 3999 Walnut Lake Rd., West Bloomfield, ☎ 248-737-8700, www.shirshalom.org.

SECULAR & HUMANISTIC

Birmingham Temple, 28611 West Twelve Mile Rd., Farmington Hills, ☎ 248-477-1410, e-mail bhamtmpl@speedlink.net.

KOSHER DINING

❖ For updates regarding kashrut designation, call the **Council of Orthodox Rabbis/Vaad Harabonim,** ☎ 248-559-5005. Several synagogues offer kosher meals, catered or carry-out, two or three nights a week.

Jerusalem Pizza, 25050 Southfield Rd., Southfield, ☎ 248-552-0087. This casual eatery features pizzas, gourmet pizzas, calzones, and sandwiches. Dine in or carry out.

New York Pizza World, 15280 West Lincoln, Oak Park, ☎ 248-968-2102. Soups, salads, and sandwiches, in addition to pizza. Dine in or carry out.

Taste of Israel, 25254 Greenfield, Oak Park, ☎ 248-967-6020. Glatt kosher Middle Eastern cuisine. Dine in or carry out.

Unique Kosher Carryout, 25270 Greenfield Rd. Oak Park, ☎ 248-967-1161. Glatt kosher, carry-out only. Pick up a Shabbat dinner with all the trimmings.

Sperber's North Kosher Catering, 6600 West Maple Rd., Jewish Community Center, West Bloomfield, ☎ 248-661-5151, e-mail sperbers@sperbers.com. Cafeteria-style meat restaurant. Limited hours.

La Difference, 7295 Orchard Lake Rd., West Bloomfield, ☎ 248-932-8934. This upscale, fine-dining restaurant features an elegant

American eclectic menu, including dishes such as angel hair pasta with salmon and asparagus and macadamia-encrusted Chilean seabass. Oh – and it just happens to be kosher. No meat or fowl on the menu.

JEWISH COMMUNITY CENTERS

Jewish Community Center of Metropolitan Detroit has two locations:

- ❖ **D. Dan & Betty Kahn Building,** 6600 West Maple Rd., West Bloomfield, 48322, ☎ 248-661-1000.

- ❖ **Jimmy Prentis Morris Branch,** 15110 West Ten Mile Rd., Oak Park, 48237, ☎ 248-967-4030.

SHOPPING

Check out the synagogue listings for more shopping opportunities. Most gift shops have limited hours of operation or require appointments, so be sure to call first.

Borenstein's Book & Music Store, 25242 Greenfield, Oak Park, ☎ 248-967-3920.

Esther's Judaica Gift World, 6239 Orchard Lake Rd., West Bloomfield, ☎ 248-932-3377.

Spitzer's Hebrew Book Store, 21790 West Eleven Mile Rd., Southfield, ☎ 248-356-6080, e-mail plotnik3@juno.com.

Jewish Community Center, 6600 West Maple Rd., West Bloomfield, ☎ 248-661-7649.

Tradition! Tradition!, 17235 Shervilla Place, Southfield, ☎ 248-557-0109 or ☎ 800-579-6340.

Aish HaTorah of Metro Detroit, 32571 Franklin Rd., Franklin, ☎ 248-737-0400, detroit@aish.edu.

EVENTS

Birmingham Temple Art Show, 28611 West Twelve Mile Rd., Farmington Hills, ☎ 248-477-1410. Each fall, juried works of Jewish and non-Jewish artists are displayed during this synagogue fund-raiser. Many of the works are of Jewish content. First weekend of November.

Birmingham Temple Book Fair, 28611 West Twelve Mile Rd., Farmington Hills, ☎ 248-477-1410, E-mail bhamtmpl@speedlink.net. In the spring, nationally known Jewish authors entertain, enlighten, and frequently challenge with controversial topics. Books are for sale and admission is free.

Jewish Book Fair, Jewish Community Center, 6600 West Maple Rd., West Bloomfield, ☎ 248-661-7649. The oldest and largest annual Jewish Book Fair in the United States is hosted each November at the JCC. Dozens of speakers, including the likes of Dr. Ruth Westheimer and playwright Wendy Wasserstein, educate and entertain attendees. The weeklong event held at both JCC locations includes programs, entertainment, and – the big draw – more than 10,000 books by Jewish authors or with Jewish content for sale.

HERITAGE TOURS

Jewish Historical Society of Michigan, 6600 West Maple Rd., West Bloomfield, ☎ 248-661-7706. Community members lead tours for groups of 25 or larger. The tour ranges in length from 1½ to three hours. The volunteer-run organization typically needs a month or more to schedule a tour. Although the group can't support smaller tours, its members are extremely knowledgeable and are typically eager to share information and offer suggestions, so a phone call is recommended. The Society also publishes the annual *Michigan Jewish History*.

RESOURCES

Jewish Federation of Metropolitan Detroit, 6735 Telegraph Rd., Bloomfield Hills, ☎ 248-642-4260.

Bais Chabad, 28000 Middlebelt Rd., Farmington Hills, ☎ 248-737-7000. A source for home hospitality and other Chabad Houses and activities.

Council of Orthodox Rabbis/Vaad Harabonim, 16947 Ten Mile Rd., Southfield, ☎ 248-559-5005. Call for suggestions of synagogues in the neighborhood where you're staying, as well as updated information about kosher dining opportunities.

The Detroit Jewish News, 27676 Franklin Rd., Southfield, ☎ 248-354-6060, www.detroitjewishnews.com. This weekly publication averages 168 pages of local, regional, national, and international Jewish news, as well as community calendar, features, and community advertising. A great resource for the Jewish visitor to Detroit.

Jewish Genealogical Society of Michigan, ☎ 248-355-4212, e-mail srosman@aol.com.

The Jews of Detroit: From the Beginning, 1762-1914, by Robert A. Rockaway (Wayne State University Press, 1986), and *Harmony and Dissonance: Voices of Jewish Identity in Detroit, 1914-1967,* by Sidney Bolkosky (Wayne State University Press, 1991), paint a detailed picture of Detroit's Jewish history.

Metropolitan Detroit Convention & Visitors Bureau, 211 W. Fort St., Suite 1000, ☎ 800-338-7648 (DETROIT) or ☎ 313-202-1800, www.visitdetroit.com.

❖ DID YOU KNOW?

I Was a Teenage Werewolf (1957), starring Michael Landon, was produced by Detroiter **Herman Cohen.**

L OS ANGELES

LOS ANGELES

Everyone knows Mann's Chinese Theater is the spot where the handprints and footprints of movie stars and Hollywood giants mark the sidewalk. And *most* everyone knows that Jews have been well-represented in Hollywood from the earliest days. But the imprint of Jewish life on other facets of Los Angeles life may not be as familiar. In the sprawling stretch of Southern California that has become the Greater Los Angeles area, evidence of immigrant neighborhoods is in stars of David in stained-glass and synagogues-turned-churches. Farther out are world-class museums that command several return visits. Peaceful cemeteries, children's museums, and haimische neighborhoods offer a diverse sightseeing agenda.

And why shouldn't the sightseeing attractions of Jewish LA reflect diversity? Its population certainly does. With some 650,000 Jews in the Greater Los Angeles area, it is the second-largest Jewish community in the United States and one of the largest in the world. Within that number are significant populations of Israeli, Russian, South African, Moroccan, South American, and Persian Jews. In fact, Los Angeles is home to the largest population of Persian Jews (35,000) in the world.

Although Jews began migrating to Southern California as early as the 1850s, it's rare to find evidence of these early days. Few pre-20th-century structures survive. But synagogues, landmarks, and neighborhoods that grew and thrived from the 1920s to the 50s abound. As in other communities, it's possible to trace the Jewish migration from one part of the city to other neighborhoods – as

89

can be done from the Boyle Heights neighborhood (once 90% Jewish) to Fairfax and out into the Valley.

Today, LA's Jewish community is concentrated in a few areas; nearly half living on the west side in well-settled neighborhoods such as Beverly-Fairfax, Pico-Robertson/Beverlywood, and West Hollywood. Another near 50% reside in the Valley, in communities such as Sherman Oaks, Woodland Hills, Encino, and Tarzana. Within these areas are pockets of Orthodox communities.

Because Los Angeles is so expansive – and because neighborhoods are often run-down and sites obscured or boarded up – a guided tour of historic neighborhoods and attractions is suggested. A driving tour of Los Angeles Jewish neighborhoods is a good five-hour commitment, with perhaps a Hollywood tour left for another day.

SIGHTSEEING HIGHLIGHTS

MUSEUMS & GALLERIES

Museum of Tolerance, The Simon Wiesenthal Plaza, 9786 W. Pico Blvd., ☎ 310-553-8403, www.wiesenthal.com. As visitors enter the Holocaust Section of the museum, they're given a passport – and the identity of a child who actually lived during the Holocaust. At the conclusion of their tour, they learn whether that child survived – or perished. The Museum of Tolerance uses high-tech exhibits to bring the message of tolerance and the horrors of bigotry to a human and personal level. For example, the "Point of View" diner features a juke box where visitors can select an issue, input an opinion, and get instant analysis of their response. In another exhibit, the curious can "try on" another person's skin color. Nearly 35 hands-on, interactive exhibits spotlight the issues of intolerance that have haunted human history. Other highlights are a 16-screen video presentation of the civil rights movement, and focus on current examples of bigotry throughout the world. Hours: Monday-Thursday, 10-4; Friday, 10-1 (November-March), 10-3 (April-October); Sunday, 11-5. Admission: $8.50 adults, $6.50 seniors, $5.50 students; $3.50 children three-10.

Skirball Cultural Center, 2701 N. Sepulveda Blvd., ☎ 310-440-4500, www.skirball.com. "Go forth... and be a blessing to the world." This message greets visitors from a display case, where a Torah scroll is opened to Genesis 12:1-3. The museum reflects the fruits of that going forth, retelling the Jewish experience from its beginnings. The Journeys galleries, connected by corridors of Jerusalem stone, explore Jewish culture – focusing on the Roman destruction of Second Temple (70 CE), the 1492 expulsion of Jews from Spain, and the rise of pogroms that swept Russia beginning in 1881. The museum galleries are undergoing a redesign and expansion that will result in new exhibits showcasing the relationship of the Jewish community to George Washington and Abraham Lincoln, among other additions. Hours: Tuesday-Saturday, noon-5; Sunday, 11-5. Admission: $8 adults; $6 seniors and students; children 12 and under free.

Zimmer Discovery Children's Museum, JCC Association of Los Angeles, 6505 Wilshire Blvd, ☎ 323-761-8989. This hands-on museum is designed for children ages three to 11, and involves lots of action. A visit to Israel, for example, begins with a simulated El Al flight and includes work on a kibbutz, a hike to Mt. Sinai, and a trek across the Red Sea. Through lively exhibits, children have the chance to meet famous Jewish heroes, dress up in medieval Spanish costumes, and participate in a Sabbath dinner. Pint-sized recreations are impressive – kids crawl in and out of a Sephardic temple, the Western Wall, Noah's Ark, and a 10-foot-tall Statue of Liberty. Call ahead for information on programs, concerts, and workshops. Hours: Tuesday-Thursday, 12:30-4; Sunday, 12:30-5. Admission: $3 for adults and children seven and older; $2 children ages three-seven.

Finegood Art Gallery, Jewish Community Center, 22622 Vanowen St., West Hills, ☎ 818-587-3200. The site of changing art exhibits scheduled year-round features works of Jewish content or by Jewish artists – particularly those from Southern California. In addition, the Art Council of the Jewish Federation Council, which sponsors the exhibits, also offers a tour program that visits private galleries and homes.

Jewish Federation's Los Angeles Museum of the Holocaust, 6006 Wilshire Blvd., ☎ 323-761-8175. Displays of memorabilia are small, intimate, thus underlining the losses of the Holocaust on a personal level. A 1930s Shabbat table set with fine linens and best china. A dress worn at Liberation. Photos of American soldiers as they enter the camps. The museum shares the building, known as the Jewish Heritage Center, with the Jewish Historical

Society and Jewish Library. Hours: Monday-Thursday, 10-4; Friday, 10-2; Sunday, 11-2. No admission charged.

HISTORIC SITES

Wilshire Boulevard Temple, 3663 Wilshire Blvd., ☎ 213-388-2401. This landmark structure, modeled after the Great Synagogue in Florence, Italy, is perhaps one of the most important historical sites in the city. Since 1928, the Reform temple served as the heart of the community and remains a vibrant and active congregation. Its origins are rooted in Los Angeles' earliest days – in 1862 established as Congregation B'nai B'rith, and located on what is now a parking structure for *The Los Angeles Times*. Its permanent history photo exhibit is "one of the best local history exhibits anywhere," according to Jerry Freedman Habush, tour operator and vice president of the Southern California Jewish Historical Society. The structure is listed on the National Register of Historic Places.

When you're in the neighborhood, swing past the **Korean Presbyterian Church,** at 4th and New Hampshire. This was the second site of the Sinai Temple, from 1925 to 1961. Today, Korean calligraphy appears below the Hebrew-inscripted tablets on the outside of the building.

Breed Street Shul, 247 N. Breed St., no telephone. At press time, the historic building is not much to look at. Located in the heart of the Boyle Heights neighborhood, it's defaced with graffiti, littered with broken bottles and trash, boarded up, and padlocked shut to keep out drug users. But this once-vibrant synagogue, so important to the Jewish community's past, is slated for a more promising future. The Breed Street Shul was built in 1923, and known as Congregation Talmud Torah. For nearly three decades, the synagogue served as the focal point of the neighborhood (at that time, 90% Jewish). Some sources claim that it was the setting for scenes from the first talking movie, *The Jazz Singer*. Recently, the Southern California Jewish Historical Society took ownership of the property. Efforts are in the works to raise money to restore the building, turning it into a museum or community center in the now-predominantly Latino neighborhood.

Welsh Presbyterian Church, 12th and Valencia, ☎ 323-761-8950 (Jewish Historical Society). In the Pico-Union District stands the site of the first Conservative synagogue west of Chicago, Sinai Temple, built in 1909 and serving the congregation until 1925. stars of David adorn the large stained-glass windows as well as the masonry. This is definitely a stop that requires an arranged tour.

Original site of Cedars Sinai Medical Center, 1441 Carroll Ave., no telephone. In 1902 the Kaspare Cohn Hospital opened to serve tuberculosis patients. This drive-by site in a grand Victorian structure is surrounded by stately homes. Nearby is a marker designating the historic spot.

MONUMENTS, MARKERS & MEMORIALS

Home of Peace Memorial Park, 4334 Whittier Blvd., ☎ 323-261-6135. It's smaller than many of the celebrity-filled cemeteries in Los Angeles, but this burial site contains its share of Hollywood movers and shakers, including some of the Warner brothers (of Warner Bros.), as well as gangster Bugsy Siegal. Perhaps of greater note, the cemetery is historically significant. Home of Peace wasn't established until the 20th century, but the graves of Southern California's earliest Jewish settlers were moved here. The oldest stones, dating to the 1850s, are weathered away, but it's possible to read the inscriptions on headstones from the 1870s.

Site of first synagogue, 218 Broadway. A small, sidewalk plaque, easily missed, marks the spot where the first synagogue in Southern California was built in 1873 by Congregation B'nai Brith. The structure was torn down more than a century ago. But the congregation still thrives, and worships at the Wilshire Boulevard Temple.

Chavez Ravine, near Dodger Stadium. It's a challenge to find. But in this hilly area, on city land just a little west of Lilac Terrace and Lookout Drive, is a state marker designating the spot where early Jewish settlers established a cemetery. Here the former Hebrew Benevolent Society Cemetery served the community from 1855 to 1910.

Fairfax Community Mural, on the wall of the People's Market Building, Fairfax and Oakwood Ave. Seven panels tell the story of Jews in Los Angeles from the early 1800s. Look for celebs and heroes from Al Jolson to Sandy Koufax.

LOS ANGELES

Neighborhoods

Fairfax. There are no museums, monuments, historical sites, or other markers testifying to the area's Jewish roots. But there's no doubt that the Fairfax area of Los Angeles has an energetic and visible Jewish – predominantly Orthodox – population. Arriving in greater numbers are Israelis and Russians. The residential neighborhoods and commercial areas along Beverly and Fairfax avenues bustle with activity, as shoppers, merchants, and strollers weave in and out of shops, restaurants, and synagogues. Surprisingly, one of the most popular stops for tourists and other Angelenos is **Canter's**, a kosher-*style* deli flaunting pickle barrels, hanging salamis, and a boisterous ambiance. The place, which includes a bar and a band, is open 24 hours a day, 363 days a year. It closes for Yom Kippur and Christmas. Go figure.

Boyle Heights. From the 1910s until the 1950s, Boyle Heights, just east of downtown, was known as the "Lower East Side of Los Angeles." In fact, the main artery was called Brooklyn Avenue (today it's Cesar Chavez Boulevard). Here the neighborhoods were filled with Jewish-owned shops, kosher butchers and bakeries, and houses of worship from small shuls to grand synagogues such as the **Breed Street Shul**. Even into the 1950s, Boyle Heights was the place to find barrels of pickles and live chickens for a Shabbat dinner. At this time, 90% of the residents were Jewish. Today, the neighborhood is rundown and the Breed Street Shul, once the "queen of shuls," is in disrepair. A tour by a knowledgeable guide will identify other sights of Jewish interest, such as the **Soto-Michigan JCC**, the **Jewish Home for the Aged**, and more.

Pico-Robertson/Beverlywood. Along Pico Boulevard, quick-stop felafel stands and kosher pizza and grill restaurants line the busy street. It is in this neighborhood that the Museum of Tolerance (see page 90) stands. Among the numerous synagogues is the **Kabbalah Center**, a former church that seems to be getting a lot of attention of late, as celebrities such as Madonna seek out spiritual direction. On the west side of Robertson is **Beverlywood**, an area described by locals as more upscale, and attracting a growing Persian Jewish community.

> ### ❖ DID YOU KNOW?
>
> It's no big news that Jews have played a major role in the movie industry from its earliest beginnings. In fact, a tour might start at historic Gower Gulch at Selma and Vine. This was the site of Hollywood's first movie, *Squaw Man*, by Jesse Lasky, Sam Goldfish (who later changed his name to Goldwyn), and Cecil B. DeMille (his mother was Jewish). The tour takes in sites such as Mann's Chinese Theater and Grauman's Egyptian Theater. Revealing the names of Jewish actors – before they changed them – is one of the most popular segments of the tour. Learn how Betty Joan Perske, Bernie Schwartz, and Melvin Kaminsky rose to stardom. Call Freedman Habush Associates (see *Heritage Tours*, page 102) for more about tours.

COLLEGES & UNIVERSITIES

University of Judaism, 15600 Mulholland Dr., Bel Air, ☎ 310-476-9777. The university offers fully accredited undergraduate and graduate degree programs in arts and science, education, and rabbinic studies, but the campus is also a great place for continuing education in the community. Visitors should explore the **Smalley Family Sculpture Garden.** Here, terraces, walkways, and plazas lead to serene views of the Santa Monica Mountains, not to mention striking and evocative sculpture by preeminent contemporary artists, including Jenny Holzer, Fletcher Benton, Aldo Casanova, and George Rickey. Indoors, the **Platt Gallery** showcases Jewish art and artists, expressing a variety of themes and media. Major exhibitions are scheduled throughout the year. Hours: Sunday-Thursday, 10-4; Friday, 10-2.

SYNAGOGUES

There are nearly 165 synagogues in the Los Angeles metropolitan area, with a mix of tiny neighborhood Orthodox shuls to some of the largest congregations in the world.

Orthodox

B'nai David-Judea Congregation, 8906 West Pico Blvd., ☎ 310-276-9269.

Congregation Beth Israel, 8056 Beverly Blvd., ☎ 213-651-4022.

Congregation Beth Jacob, 9030 W. Olympic Blvd., Beverly Hills, ☎ 310-278-1911.

Congregation Etz Jacob, 7659 Beverly Blvd., ☎ 213-938-2619.

Ohev Shalom, 525 S. Fairfax Ave., ☎ 213-653-7190.

Shaarey Zedek Congregation, 12800 Chandler Blvd., North Hollywood, ☎ 818-763-0560

Young Israel of Beverly Hills, 8701 West. Pico Blvd., ☎ 310-275-3020.

Conservative

Valley Beth Shalom, 15739 Ventura Blvd., Encino, ☎ 818-788-6000.

Adat Ari El, 12020 Burbank Blvd., North Hollywood, ☎ 818-766-9426.

Adat Shalom, 3030 Westwood Blvd., ☎ 310-475-4986.

Hollywood Temple Beth El, 1317 N. Crescent Heights, ☎ 213-656-3150.

Sinai Temple, 10400 Wilshire Blvd., ☎ 318-474-1518.

Shomrei Torah, 7353 Valley Circle Blvd., West Hills, ☎ 818-346-0811.

Temple Aliyah, 6025 Valley Circle Blvd., Woodland Hills, ☎ 818-346-3545.

Valley Beth Shalom, 15739 Ventura Blvd., Encino, ☎ 818-788-6000.

Reform

Kol Tikvah, 20400 Ventura Blvd., ☎ 818-348-0670.

Leo Baeck Temple, 1300 Sepulveda Blvd., ☎ 310-476-2861.

Stephen S. Wise Temple, 15500 Stephen S. Wise Dr., ☎ 310-476-8561.

Temple Beth El, 1435 West Seventh St., San Pedro, ☎ 310-833-2467.

Temple Beth Hillel, 12326 Riverside Dr., North Hollywood, ☎ 818-763-9148.

Temple Emanuel, 8844 Burton Way, Beverly Hills, ☎ 310-288-3742.

Temple Isaiah, 10345 West Pico Blvd., ☎ 310-277-2772.

Temple Israel of Hollywood, 7300 Hollywood Blvd., ☎ 213-876-8330.

Wilshire Boulevard Temple, 3663 Wilshire Blvd., ☎ 213-388-2401. Historic congregation and structure (see *Historic Sites*, page 92).

KOSHER DINING

❖ A healthy menu of kosher food establishments can be found in the Fairfax area, as well as other neighborhoods of west Los Angeles and the Valley. For up-to-the-minute status, call the **Rabbinical Council of California** at ☎ 213-489-8080, or check online at www.rccvaad.org.

FAIRFAX AREA

Café Et Lait, 7115 Beverly Blvd., ☎ 323-936-2861. Lox and eggs, omelettes, and bagels are breakfast highlights; lunch features fish, pasta, and other dairy dishes. Outdoor seating is perfect for an espresso and pastry.

Elite Cuisine Restaurant, 7119 Beverly Blvd., ☎ 323-930-1303. A new Chinese chef is adding an Asian twist to the menu, featuring traditional deli sandwiches and grilled items. The menu includes vegetarian entrées, pasta, and salads, as well. Open for lunch and dinner.

Grill Express, 501 N. Fairfax Ave., ☎ 323-655-0649. Mediterranean specialties, grilled meats, and Chinese items are featured. Breakfast, lunch, and dinner are served daily.

Shalom Hunan, 5651 Wilshire Blvd., ☎ 323-934-0505. A meat menu features Chinese favorites for lunch and dinner.

Simon's La Glatt, 446 N. Fairfax, ☎ 323-658-7730. Roast beef, prime rib, and deli sandwiches, not to mention schnitzel, stuffed cabbage, and kugels, attract patrons who love traditional dishes. Eat in or order carry-out for lunch and dinner.

WEST LOS ANGELES

Cohen Restaurant, 316 E. Pico Blvd., ☎ 213-742-8888. Lunch draws crowds ordering shish kebab, chicken, ribs, and burgers.

Elat Burger, 9340 W. Pico Blvd., ☎ 310-278-4692. This quick-stop features burgers, shwarma, chicken sandwiches or nuggets, and more meat standards. Open for lunch and dinner, and Saturday after Shabbat.

Glatt Hut, 9303 W. Pico Blvd., ☎ 310-246-1900. Lamb, chicken schnitzel, teriyaki chicken, and stuffed cabbage are popular items for lunch or dinner.

Milk N' Honey Restaurant, 8837 W. Pico Blvd., ☎ 310-858-8850. Described as "upscale," this dairy restaurant offers pasta, fish, and gourmet pizza, open for lunch, dinner, and after Shabbat.

Milky Way, 9108 W. Pico Blvd., ☎ 310-859-0004. Everyone knows by now that this dairy restaurant is owned by Steven Spielberg's mom, Leah Adler. Posters of Spielberg films decorate the place.

Nessim's Restaurant, 8939 W. Pico Blvd., ☎ 310-859-9429. Sushi is a highlight on this meat menu. The restaurant also offers an ample Shabbat take-out package. Open for lunch, dinner, and after Shabbat.

Pico Deli, 8826 W. Pico Blvd., ☎ 310-273-9381. Owner Max Hecht is proud of a reputation that brings customers from overseas on referrals. His deli menu features ample portions of traditional favorites for lunch and dinner.

Shalom Pizza, 8715 W. Pico Blvd., ☎ 310-271-2255. Mediterranean, Israeli, and Iranian fare – and pizza – attract a lunch and dinner business. The dairy restaurant is also open after Shabbat.

VALLEY

Falafel Village, 16060 Ventura Blvd., ☎ 818-783-1012. Diners order felafel, shwarma, and other fast-food Middle Eastern fare at the counter and find a seat for lunch or dinner. Closed Sunday.

Golan, 13075 Victory Blvd., ☎ 818-763-5375. The restaurant offers a well-rounded meat menu, ranging from Israeli favorites such as shwarma and felafel, to traditional dishes such as shnitzel and stuffed cabbage, to a complete Chinese menu. The restaurant is open for breakfast, lunch, and dinner.

Rami's Pizza, 17736½ Sherman Way, ☎ 818-342-0611. There's something for everyone – in addition to pizza, the restaurant offers Middle Eastern, Mexican, and Italian specialties for lunch and dinner. Diners with special diets (diabetics, vegans, etc.) can have their meals prepared to their needs.

Sharon's, 18608 1/2 Ventura Blvd., ☎ 818-344-7472. This small, casual restaurant serves basic meat dishes for lunch and dinner.

Tiberias, 18046 Ventura Blvd., ☎ 818-343-3705. The perfect place to go when you have a killer appetite. Brisket, moussaka, goulash, veal chops – all main dishes come with two sides. Open for lunch and dinner.

LOS ANGELES

❖ DID YOU KNOW?

Not that you'd guess from Aaron Spelling's spin on high school life in the early seasons of "Beverly Hills 90210," but tony Beverly Hills High School has served a large Jewish adolescent population for generations. Says Jewish Historical Society leader Jerry Freedman Habush, Jews have accounted for half or more of the student population since the 1940s.

JEWISH COMMUNITY CENTERS

Jewish Community Centers of Greater Los Angeles, 5700 Wilshire Blvd., 2nd Fl. ☎ 323-761-8761. This is the headquarters for area JCCs – and there are several. Smaller facilities, including North Valley in Granada Hills, Silverlake Los Feliz in Hollywood, and Valley Cities in Sherman Oaks, have plenty of programming and services, but perhaps less in the way of health clubs and attractions for the visitor. The following are recommended for continuing your workout regimen while visiting LA.

Westside Jewish Community Center, 5870 W. Olympic Blvd., ☎ 323-954-2288. The biggest JCC in the Greater LA area features two pools (allowing separate-sex swimming for Orthodox members), a fully equipped gym, playground, basketball, racquetball, jacuzzi, and sauna – not to mention scheduled events and a legendary theater (Richard Dreyfuss performed here in the 1960s).

Bernard Milken Jewish Community Campus, 22622 Vanowen St., West Hills, ☎ 818-587-3300. In addition to a full-service fitness center, complete with pool, sauna, jacuzzi, steam room, and gym, this facility holds the Finegood Art Gallery.

SHOPPING

Abi's Judaica & Gifts, 18369 Ventura Blvd., Tarzana, ☎ 818-705-4573 and 5891 Kanan Rd., Agoura Hills, ☎ 818-991-0092. Abi is a trained scribe who creates ketubot and Torahs.

Audry's, Skirball Cultural Center, 2701 N. Sepulveda Blvd., ☎ 310-440-4505. Museum-quality fine-art objects, traditional and contemporary Judaica, handcrafted Judaica, books, music, and children's gifts.

Mitzvahland – The Judaica Center, 16733 Ventura Blvd., ☎ 818-705-7700.

Hatikvah Music International, 436 N. Fairfax, ☎ 213-655-7083.

Treasures of Judaica Gift Shop, University of Judaism, 15600 Mulholland Dr., Bel Air, ☎ 310-476-0772. Located on the campus of the University of Judaism, the gift shop offers standard inventory, and provides a complimentary service of personal shoppers who can assist you.

EVENTS

Israel Film Festival, Laemmle's Music Hall Theatre (Wilshire and Doheny), ☎ 323-966-4166, www.israelfilmfestival.com. The festival has been operating for more than 16 years, and is usually held in early April. Nearly two weeks of showings and events are on the schedule. Israeli directors, producers, and stars attend most showings during the first week.

Valley Jewish Festival, ☎ 818-464-3227 and 464-3200. Billed as the "largest outdoor Jewish gathering west of Chicago," the event is a biennial extravaganza for the Jewish community. The kickoff celebration was held on the campus of California State University, Northridge. Organized by the Jewish Federation/Valley Alliance, the festival focused on family activities including arts and crafts, carnival rides, entertainment and music, food, and more in a pleasant parklike setting. Call for details, locations, and admission fees.

Hanukkah Festival, Skirball Cultural Center, 2701 N. Sepulveda Blvd., ☎ 310-440-4500. The annual holiday event features musical performances and plenty of activities for children including games, treasure hunts, art workshops, and dreidel spins.

Brandeis-Bardin Institute, 1101 Peppertree Lane, Brandeis, ☎ 805-582-4450, www.brandeis-bardin.org. A concert series as well as a schedule of festive events make a 40-minute drive out of LA well worth it. The Institute is in a beautiful setting in Simi Valley and attracts attendees from all over the country with its retreats, camps, institutes, lectures, and continuing education programs for people of all ages. The musical programs feature Jewish music from popular performers to classical to cabaret. And events such as a tree-planting festival for Mother's Day fill the calendar. Also for the short-term visitor are a number of weekend and one-day programs for the whole family to take advantage of. Topics range from issues of Jewish practice to Jewish healing services to Israel.

HERITAGE TOURS

Freedman Habush Associates Jewish Tours, 6200 Mammoth Ave., Van Nuys, ☎ 818-994-0213. Jerry Freedman Habush has led tours of Jewish Los Angeles for more than 15 years – on his own and as representative for the University of Judaism and the Jewish Historical Society. His "Hollywood and the Jews" tour, incorporating stops at Paramount Studios and Hollywood, is one of the most popular requests. He also leads groups to Tijuana, Santa Fe, and other surprising destinations. He will arrange tours for groups of any size, but does not provide transportation.

RESOURCES

Jewish Federation, 5700 Wilshire Blvd., 2nd Fl., ☎ 323-761-8207, www.jewishla.com.

Rabbinical Council of California Kashrut Division, 617 S. Olive St., Ste. 515, ☎ 213-489-8080, www.rccvaad.org.

Jewish Historical Society of Southern California, 5700 Wilshire Blvd., Rm. 2512, ☎ 323-761-8950.

Jewish Genealogical Society of Los Angeles, no address, ☎ 818-501-5951.

The Jewish Journal of Greater Los Angeles, 3660 Wilshire Blvd., Ste. 204, ☎ 213-368-1661, www.jewishjournal.com. Published weekly, the magazine features local, national, and international news of Jewish interest, and features an area calendar of events.

The Jewish News, 11071 Ventura Blvd., Studio City, ☎ 818-786-4000.

The Los Angeles Jewish Times, 5455 Wilshire Blvd., #903, ☎ 323-962-8014.

Jewish Television Network (cable), 8383 Wilshire Blvd., Ste. 1010, Beverly hills, ☎ 323-852-9494.

The Web site **www.californiasedge.com** leads visitors on a near step-by-step tour of the Jewish neighborhoods, past and present, in San Diego, San Francisco, and Los Angeles.

Los Angeles Convention & Vistors Bureau, ☎ 312-988-3312.

M IAMI

Moses Elias Levy failed to convince Jews to move to southern Florida in the early 1800s. His plan to populate the unsettled swamplands with immigrants from Europe fizzled shortly after the Moroccan-born merchant launched his scheme. If Levy were able to time-travel to modern-day Miami, he might experience a certain sense of irony. Strolling down the bustling stretch of South Beach, where Art Deco synagogues blend into the pastel architecture, or wandering past delis and hotels that advertise kosher menus on Collins Avenue, he would indeed scratch his head in wonder – especially to learn that the Jews of the 20th century were lured to this coastal community not by economic opportunities but sun, sand, and sea.

Jews were not permitted to live in the territory that is today the state of Florida until 1763. But even after, restrictive laws and discrimination did not offer a friendly welcome. Although Jewish settlers slowly trickled into St. Augustine, Jacksonville, and other parts of the state, South Florida was one of the last places Jews moved to.

It wasn't until the turn of the century that Jews began to settle in Miami Beach and South Florida. Restrictive covenants continued to keep Jews out of residential areas and the job market. Even the forces of nature seemed to discourage growth. In fact, shortly after the establishment of Miami Beach's first congregation, Beth Jacob in 1926, a devastating hurricane struck during Kol Nidre services.

During the 1930s, South Florida gained popularity as a resort community. And after World War II ended, tourism skyrocketed, and the Jewish community grew as quickly. In fact, Miami Beach emerged as a near-exclusive Jewish resort area during this time. As the U.S. economy evolved to allow for retirement, the area experienced a shift to an older population of permanent residents and "snowbirds" who lived here during the winter months.

Today, South Florida, identified as Miami-Dade, North Broward, and Palm Beach counties, enjoys one of the largest concentrations of Jewish population in the country, at 645,000. While community supporters prefer to talk about "shifting populations," truth is Jewish numbers are declining. There's promise, though, as the renaissance of Miami Beach brings renewed interest in the area. There are pockets of Orthodox communities, and some evidence that younger families are moving back to Miami Beach, perhaps sustaining the declining numbers of the predominantly elderly population.

As the community struggles and triumphs with transition, there remains a strong Jewish presence in South Florida. Jews have enjoyed political representation, with several Jewish mayors elected in recent decades. There are plenty of kosher restaurants – in fact, the city of Miami Beach employs a full-time kashrut supervision department.

The area also offers a number of Jewish archives, libraries, and, particularly, Holocaust resources. The survivor community of South Florida contributes much in the way of promoting Holocaust awareness.

And despite a disproportionate elderly population, the Jews of South Florida support some two dozen day schools. In addition, several Jewish Community Centers, more than 100 synagogues, and a lively calendar of activities, classes, and events are clear evidence of a Jewish presence in the very place that Jews were first forbidden and then reluctant to come. A situation that would certainly surprise and delight Moses Elias Levy.

SIGHTSEEING HIGHLIGHTS

MUSEUMS & GALLERIES

Sanford L. Ziff Jewish Museum of Florida, 301 Washington Ave., Miami Beach, ☎ 305-672-5044, www.jewishmuseum. com. The building itself is worth the visit. The Art Deco structure, with a pink and cream cast, arched windows, stained glass, and copper dome is at home with its South Beach surroundings. Constructed in 1936 as the Congregation Beth Jacob, it is now on the National Register of Historic Places and houses the state's first Jewish museum. "MOSAIC: Jewish Life in Florida" is its core exhibit. The collection comes to life through whimsical photos (toddler Felix Glickstein astride an alligator in 1916), curious artifacts (a plate koshered in the Gulf of Mexico in 1865), and historical displays (Jewish Cuba before Castro). A timeline wall tells the story of Jewish history from ancient times to arrival in Florida. Docent-led tours are available with advance reservations. Be sure to visit the synagogue next door. **Congregation Beth Jacob** (311 Washington Ave., ☎ 305-672-6150) returned to its original 1927 structure when the museum took over the landmark building in the 1980s. Though small, the congregation is still active. Hours: Tuesday-Sunday, 10-5. Admission: $5, seniors and students $4, children under six free.

❖ DID YOU KNOW?

One of the most notorious gangsters of the 20th century, Meyer Lansky, was a member in good standing at Congregation Beth Jacob for decades. He was purported to have controlled a gambling empire that stretched from Florida and the Caribbean to Las Vegas from the 1930s until his death in the 80s. Although he was denied Israeli citizenship because of his criminal connections, Lansky was apparently generous to Jewish causes.

Harold and Vivian Beck Museum of Judaica, Beth David Congregation, 2625 Southwest Third Ave., Miami, ☎ 305-854-3911. The museum's holdings range from an 18th-century chanukiah to a 20th-century Torah breastplate. A second-floor gallery holds art and sculpture by Jewish artists or of Jewish content. The collection is housed at the Beth David synagogue, Miami's pioneer congregation founded in 1912. No admission charged. Hours are irregular; call ahead to schedule a visit.

Molly S. Fraiberg Judaica Collections, Wimberly Library, Florida Atlantic University SE, Boca Raton, ☎ 561-297-3742. This collection is only open to the public on a limited basis during weekday hours. But it's worth the effort to see the memorabilia of Isaac Bashevis Singer – his writing table and chair are on display – as well as archives and artifacts of the Holocaust, Yiddish, Hebrew, and cantorial music.

Nathan D. Rosen Gallery at the Levis JCC, 9801 Donna Klein Blvd., Boca Raton, ☎ 561-852-3200, www.levisjcc.org. Not all the works at this JCC gallery are Judaic in nature – the changing exhibits feature contemporary art, folk art, mixed-media shows, and collections of historical significance. Check for a schedule of related events, including seminars, speakers, and workshops. Hours: Monday-Friday, noon-5. No admission charged.

Temple Israel of Greater Miami, 137 NE 19th St., Miami, ☎ 305-573-5900, www.templeisrael.net. The Nathan and Sophie Gumenick Chapel has won awards for its three-dimensional sculptured windows depicting a history of the Jewish experience. The chapel's architecture is quite unusual – forget geometric sensibilities. The structure is reminiscent of a desert shelter, a refuge carved out of cliffs. The synagogue's garden contains all the plants mentioned in the Bible.

The Shul at Bal Harbour, 9540 Collins Ave., ☎ 305-868-1411. There isn't a museum or gallery on site, but the architecture of this new synagogue replicates the look of Eastern European synagogues that were destroyed during the Holocaust. Built of Jerusalem stone, the structure shelters a traditional interior, with bimah in the center, and a women's balcony. The Lubavitch congregation is welcoming of visitors who come to tour or attend services.

My Jewish Discovery Place, Soref JCC, 6501 W. Sunrise Blvd., Ft. Lauderdale, ☎ 954-792-6700. A kid-friendly facility teaches Jewish children (and their parents) about their history, customs, holidays, and heroes. Open Tuesday-Friday, 10-4; Sunday, 1-5. Admission $3 adults; $2 children ages two to six; free to JCC members.

HISTORIC SITES

Cardozo Hotel, 1300 Ocean Drive, South Beach, Miami Beach, ☎ 305-538-7881 or ☎ 800-782-6500, www.cardozohotel.com. Named after Supreme Court Justice Benjamin Cardozo, the pastel-tinted Art Deco hotel was built in 1939. The architect was

Henry Hohauser, the same man who designed the Beth Jacob synagogue, which now houses the Jewish Museum of Florida. The hotel has been the setting for movies as old as Frank Sinatra's 1940s *A Hole in the Head* to the more recent irreverent hit *There's Something About Mary.*

Cuban Hebrew Congregation, 1700 Michigan Ave., Miami Beach, ☎ 305-534-7213. This Conservative congregation, also known as Temple Beth Shmuel, was established in 1961 by Jews who fled Castro's Cuba. The Spanish-speaking congregation follows the Ashkenazi tradition (its founders were from Eastern Europe). The structure is architecturally noteworthy. Its unusual facade resembles a cliff-dwelling. Twelve stained-glass windows, spanning two sides, represent the 12 tribes. For those intrigued to participate in services with a Cuban/Sephardic influence, also check out **Temple Moses** (1200 Normandy Dr., Miami Beach, ☎ 305-861-6308) and **Temple Menorah** (620 75th St., Miami Beach, ☎ 305-866-0221).

MEMORIALS, MONUMENTS & MARKERS

Holocaust Memorial, 1933-1945 Meridian Ave., Miami Beach, ☎ 305-538-2423. An outdoor plaza paved in Jerusalem stone surrounds a lilly-filled reflection pond. In the center, a large bronze hand reaches out and stretches skyward. Sculptured people climb and struggle upward. The memorial was designed by acclaimed sculptor Kenneth Treister. Two semi-circular walls of black granite provide a backdrop, one etched with a pictorial record of the time and the other inscribed with the names of those who perished. Hours: Daily, 9-9. No admission is charged. Guide tours on request.

Mania Nudel Holocaust Learning Center, David Posnack JCC, 5850 S. Pine Island Rd., Davie, ☎ 954-434-0499. Primarily an educational resource, the learning center does offer some Holocaust exhibits. Hours: Monday-Wednesday, 9-5. No admission charged.

NEIGHBORHOODS

Miami Beach. The length of 41st Street, also called Arthur Godfrey Road, is one nerve center of Jewish life in Miami Beach. Here, synagogues and businesses draw community members to shop, worship, and socialize. Fanning out from the artery are neighborhoods where Jewish families reside. Other streets with a strong Jewish flavor are Collins Avenue, Washington Avenue, and Ocean Drive, all running parallel to each other, north-south. Locals remember that the area was much livelier during the 1950s and 60s – when places such as Lummus Park on Ocean Drive were magnets for social activity. Flamingo Park, in fact, is said to have been a favorite hangout of Isaac Bashevis Singer. In the revitalized beach strip of South Beach, many of the Art Deco landmark structures were designed by Jewish architect Harry Hohauser (he's said to have designed up to 300 buildings), responsible for the Jewish Museum, formerly Congregation Beth Jacob. Hohauser often gave his structures names with Jewish resonance – such as the Cardozo Hotel and the Lord Balfour, on Ocean Drive.

SYNAGOGUES

ORTHODOX

B'nai Israel & Greater Miami Youth Synagogue, 16260 SW 288th St., Naranja Lakes, ☎ 305-264-6488.

Congregation Shaaray Tefilah of North Miami Beach, 971 NE 172nd St., North Miami Beach, ☎ 305-651-1562.

Young Israel of Greater Miami, 990 NE 171st St., North Miami Beach, ☎ 305-651-3601.

The Shul at Bal Harbour, 9540 Collins Ave., ☎ 305-868-1411.

CONSERVATIVE

Bet Shira Congregation, 7500 SW 120th St., Miami, ☎ 305-238-2601.

Beth David Congregation, 2625 SW Third Ave., Miami, ☎ 305-854-3911.

Temple B'nai Zion, 200 178th St., Sunny Isles Beach, ☎ 305-932-2159.

Temple Emanu-El of Greater Miami, 1701 Washington Ave., Miami Beach, ☎ 305-538-2503.

REFORM

Bet Breira, 9400 SW 87th Avenue, South Miami, ☎ 305-595-1500; www.betbreira.org.

Temple Beth Am, 5950 N. Kendall Dr., South Miami, ☎ 305-667-6667; http://betham-miami.org/ (1,400 families).

Temple Sinai of North Dade, 18801 NE 22nd Ave., North Miami Beach, ☎ 305-932-9010.

Temple Israel of Greater Miami, 137 NE 19th St., Miami, ☎ 305-573-5900.

Temple Beth Shalom, 4144 Chase Ave., Miami Beach, ☎ 305-538-7231.

Temple Beth El of Boca Raton, 333 SW 4th Ave., ☎ 561-391-8900.

KOSHER DINING

> ❖ For up-to-date status on restaurant kashruth, contact the **Rabbinical Kosher Supervisory Board, Inc.,** (☎ 305-932-2829) or the **South Palm Beach Va'ad Hakashrut** (☎ 561-394-5733).

Adams's Rib, 530 41st St., Miami Beach, ☎ 305-534-2276. No surprise to find on this menu hefty portions of beef, chicken, and ribs. The place features barbecue and is open for lunch and dinner.

China Kikar Tel Aviv, 5005 Collins Ave., Miami Beach, ☎ 305-866-3316. The all-you-can-eat buffet features Chinese favorites, soup, salad, and dessert bar, and is even open on Shabbat with advance reservations. Open for dinner only.

Embassy Peking, 4101 Pine Tree Dr., Miami Beach, ☎ 305-538-7550. An upscale restaurant with reasonable prices serves American and Chinese dinners during the week. Prepaid reservations can be made for Friday night and Saturday afternoon Shabbat meals, which showcase traditional Jewish cooking.

Famous Pita Hut, 17258 Collins Ave., N. Miami Beach, ☎ 305-945-6573. Israeli favorites such as shwarma and felafel are served, with pita baked fresh on the premises. Salads from baba-ganoush to tabouli are traditional sides; entrées feature steaks and chicken. Open for lunch and dinner.

Jerusalem Peking, Days Inn, 4299 Collins Ave., ☎ 305-532-2263. Chinese and American dishes are served for lunch and dinner in this casual eatery in the Days Inn hotel. Patrons may prepay for Shabbat meals.

Jerusalem Pizza, 761 NE 167th St., North Miami, ☎ 305-653-6662. People rave about the great pizza, reasonable prices, and good service at this casual dairy establishment open for lunch and dinner, and Saturday after sundown.

Kosher Ranch, 740 41st St., Miami Beach, ☎ 305-8KOSHER. Flame-grilled burgers, steaks, chicken – fried and barbecued, deli sandwiches, and homemade soups are the highlights here. The restaurant is closed during summer months; open for lunch and dinner fall, winter, and spring.

Miami Pita, 175 Sunny Isles Blvd., North Miami Beach, ☎ 305-940-4007. Israeli favorites with a large salad bar are featured at this reasonably priced meat restaurant near the Newport Hotel. Open for lunch and dinner.

❖ DID YOU KNOW?

No, Joe's Stone Crab is *not* kosher. But Miami Beach's renowned oceanside restaurant (tourists and residents alike willingly wait hours for a table) does have a Jewish connection. Jesse Weiss, who owns the restaurant, is descended from a pioneer Miami Beach family (arriving around 1917) – who owned the city's first restaurant.

Mr. Bean, 1205 17th St., Miami Beach, ☎ 305-672-0565. A great place for gourmet coffee, the dairy place also offers light bites – sandwiches, pastries, and cheesecake. Open throughout the day, on Sundays for breakfast, and Saturday night after Shabbat.

Pinati, 2520 NE Miami Gardens Dr., North Miami Beach, ☎ 305-931-8086. The vegetable soup is reported to be excellent. Other lunch and dinner items on the Israeli-themed menu are grilled meats, chicken, and hot dogs.

Pita Hut, 534 41st St., Miami Beach, ☎ 305-531-6090. An inexpensive stop for lunch or dinner, felafel, shwarma, and quick Middle Eastern fare are featured.

Pita Loca, 6th St. between Collins Ave. and Ocean Drive, Miami Beach, ☎ 305-673-3388. Traditional Israeli and Middle Eastern menu for lunch, dinner, and after Shabbat on Saturday evening.

Sabra, 19201 Collins Ave., North Miami Beach, ☎ 305-932-2233. As the name implies, Israeli favorites highlight the meat menu. This restaurant in the Ramada Hotel is closed during summer months.

Sara's, 1127 NE 163rd St., North Miami Beach, ☎ 305-948-7777, www.kosher-food.com. Gut-busting omelettes are a menu favorite, as well as unusual entrées such as pizza on phyllo dough at this dairy establishment that is open for breakfast, lunch, dinner, and after Shabbat.

Shalom Haifa, 1330 NE 163rd St., North Miami Beach, ☎ 305-945-2884. Steak, chicken, grilled meats, and couscous lend a Moroccan accent to this menu, also featuring Israeli favorites for lunch and dinner.

Shemtov's Pizza, 514 41st St., Miami Beach, ☎ 305-538-2123. Cheeseless pizza is one of the items served at this casual dairy eatery. In addition are pastas, fish dishes, calzone, and soy burgers. Open for lunch and dinner.

Tani Guchi's, 2224 NE 123rd St., North Miami Beach, ☎ 305-892-6744. This is the place to come for sushi, but the meat menu highlights other Japanese dishes as well. It's open for lunch and dinner.

Terrace Oceanside, 1960 S. Ocean Dr., Hallandale, ☎ 954-454-9444. Soothing ocean views are a big draw. Fish dishes are showcased on the meat menu; continental and Italian cooking are featured. The restaurant is closed during spring and summer.

Yonnie's Kosher Italian Restaurant & Pizzeria, 19802 West Dixie Hwy., North Miami Beach, ☎ 305-932-1961. A little Israeli, a little Italian, and a big menu of dairy and vegetarian dishes are available for lunch and dinner.

Yummy's Garden Café, 11155 SW 112th Ave., Miani, ☎ 305-217-9000. A varied dairy and vegetarian menu features items such as quesadillas, spinach lasagne, and stir-fried vegetables and tofu, not to mention interesting salads. Breakfast, lunch, and dinner is served.

❖ DID YOU KNOW?

National news personality Barbara Walters is from the South Florida area. In the 1950s her father, Lou Walters, owned a popular nightclub, The Latin Quarter, located on Palm Island off the Miami Beach coastline.

JEWISH COMMUNITY CENTERS

Several JCCs in the South Florida area will offer members reciprocal privileges. If you're staying in South Broward County, check out the **David Posnack JCC** (5850 S. Pine Island Rd., Davie, ☎ 954-434-0499) or the **Samuel M. & Helene Soref JCC** (6501 W. Sunrise Blvd., Ft. Lauderdale, ☎ 954-792-6700). In Boca Raton, the **Adolph and Rose Levis JCC** (9801 Donna Klein Blvd., ☎ 561-852-3200) offers sports and fitness as well as theater, a gallery, and a gift shop. The **Harold and Sylvia Kaplan JCC** in West Palm Beach (3151 N. Military Trail, ☎ 561-478-3060) also showcases art in its gallery.

Dave and Mary Alper JCC, 11155 SW 112th Ave., Miami, ☎ 305-271-9000. Fitness is the focus, with a state-of-the-art health and fitness center on this 23-acre campus. A heated outdoor pool, tennis and racquetball courts, and a regulation-sized roller hockey rink offer many action options. After a workout, enjoy a vegetarian or dairy meal at Yummy's Garden Café, located on site and open for breakfast, lunch, and dinner.

Michael-Ann Russell JCC, Sanford L. Ziff Campus, 18900 NE 25th Ave., North Miami Beach, ☎ 305-937-1793. Two swimming pools, nine lighted all-weather tennis courts, state-of-the-art equipment in fitness center, and a refurbished gym are available to JCC members. Check out the event schedule – cultural programs for children and adults highlight the calendar. There's an indoor snack bar, too.

SHOPPING

Museum Store, Sanford L. Ziff Jewish Museum of Florida, 301 Washington Ave., Miami Beach, ☎ 305-672-5044. Carries Judaica, cards, books, gifts.

Sylvia Rosen Art, Gifts, and Judaica Shoppe, Adolph and Rose Levis JCC, 9801 Donna Klein Blvd., Boca Raton, ☎ 561-852-3232, www.levisjcc.org.

LODGING

The Saxony Hotel, 3201 Collins Ave., Miami Beach, ☎ 305-538-6211. Although there are several hotels that cater to Jewish clientele, the city's Jewish Information and Referral Service reports that the Saxony is the only *year-round* kosher hotel in the area.

The Ramada Inn, 4041 Collins Ave., Miami Beach, ☎ 305-531-5771. Between January and March, the Ramada offers a kosher meal plan to hotel guests. Others may order kosher meals as well, but they pay per entrée.

Days Inn Oceanside, 4299 Collins Ave., Miami Beach, ☎ 305-673-1513. The Jerusalem Peking restaurant in the lobby of this hotel provides convenient kosher cuisine – eat in or carry out.

EVENTS

Miami Jewish Film Festival, Central Agency for Jewish Education, 4200 Biscayne Blvd., ☎ 305-576-4030. The annual, week-long event is scheduled in December and features films of Jewish interest and by Jewish artists.

HERITAGE TOURS

Sanford L. Ziff Jewish Museum of Florida, 301 Washington Ave., ☎ 305-672-5044, www.jewishmuseum.com. The museum schedules occasional walking tours as part of particular exhibits, but the staff are also a great resource for information about South Florida Jewry and local sights of interest.

JTEN Tours, ☎ 305-931-1782. Milton Heller moved to South Florida in 1977 and has learned to love his new home. In fact, he's become so "at home" here, he leads tours of various Jewish neighborhoods. Heller's group tours focus on various aspects of the community, from its Art Deco synagogues to the neighborhoods he calls the area's "Lower East Side of the 1950s and 60s." Although he only schedules group tours, he advises that a family might want to contact him to find out if they can join a scheduled group.

RESOURCES

Greater Miami Jewish Federation, 4200 Biscayne Blvd., ☎ 305-576-4000; South Dade office: ☎ 305-595-5151; North Dade Office ☎ 305-705-0800.

Jewish Genealogical Society of Greater Miami, 8340 SW 151st St., ☎ 305-253-1207.

Jewish Living, 525` NW 33rd Ave., Fort Lauderdale, ☎ 954-252-9393. The annual guide lists synagogues, services, and other resources of value to the Jewish community.

Jewish Arts Foundation, 230 Royal Palm Way, Ste. 207, Palm Beach, ☎ 561-659-7264.

Miami Beach Visitor and Convention Center, ☎ 305-539-3000.

Miami Beach Chamber of Commerce, ☎ 305-672-1270.

❖ DID YOU KNOW?

Larry King (nee Larry Zeiger) started his broadcast career in Miami Beach. In 1956, he launched his first radio talk show from Pumpernicks, a popular kosher-style deli. He left the area in 1978 and, of course, went on to contribute his well-known show "Larry King Live" to popular culture.

M ONTREAL

The completion of a $30 million expansion in 2001 will bring services, agencies, and community activities to one convenient Jewish campus. Visitors to the YM-YWHA Ben Weider Jewish Community Centre – which has indoor parking – will be delighted to find in one spot so many attractions, including recreational facilities, an art gallery, Yiddish Theatre, and a place to eat. Across the street are the Holocaust Memorial Centre and the Jewish Public Library.

What's more, the campus is within a walk to other Jewish sights, institutions, and synagogues. A nearby hotel makes the location the perfect base for a Jewish exploration of Montreal. See pages 116 and 125 for more information on the Holocaust Memorial Centre and the Jewish Community Centre.

But there's more to Montreal's Jewish component than this modern suburb. A member of the community claims, "Montreal is to Canada what New York City is to the United States – a city where it's very easy to be Jewish." Downtown neighborhoods hum with Jewish life. Students from nearby McGill University attend services at a historic shul, observers of kashrut are overwhelmed with restaurant choices, and names of internationally successful Jews mark buildings and institutions, both Jewish and non-Jewish.

The city's Jewish history stretches back to the late 1700s, when Aaron Hart arrived from London to open a trading business. The first congregation was established in 1768. Shearith Israel was modeled after the same-named synagogue in New York City, and is known today as the Spanish and Portuguese Synagogue.

The first Jews in Montreal were from Britain. Unlike in the United States, few Spanish, Portuguese, or Germans migrated to this area during the 18th and 19th centuries. But the Eastern European waves of immigration did wash over Montreal as they did the rest of North America, resulting in teeming neighborhoods and thriving Jewish life from the 1880s and into the 20th century. Boulevard St. Laurent and surrounding streets bustled with bookstores, kosher restaurants, newspapers, and pushcart peddlers. This area remained the heart of the community until the 1950s.

❖ DID YOU KNOW?

St. Urbain Street, an artery that pulsed with Jewish life, was where internationally known author Mordecai Richler grew up in the 1930s and 40s. His novels include *Joshua Then and Now, St. Urbain's Horseman,* and *The Apprenticeship of Duddy Kravitz,* made into a movie in the 1970s, starring Richard Dreyfuss. Many of the scenes were filmed in Montreal, at locations such as the Wilensky Deli on Fairmount and Clark.

Immigrant growth was stunted, though, in the 1930s with restrictive policies and discrimination, exacerbated by the Depression. After World War II, the anti-Semitism subsided and Jews from Europe as well as from Morocco and other Sephardic communities flooded into the city.

Today, Jews of Sephardic origin make up more than 25% of Montreal's Jewish population. The community of some 100,000 Jews is widely diverse. A number of Chasidic sects live and work in areas such as Outrement. Other suburbs with large Jewish populations are Westmount, Côte St. Luc, and Chomeday.

SIGHTSEEING HIGHLIGHTS

MUSEUMS & GALLERIES

Montreal Holocaust Memorial Centre, Cummings House, 1 Cummings Square, ☎ 514-345-2605. As part of the $30 million expansion of the Montreal Jewish Community Centre campus, the Holocaust Memorial Centre, too, is renovating and doubling the size of its space, to launch in 2002 a new, permanent exhibit. In the meantime, the temporary exhibit, *Children of the Holocaust: The Legacy*, is open for visitors. Hours: Sunday-Thursday, 10-4. No admission charged; donations appreciated.

Aron Museum, Temple Emanu-el Beth Sholom, 4100 Sherbrooke West, ☎ 514-937-3575. Located near Shaar Hashomayim on the fringes of Montreal's downtown, Temple Emanu-El is Canada's first Reform congregation and the city's only remaining Reform synagogue. The facility is modern, but the museum displays more than 200 pieces of Judaica and ritual objects, from old Torah scrolls to 19th-century chanukiot, as well as part of the Rothschild collection. It's open before services on Friday, or by appointment.

Spanish and Portuguese Synagogue, 4894 St. Kevin, ☎ 514-737-3695. From the outside, little about the Orthodox synagogue hints at its history. But inside, artifacts and displays attest to its origins as Montreal's oldest congregation. Sadly, none of its previous three homes exists today (the first structure was built in 1777). But the unique, dark-wood, round Ark dates to the Chenneville building, established in 1838. Throughout the large structure are display cases showcasing historic artifacts, including jewelry, samovars, Judaica, and other items collected and donated by congregants. The synagogue does not schedule tours, but those who call in advance may be accommodated.

Liane and Danny Taran Gallery, Saidye Bronfman Centre for the Arts, 5170 Côte Ste. Catherine, ☎ 514-739-2301. Housed in the Saidye Bronfman Centre of the YM-YWHA, the Gallery hosts changing exhibits of contemporary art. The shows are not always Jewish in content, but frequently feature Jewish artists and themes. Hours: Monday-Thursday, 9-9; Friday, 9-3 (winter), 9-5 (summer); Sunday 10-5. No admission charged.

HISTORIC SITES

Congregation Temple Solomon, 3919 Clark St., ☎ 514-288-0561 or ☎ 514-845-7700. Joseph Brick, self-described custodian, president, and financial secretary, is a good-natured source of stories about this history-rich congregation. Also known as Bais Shloima or the Bagg Street Shul, it's the only remaining synagogue

MONTREAL

in a neighborhood of 30 or more in the 1940s. In 1922, Eastern European immigrants purchased a Victorian townhome and converted it into a synagogue, complete with center bimah, a skylight, and a women's gallery. Its Ark, bimah, and seating came from Shaar Hashomayim and date back to the 1880s. A handpainted mural of the Hebrew calendar in the women's gallery is captivating. The synagogue is still active, attracting students from nearby McGill University to its Sephardic-style Shabbat and holiday services. From time to time, movies and television productions are filmed in this Religious Heritage Site. To visit, call for an appointment. Joseph Brick will happily be your guide. "On the outside, it may not look like much," he says, but assures visitors that once you enter the Bagg Street Shul, "you'll fall in love with it."

❖ DID YOU KNOW?

Congregation Temple Solomon has played a supporting role in a few Hollywood films. The charming, old-world synagogue may be best-known as the setting of the wedding in *Enemies: A Love Story*. Temple Solomon is slated to appear again in an upcoming movie about sports legend Jackie Robinson.

Shaar Hashomayim Congregation, 450 Kensington, Westmount, ☎ 514-937-9471, www.shaarhashomayim.org. Today the congregation is Traditional, but its founders were proud to claim themselves as the first Ashkenazi Orthodox congregation in Canada. A splinter group from the Spanish and Portuguese synagogue established in 1846. The congregation has worshiped at its current site since 1922. The large, stone structure is typical of 1920s synagogues, with Moorish influences, arched windows, and a large dome. The sanctuary is grand, with story-telling stained-glass windows.

Sir Mortimer B. Davis Jewish General Hospital of Montreal, 3755 Côte Ste. Catherine, ☎ 514-340-8222. The renowned hospital is the result of a community-wide campaign launched in 1929 to build an institution where Jews could practice medicine without discrimination. (An anti-Semitic environment restricted, among other things, Jewish employment in hospitals during this time.) The hospital was named for Davis, founder of the Imperial Tobacco company. Today, it's a McGill University teaching hospital just a 10-minute walk from the Montreal YM-YWHA campus. The names of the community's Jewish contributors can be seen on plaques throughout. The cafeteria is, of course, kosher, and open to the public.

Bronfman homes, Westmount. Westmount is a downtown neighborhood graced with mansions built by the wealthy, from Victorian times to the 1930s. The castle-like home at **15 Belvedere** commands a mountainside setting and breathtaking view. The home, built in 1906, was bought by Sam Bronfman, of the Seagram dynasty, and his wife Saidye in the 1920s. Saidye, for whom the city's YM-YWHA Centre for the Arts is named, lived here until her death just a few years ago. The Bronfman family still owns the home. Nearby, the house at **4363 Westmount Ave.** (corner of Carlton) was owned by Sam's brother Abe Bronfman. The white stone, three-story structure with a magnificent balcony was built in the early 1930s by architect Robert Findley. The home is no longer in the Bronfman family, however. Nor is the large Tudor at **3617 de Boulevard**, once owned by yet another Bronfman brother, Harry.

❖ DID YOU KNOW?

Before shooting into folk-music fame with his 60s hit, "Suzanne," musician and songwriter Leonard Cohen studied English at McGill University, not far from where he grew up in the Westmount neighborhood of Montreal.

MONUMENTS, MARKERS & MEMORIALS

Rabin Memorial Park, Beth Zion Synagogue, 5740 Hudson Ave., Côte St. Luc, ☎ 514-489-8411. On the grounds of Beth Zion Synagogue, the small park offers a place of reflection and solitude. A bust of the slain Israeli leader stands in his memory, and a large Holocaust wall lists the names of concentration camps.

Louis Rubinstein Fountain, near Fletcher's Field at the corner of Parc and Mont Royal. A small fountain is dedicated to Montreal native Louis Rubinstein. He was the 1890 winner of the Ice Skating World Championships held in St. Petersburg, Russia.

MONTREAL

Rubinstein was active in the city's Jewish community, serving as president of the YM-YWHA, as well as city alderman.

NEIGHBORHOODS

The Immigrant Neighborhood. Radiating from St. Laurent Boulevard and bounded roughly by Sherbrooke to the south and St. Viateur at the north end, are historic neighborhoods still sprinkled with Jewish businesses and institutions. It's a wonderful area to walk through – especially with a knowledgeable guide who knows the Jewish history. Although many former synagogues and Jewish businesses and institutions have been torn down, dozens of structures remain – often revealing their origins with telltale Hebrew inscriptions or stars of David carved into the facade. For example, at 172 Fairmount W., the College Francais was formerly the **B'nai Jacob Synagogue,** now a national historic site. The **Popliger Building** (Clark St. north of Milton St.), erected in 1909, has historic landmark status. Its innovative design allowed all apartments to open to the outdoors instead of to an inside hall. Today, the facade still shows the name of Popliger, the structure's Jewish designer, bordered by stars of David and the Hebrew date. The Portuguese Association of Canada, 4170 St. Urbain, was once the **Beth Hamedrash Hagadol,** an Orthodox congregation active from the 1920s to mid-century. Just up the street, the Sun Youth Organization 4251 St. Urbain, ☎ 514-842-6822, was once the **Baron Byng High School,** built in 1923. The student body remained more than 90% Jewish during its peak years in the 1930s and 40s. Alumni are writers Mordecai Richler, A. M. Klein, and Irving Layton.

In the neighborhood, institutions such as **Moishe's** (3961 St. Laurent, ☎ 514-845-3509) and **Schwartz's** (3895 St. Laurent, ☎ 514-842-4813) are renowned for their traditional Jewish delicacies – although neither are kosher.

COLLEGES & UNIVERSITIES

Canadian Jewish Studies, Concordia University, 1590 Ave. Docteur Penfield, ☎ 514-931-7531. The modern structure, built by the Bronfman family, houses genealogical archives and some interesting collections of Judaica, paintings, sculpture, and an Israeli stamp and coin collection. The artifacts are not on public display, but you can make an appointment to visit.

A McGill University Home Tour. Sir Mortimer B. Davis, founder of Imperial Tobacco, was to the tobacco industry what the Bronfman family was to whiskey. His home at 1020 Pine Avenue was designed by well-known architect Robert Findley in 1905-1906 (he also designed Abe Bronfman's home in Westmount). The curious can roam the building today – it's university-owned Purvis Hall. Just down the street, at 1374-1380 Pine Avenue West, is the former home of **Clarence de Sola**, son of Abraham de Sola, who served as rabbi for the Spanish and Portuguese Synagogue in the late 1800s. The home, built in 1913, is privately owned today, but the Moorish-style, seven-story, cliffside structure is still worth a walk-by.

❖ DID YOU KNOW?

William Shatner grew up in Montreal and attended McGill University before his acting career was launched into celebrity orbit with the television series *Star Trek.*

GENERAL-INTEREST SIGHTS WITH JEWISH CONNECTION

Habitat, Route 10, Bonaventure (Rue University), no telephone. On the site of Montreal's Expo 67, the building-block complex has a cubist, futuristic look. It was, however, the project that launched internationally acclaimed architect Moshe Safdie in the 1960s. The McGill-trained Israeli architect designed the complex to be functional and visually pleasing. He was evidently successful – the modernistic complex is still used today as residential apartments.

SYNAGOGUES

ORTHODOX

Beth Zion Congregation, 5740 Hudson Ave., Côte St. Luc, ☎ 514-489-8411.

MONTREAL

Congregation Temple Solomon, 3919 Clark St., ☎ 514-288-0561.

Congregation Shomrim Laboker, 5150 Plamandon, ☎ 514-731-6831.

Spanish and Portuguese Synagogue, 4894 St. Kevin, ☎ 514-737-3695.

Young Israel of Chomeday, 1025 Elizabeth, Laval, ☎ 514-681-2571. Mikvah on site.

CONSERVATIVE

Congregation Beth El, 1000 Lucerne, Town of Mount Royal, ☎ 514-937-3575.

Congregation Shaar Shalom, 4880 Notre Dame, Chomeday, ☎ 514-688-8100.

Shaare Zedek Congregation, 5305 Rosedale Ave., ☎ 514-484-1122.

Shaare Zion Congregation, 5575 Côte St. Luc, ☎ 514-481-7727.

REFORM

Temple Emanu-El Beth Shalom, 4100 Sherbrooke West, ☎ 514-937-9471.

TRADITIONAL

Shaar Hashomayim, 450 Kensington, Westmount, ☎ 514-937-9471.

RECONSTRUCTIONIST

Dorshei Emet, 18 Cleve Rd., Hampstead, ☎ 514-486-9400.

o Jerusalem, Montreal Jewish
ury Ave., ☎ 514-737-6551. The
off with the March to Jerusalem
early 20,000 with live stage per-
reet entertainment, crafts, food,
han 25 years old, the free street
ation, with the March serving as
wish Cultural Association.

an Centre for the Arts, 5170 Côte
, ext. 323. Founded more than 40
n Montreal claims to be the only
esidence in North America. The
language plays a year, and each
tand Yiddish? Not to worry – si-
rts the dialogue into English,
n.

352 Emery St., Fifth Floor, ☎ 514-
s selected for the Montreal Jewish
, whether they're documentaries,
t is held the second week in May
festival has gained a growing fol-
the United States, Israel, and Eu-
vents surrounding the films draw
y.

A/Ben Weider Jewish Community
4-737-6551. The celebration of
ther year during June or July at the
ations around Montreal. The two-
tures and seminars as well as mu-
t. Admission varies from event to

é Cummings Square., ☎ 514-345-
ith children in tow, the children's
ch as a Sunday morning story hour,
concerts. Established in 1914, the
000 books and periodicals in Eng-
and Russian.

KOSHER DINING

❖ For the latest information on kosher restaurants in Montreal, contact the **Vaad Ha-ir/The Jewish Community Council,** ☎ 514-739-6363.

Casalinga Ristorante, 5095 Queen Mary, ☎ 514-737-2272. This upscale dairy establishment features brick-oven pizzas and gourmet pasta as well as classic French cuisine, for lunch and dinner. The restaurant opens after Shabbat on Saturday evening. Same for the **Bistrot Chez Raymond** (☎ 514-738-5772), at the same address but on the lower level. This restaurant features a fancy French meat menu.

Mousseline Caviar, 3779 Jean Talon West, ☎ 514-731-4847. A deli menu attracts crowds for lunch, but patrons are always streaming in for carry-out meals, including complete Shabbat dinners.

Chez Babis Kosher, 6136 Chemin Côte St. Luc, ☎ 514-486-1414. An expansive meat and fish menu offers filling entrées from rib steak and veal cutlet to salmon steak and red snapper. The restaurant offers a full bar, and is open for lunch, dinner, and after Shabbat.

Chez Benny, 4999 Queen Mary Rd., ☎ 514-735-1836. Israeli favorites are featured at this casual, sit-down meat restaurant. Grilled meats, shwarmas, felafel, and a variety of salads are offered for lunch and dinner, and the establishment opens after Shabbat on Saturday nights.

El Morocco II, 3450 Drummond, ☎ 514-844-6888. Exotic ambiance (think Marrakech) and authentic Moroccan meat dishes such as pastilla, a variety of couscous dishes, chicken, beef, and lamb. The restaurant serves lunch and dinner, and opens Saturday after Shabbat.

Ernie & Ellie's Restaurant, 6900 Decarie Blvd., ☎ 514-344-4444. A traditional deli atmosphere is reflected in touches such as the bottle of soda water on each table and hefty meat sandwiches with a slice of pickle. But the menu also features Chinese entrées. The restaurant serves lunch and dinner, and opens after Shabbat on Saturday night.

Foxy's, 5987 Victoria, ☎ 514-739-8777. A casual and homey mosphere attracts lunch and dinner business for pizza, felafel, other favorites at this dairy restaurant. Open after Shabbat on [...] urday evening.

Gan Eden Restaurant, 3429 Peel St., ☎ 514-987-9875. The [...] taurant, located inside the Chabad Center, boasts a Middle E[...] ern meat menu featuring favorites such as shwarma, gril[...] meats, and couscous (call ahead to order). But more unusual ite[...] for a glatt kosher restaurant are available as well, including ocean salad with mock shrimp and crab. Prices are extremely re[...] sonable. The restaurant is open for lunch and dinner.

Hillel Jewish Student Center, 3460 Stanley, ☎ 514-845-917 www.hillel.montreal.qc.ca/rabbif.html. On the campus of McG[...] University, Hillel offers meat and vegetarian meals that are al[...] available to the public. The center is open for lunch and dinn[...] Monday through Friday.

Majestic, 5415 Royalmount, Town of Mount Royal, ☎ 514-73[...] 7911. During lunch, the atmosphere is more casual, serving quic[...] meat and fish meals. In the evening, the tablecloths and candle[...] come out, and the Majestic offers finer dining. The restaurant ha[...] a liquor license.

Mitchell's, YM-YWHA/Ben Weider Jewish Community Centre, 5500 Westbury, ☎ 514-737-8704. In the morning it's dairy, serving bagels, cream cheese, and breakfast fare for those who schedule early workouts. At 10:30, Mitchell's switches over to meat, serving sandwiches, soups, and a changing menu for lunch and dinner. The restaurant is open Monday through Thursday.

Pizza Pita, 5710 Victoria, ☎ 514-731-7482; 2145 St. Louis, Ville St. Laurent, ☎ 514-736-7482. At first glance, you may think you're in the wrong place – what appears to be hot dogs topped with cheese, chicken parmesan, and even shrimp, are menu highlights. But everything is kosher. The menu features several vegetarian "meat" items. Veggie-burgers are a favorite. Also popular are Tunisian tuna subs and *poutine*, French fries with cheese. Open for lunch and dinner, and after Shabbat, Saturday evening.

EVENTS

Israeli Street Festival/March [...]
Community Centres, 5500 West[...] annual May event, which kicks [...] walk, typically draws crowds of [...] formances, dancing, concerts, s[...] and children's activities. More [...] festival is sponsored by the Fede[...] a fund-raiser, organized by the J[...]

Yiddish Theatre, Saidye Bronfm[...] Ste. Catherine, ☎ 514-739-2301[...] years ago, the Yiddish Theatre i[...] one of its kind in permanent r[...] Theatre produces two Yiddish-[...] runs for a month. Don't under[...] multaneous translation conv[...] French, and occasionally Russi[...]

Montreal Jewish Film Festival, [...] 987-9795. All the 30-some film[...] Film Festival tell a Jewish stor[...] features, or animated. The eve[...] over a period of seven days. Th[...] lowing, with fans flocking from[...] rope to attend. A number of [...] attendance. Admission fees va[...]

Quizaine Sepharade, YM-YW[...] Centre, 5500 Westbury, ☎ 5[...] Sephardic culture is held every[...] Ben Weider JCC and other loc[...] week event includes serious le[...] sic, theater, and entertainme[...] event.

Jewish Public Library, 1, Ca[...] 2627. For the out-of-towner [...] libary offers great programs, s[...] arts and crafts, workshops, an[...] library boasts more than 100[...] lish, French, Hebrew, Yiddish[...]

HERITAGE TOURS

Jewish Walking Tour, Jewish Public Library, 5151 Côte Ste. Catherine, ☎ 514-345-2627. Reference librarian Ron Finegold reports that walking tours or bus tours are scheduled during the summer and fall months. Knowledgeable guides, born and brought up in Montreal, escort groups to Jewish heritage sites in areas such as St. Laurent Boulevard, the Chasidic neighborhoods, and the new campus area.

Allan Raymond, 4660 Bonavista Ave., Apt. 504, ☎ 514-489-8741. Raymond is a historian whose personal interest is the history of Jews in Montreal. He offers freelance tours, customized to the interest and size of the group. A typical tour is less than a half-day, and usually involves driving to various locations.

RESOURCES

Federation CJA, Federation of Jewish Community Services of Montreal, 5151 Côte Ste. Catherine, ☎ 514-735-3541, www.federationcja.org.

Jewish Information and Referral Service, ☎ 514-737-2221.

Montreal Jewish Historical Society, ☎ 514-489-8741.

Jewish Genealogical Society of Montreal, 5599 Edgemore Ave., ☎ 514-484-0100, www.gtrdata.com/jgs-montreal/.

Canadian Jewish News, 6900 Decarie, ☎ 514-735-2612. A weekly tabloid-format newspaper published in Montreal and Toronto.

The Jewish Community in Quebec, published by the Interculturel Institute of Montreal, 1987.

Tourism Montreal, 1555 Peel St., Ste. 600, ☎ 514-844-5400, www.tourism-montreal.org.

Tourist Information Centre, 1001 Dorchester Square, ☎ 514-873-2015.

NEW YORK CITY

"To me, if you live in New York or any other big city, you are Jewish. It doesn't matter even if you are Catholic; if you live in New York you're Jewish." – Lenny Bruce

Outside of Israel, New York City harbors the largest concentration of Jews anywhere in the world. And indeed the Jewishness of the community blends into the fabric of urban life as it does nowhere else – where bagels, knishes, and felafel are as generic as fast-food gets and you can get kosher Chinese, Thai, Iranian, Japanese, and haute cuisine. Where it is as common to find businesses closed for the High Holy Days as for Thanksgiving. Where the New York Public Library has a special Jewish division.

This was the starting point for Jews in America: In 1654, a small group just shy of two dozen sailed into New Amsterdam, more by accident than intent. The Jews from Brazil, bound for shores more secure than the Spanish-controlled colonies where the Inquisition still threatened, found a safe, if not welcome, harbor.

Jews continued to come to America through New York City. At first a mere trickle through the 18th century and first part of 19th century, then a flood, triggered by the Eastern European pogroms of the 1880s. Between the years 1880 and 1920, more than three million Jews poured into the United States, the vast majority entering through Ellis Island.

Today most American Jews – from the toddlers in a Southern California synagogue day-care, to the teenagers competing at a Macabbi tournament in Columbus, Ohio, to the Golden Agers who gather for Bingo at an Indianapolis JCC – can trace their origins in the United States to this gateway.

Plenty, though, traveled no farther than the nearest Jewish neighborhood. They spilled into the tenement area of Manhattan's Lower East Side, and as they became more integrated and successful spread into the west-side neighborhoods that bordered Central Park. They fanned out into the other boroughs – Brooklyn, Queens, the Bronx, Staten Island. Thus, New York City – where most of today's Jews can find their beginnings – remains the single most Jewish enclave outside of Israel, numbering two million if you include surrounding suburbs.

In most American cities, Jewish travelers must seek out the Jewish community; in New York City, Jewish life is ever-present. It's in a community center in the heart of an uptown museum and boutique area, it's in a historic immigrant neighborhood that is far from being a ghost town; it's in synagogues that draw Friday night crowds so large that the services often spill out into the streets with singing and dancing.

Indeed, the world-class museums and collections found throughout Manhattan are not to be missed. The historic synagogues should be toured. But in New York City, Jewish life is just a walk down the street.

SIGHTSEEING HIGHLIGHTS

MUSEUMS & GALLERIES

The Jewish Museum, 1109 Fifth Ave. (northeast corner of 92nd St.), ☎ 212-423-3200, www.thejewishmuseum.org. Its mission – "dedicated to presenting the remarkable scope and diversity of Jewish culture" – is an understatement. When you can observe ancient coins and pottery from the first century BCE in one exhibit, and watch a comedy skit with Jack Benny and George Burns in another, that's diversity. The Jewish Museum, situated on Manhattan's Museum Mile on upper Fifth Avenue, completed a major expansion in 1993. The original space, the imposing Warburg Mansion in all its French Gothic glory, now connects with the List Building, doubling its size. The permanent exhibit includes a recreation of an ancient synagogue and a haunting Holocaust sculpture. Under the auspices of the Jewish Theological Seminary, the museum provides programming, films, and family events. The Cooper Shop has been enlarged and sells exhibit-related merchandise (currently kitschy Freud-themed items such as Freudian Slip notepaper and Freudian slippers), as well as museum reproductions, jewelry, and ceremonial objects. The Jewish Museum Design Shop sells artists' works. Hours: Sunday, Monday, Wednesday, and Thursday, 11-5:45; Tuesday, 11-8. Tickets: $8 adults; $5.50 students and seniors; children 12 and under free. Free on Tuesday from 5-8.

Center for Jewish History, 15 West 16th St.,☎ 212-294-8301, www.centerforjewishhistory.org. A year-long schedule of events was launched with the grand opening on October 26, 2000, as five major Jewish institutions moved into a single center, offering one of the greatest concentrations of Jewish archives, educational resources, programming, and collections in the world. The five-building, 125,000-square-foot complex houses the American Jewish Historical Society, Leo Baeck Institute, American Sephardi Foundation, Yeshiva University Museum, and YIVO Institute for Jewish Research. A two-story reading room, theater, children's discovery area, and four exhibition galleries allow visitors to take advantage of some of the more than 100 million archival items, in excess of 500,000 library volumes, and some 10,000 art works and artifacts. Call for hours and information on admission fees.

- ❖ **American Sephardi Federation,** ☎ 212-294-8350. Representing more than 25 organizations, the ASF serves to unify, strengthen, advocate for, and educate the greater Jewish community about the Sephardi community through cultural and social programs. Its archives and special displays are of interest to the public.

- ❖ **Yeshiva University Museum,** ☎ 212-294-8330, www. yu.edu/museum. A hallmark exhibit is the recreation of a Jewish home of Biblical times. Museum-goers are invited to walk through the home and touch the items within. A film, "A Day in the Life," details the routines and rhythms of Jewish life in ancient times. The museum offers workshops, programming for children, and changing and permanent exhibits. On permanent display is the 15th-century Trent Manuscript, accusing the Jews of Trento, Italy of ritual murder.

NEW YORK CITY

* ❖ **Leo Baeck Institute,** ☎ 212-744-6400, www.lbi.org. The Institute is devoted to the study of German-speaking Jewry. In addition to a 60,000-volume library, genealogical records, and archives that include more than 12,500 photographs, the art collection features Judaica paintings, sculpture, drawings, and prints – as well as an extensive collection of drawings by inmates of concentration camps.

* ❖ **YIVO Institute for Jewish Research,** ☎ 212-246-6080, www. baruch.cuny.edu. Specializing in Eastern European Jewry, YIVO has been collecting documents, artifacts, and archival records of hundreds of Jewish communities since 1925. A collection of posters conveys the color of Jewish life in pre-Holocaust Eastern Europe, illustrating subject matter as diverse as breast-feeding, Yiddish theater, and politics.

* ❖ **American Jewish Historical Society,** ☎ 212-294-6160, www. ajhs.org. The headquarters for the country's first ethnic or religious historical organization has returned to New York City. Since 1968, the Society has been located near Brandeis University in Waltham, Mass., and will retain a museum there. Highlights of its holdings are the oldest surviving group of American family portraits from the 1730s.

Lower East Side Tenement Museum, 90 Orchard St., ☎ 212-431-0233, www.wnet.org/tenement or www.nationaltrust.org. Visitors to the Confino family apartment are welcomed by 13-year-old Victoria, who eagerly shares details of her daily life. She teaches them to fox-trot as she winds up the Victrola. She brings out a bag of marbles and suggests a game. Guests crowd into the cramped space where Victoria, her parents, four brothers, and other boarders live. Victoria may seem a curious if not gracious hostess – until visitors remember that they're at a museum, and that Victoria is an actress portraying a young Turkish-Jewish immigrant of 1916. The Lower East Side Tenement Museum, now a National Historic Landmark and a property of the National Trust for Historic Preservation, offers a unique and rare look into immigrant life. The Confino family quarters is but one of several permanently recreated apartments that portray life as it was for Jewish, German, Italian, Chinese, and other immigrant families during the immigration wave between 1870 and the 1920s. The Visitor Center holds a model of the tenement as it was in 1870 and 1915. There are a number of special programs, theme tours, and frequent theatrical performances. Hours: Tuesday-Friday, noon-5; Saturday-Sunday, 11-5. Admission: Tours are $8 adults; $6 seniors, students.

Museum of Jewish Heritage, 18 First Place, Battery Park City, New York, ☎ 212-968-1800, www.mjhnyc.org. Distinctive architecture sets it apart in the Battery Park City area. The harsh, hexagonal structure with a six-tiered roof has been described as tomblike. Inside the museum unfolds the story of the Holocaust in three phases: "Jewish Life a Century Ago," "The War Against the Jews," and "Jewish Renewal." This chapter in Jewish history is told through a collection of photos and touching artifacts, such as children's drawings and cards to loved ones, as well as wrenching personal testimonies recorded from survivors. The three-floor, circular structure allows for a tour that spirals forward without backtracking. The museum's intent is to memorialize the victims by celebrating their lives, much as the Kaddish honors the dead by praising God. Hours: Sunday-Wednesday, 9-5; Thursday, 9-8, Friday and eve of Jewish holidays, 9-2. Admission is $7, $5 students and seniors, children five and younger free.

Ellis Island Immigration Museum, Ellis Island, ☎ 212-269-5755, www.nps.gov/stli. The light-flooded Great Hall is a welcoming introduction to the museum. Immigrants who once waited hours and even days to proceed through medical and legal processing may not have received such a warm introduction to America. Yet immigrants, including an estimated 3.5 million Jews, swelled the New York population between the 1880s and the 1920s. Their gateway into the *goldena medina* between 1892 and 1954 was Ellis Island.

The museum tells the story of the immigrant experience through exhibits, artifacts, and photos, as well as interactive devices such as computers and taped accounts from immigrants. Two theaters feature the award-winning film, "Island of Hope, Island of Tears." Self-guided permanent exhibits, including *Through America's Gates,* walk visitors through the immigration process – and depicts experiences that are sometimes inspiring and sometimes tragic, such as new arrivals who were forced to return because of alleged diseases or mental conditions. "Treasures from Home," is a poignant collection of cherished heirlooms – family portraits,

NEW YORK CITY

jewelry, and religious items. The American Immigrant Wall of Honor contains the names of more than 500,000 immigrants.

Access to Ellis Island is via the Circle Line Statue of Liberty Ferry, which leaves from two locations: Battery Park in Lower Manhattan and Liberty State Park in New Jersey. The ferry makes trips to both the Statue of Liberty and Ellis Island. Ferry tickets at press time are $7 adults, $6 seniors, and $3 children. No admission charged for museum. Hours: Daily, 9:30-5; during summer, 8:30-4:30.

The Judaica Museum, Hebrew Home for the Aged at Riverdale, 5961 Palisade Ave., Bronx, ☎ 718-548-1006, www.jewishculture. org/jewishmuseums/bronx.htm. Ralph and Leuba Baum wanted to keep their art collection intact, so they donated the more than 800 objects to the Hebrew Home for the Aged. Among works by Chagall, Picasso, and Warhol are artifacts ancient and contemporary. A small amulet that dates back to the 1100s and a Torah scroll that survived Kristallnacht represent the diversity. In one exhibition, contributors of artifacts included Calvin Klein, Beverly Sills, and Alan King – each had parents who lived at the Hebrew Home for the Aged. Hours: Monday-Thursday, 1-4:30; Sunday, 1-5. No admission charge.

HISTORIC SITES

Eldridge Street Project, 12 Eldridge St. (between Canal and Division), ☎ 212-219-0888, www.eldridgestreet.org. Just a few blocks from where Chinatown encroaches, the Moorish structure dating from 1887 stands. The National Historic Landmark is in the process of a multimillion-dollar restoration, but throughout the transition, the schedule is packed with programming, special events, concerts, lectures, and more. Visitors are enthralled with the 70-foot vaulted ceiling and Victorian fixtures of the synagogue. Congregants of note include actors Paul Muni and Edward G. Robinson, as well as scientists Dr. Jonas Salk and Linus Pauling. Although the active congregation has been sparse since the 1930s, regular worship services are still scheduled. Tours: Sunday, 11 and 4; Tuesday and Thursday, 11:30 and 2:30. Admission: $4 adults, $2.50 students and seniors.

Shearith Israel, 8 West 70th St. (Central Park West), ☎ 212-873-0300. The current home of Shearith Israel, known as the Spanish and Portuguese Synagogue, was built in 1897 – but the congregation is the oldest in North America. It was founded in 1654. The Orthodox congregation is still thriving, and visitors are welcome for Shabbat worship. The building is constructed in the style of Spanish and Portuguese synagogues, and services are conducted according to those traditions. Highlights are the Tiffany stained-glass windows and marble steps and wall surrounding the Ark. Within the building is the Little Synagogue, where daily morning and evening services are still held. Worshipers will find themselves surrounded by treasures from earlier congregations – including the reader's desk, candlesticks, the Ner Tamid, Ten Commandment tablets, benches, and more from the 1730 Mill Street Synagogue. The congregation boasts an illustrious roster of past members: Emma Lazarus, Justice Benjamin Nathan Cardozo, and Commander Uriah Phillips Levy, to name a few. The synagogue is open for services. Tours are by appointment only and must be arranged in advance.

Temple Emanu-El, Fifth Ave. at 65th St., 1 East 65th St., ☎ 212-744-1400, www.emanuelnyc.org. With seating in its main sanctuary for 2,500, Emanu-El claims to be the world's largest Reform congregation and synagogue. The synagogue was completed in 1929, and the first services were held just weeks before the crash of the stock market that heralded the Depression. The architecture, a mix of Romanesque and Gothic details, is reminiscent of centuries-old cathedrals of Europe, but some Art Deco touches reveal its 20th-century origins. Its museum collection displays ritual objects, some from the 14th century. A Moroccan wedding ensemble is noteworthy. The synagogue is open for services and the sanctuary is open daily. Tours are available Sunday to Friday. Call in advance.

Central Synagogue, 650 Lexington Ave., ☎ 212-838-5122. Its onion-shaped copper cupolas have been a part of the New York City landscape since 1872. A devastating fire in 1999 damaged the city and National Historic Landmark – the colorfully stenciled walls and tiled floors of the Moorish Revival structure were destroyed. But the structure is scheduled to be completely restored and updated by the end of 2001. In the meantime, services are held in the congregation's Community House, across the street at 123 E. 55th St. In the lobby is a collection of silver spice boxes, Torah decorations, and needlepoint and wall hangings depicting Biblical scenes.

NEW YORK CITY

Bialystoker Synagogue, 7 Bialystoker Place, ☎ 212-475-0165. The building dates to 1826 and was originally a Methodist church. Call ahead to arrange a tour of this historic building that still serves an active congregation on the Lower East Side.

MONUMENTS, MARKERS & MEMORIALS

First Shearith Israel Cemetery, 55th St. James Pl., ☎ 212-873-0300. Sadly, the cemetery is never open to the public except for Memorial Day. But the small burial ground, dating to 1683, served as the final resting place for the first Jewish settlers who came in 1654 from South America. Two other congregational cemeteries not open to the public are at 76 W. 11th St. and at 21st St. between 6th and 7th Ave.

NEIGHBORHOODS

The two primary neighborhoods, the Lower East Side and Upper West Side, are detailed here. But don't miss visits to other places, including commercial areas, such as the **Diamond District** at West 47th Street between Fifth Avenue and Avenue of the Americas. It's an energetic, open-market atmosphere, buzzing with Chasidic diamond merchants and businesspeople – several kosher restaurants are located in the area. Go with those who know the past for a fascinating tour of neighborhoods such as **Harlem** – the 92nd Street Y offers a walking tour to sites of once-grand synagogues and homes of former residents.

Lower East Side, between Houston and Canal. Narrow streets darkened by looming tenement buildings teemed with activity during the decades preceding and following the turn of the last century. At that time the Lower East Side bustled with Jewish life – some 300 synagogues drew worshipers, seven daily Yiddish papers kept newcomers informed and connected to their old worlds, and pushcart merchants peddled goods from clothing to pickles.

Although the descendants of these early settlers have moved on, the Lower East Side is far from being a ghost town of Jewish life. The area still supports 11 synagogues. While the pushcarts have disappeared, streets such as Essex, Orchard, and Hester still fill with sidewalk tables on Sundays. Jews in the outlying suburbs still head for the neighborhood when they want to bargain for a tefillin set. Uniquely Jewish enterprises such as **Streit's Matzoh Bakery** (150 Rivington St., ☎ 212-475-7000) and **H&M Skull Cap Co.** (46 Hester St., ☎ 212-777-2280) draw customers. **Schapiro's Kosher Winery** (126 Rivington St., ☎ 212-674-4404) offers free tours on Sundays that conclude in wine-tasting. And you can still get a good half-sour pickle from a brine-filled barrel at **Guss's** (35 Essex St., ☎ 212-254-4477) – though the price has skyrocketed from its original nickel a pickle to 50¢.

The Lower East Side is packed with sights – some offering tours, such as the **Lower East Side Tenement Museum** (see page 132) and the **Eldridge Street Synagogue** (see page 134). Others worth a walk-by are the **Educational Alliance** (197 East Broadway), where Jewish immigrants transitioned into American society, the **Henry Street Settlement** (263-267 Henry St.), and the one-time site of offices for the *Jewish Daily Forward* (175 E. Broadway).

Upper West Side, between Central Park West and the Hudson River, 59th St. to 125th St. As the immigrant families from the Lower East Side gained a foothold into American prosperity, many moved to the Upper West Side. Because discrimination excluded them from the neighborhoods of Fifth Avenue at the time, the wealthy Jewish families built their mansions on the other side of Central Park. Congregations began moving in during the 1920s.

Today, some 90,000 Jews live in the area, supporting nearly two dozen synagogues, day schools, kosher restaurants, butchers, and bakeries. Places like **Drip** (489 Amsterdam Ave., ☎ 212-875-1032) draw Jewish clientele who meet for coffee and dessert (kosher-certified and otherwise), perhaps even signing up for the on-site dating service. Historic congregations, such as **Shearith Israel** (page 138) and **B'nai Jeshuran** (page 139), draw more worshipers than ever.

NEW YORK CITY

> ### ❖ DID YOU KNOW?
>
> Notable neighborhood residents of the Upper West Side have included Isaac Bashevis Singer, who lived at 86th between Broadway and Amsterdam, and Leonard Bernstein. Today, Itzhak Perlman, Letty Cottin Pogrebin, Tony Randall, Mandy Patinkin, and Dustin Hoffman, not to mention the *fictional* Jerry Seinfeld, call the Upper West Side home.

IN BOROUGHS BEYOND

A short drive from the Lower East Side across the Williamsburg Bridge is Brooklyn – and a number of Jewish neighborhoods. Three to see are **Williamsburg**, where the strictest of Chasidic sects live, **Borough Park**, home to the largest Chasidic community in the world, and **Crown Heights**, where a Lubavitch neighborhood thrives. Be sure to dress appropriately – women should wear skirts or dresses, men should bring head-coverings. Also in Brooklyn is **Brighton Beach**, where a large Russian Jewish population is growing in the boardwalk community. In the Bronx, the **Riverdale** neighborhood harbors an active Jewish community and includes some historic synagogues that now serve as churches. Check with the 92nd Street Y for the tour, "When the Bronx was Jewish."

SYNAGOGUES

ORTHODOX

The Carlebach Synagogue, 305 W. 79th St. (between West End and the Hudson), ☎ 212-580-2391.

Civic Center Synagogue, 49 White St., ☎ 212-966-7141.

Eldridge Street Synagogue, 12 Eldridge St., ☎ 212-219-0888 (see *Historic Sites*, page 134).

The Jewish Center, 131 W. 86th St., ☎ 212-724-2700.

Lincoln Square Synagogue, 200 Amsterdam Ave., ☎ 212-874-6100.

Park East Synagogue, 164 East 68th St., ☎ 212-737-6900.

Shearith Israel, 2 West 70th St., ☎ 212-873-0300 (see *Historic Sites*, page 134).

Wall Street Synagogue, 47 Beekman St., ☎ 212-227-7543.

Young Israel Synagogue of Manhattan, 225 E. Broadway, ☎ 212-732-0966.

CONSERVATIVE

Ansche Chesed, 251 W. 100th St., ☎ 212-865-9588 or 865-0600.

B'nai Jeshuran, 257 W. 88th St. (between West End Ave. and Broadway), ☎ 212-787-7600. It's a historic congregation (the oldest Ashkenazi congregation in the city) and the 1918 structure is impressive. But because there are no tours offered, the best way to see B'nai Jeshuran is to attend services. Friday evening's Shabbat services are spirited and renowned for music and dancing, making it a popular stop for out-of-town synagogue groups. Except for summer months, the services draw such large crowds that a second service is held at the Church of St. Andrew and St. Paul at West End Drive and 86th Street.

Congregation Shaare Zedek, 212 W. 93rd St., ☎ 212-874-7005.

Ezrath Israel, the Actor's Temple, 339 W. 47th St., ☎ 212-245-6975.

Park Avenue Synagogue, 50 E. 87th St., ☎ 212-369-2600. Art gallery on site.

Town and Village Synagogue, Tifereth Israel, 334 E. 14th St., ☎ 212-677-8090.

REFORM

Central Synagogue, 123 E. 55th St. (at Lexington Ave.), ☎ 212-838-5122. Services are being held in the Beir Chapel here until the Historic Landmark structure is restored after fire damage. A Judaica gallery is on site (see *Historic Sites,* page 135).

Metropolitan Synagogue of New York, 40 East 35th St. (Park and Madison), ☎ 212-679-8580. Scheduled the first Wednesday of each month are meditative jazz services at the synagogue where Leonard Bernstein was honorary founding musical director.

Rodef Shalom, 7 West 83rd St., ☎ 212-362-2300.

Temple Emanu-El, 1 East 65th St. (at Fifth Ave.), ☎ 212-744-1400, www.emanuelnyc.org (see *Historic Sites,* page 135).

Temple Shaaray Tefila, 250 E. 79th St., ☎ 212-535-8008.

The Village Temple, 33 E. 12th St., ☎ 212-674-2340.

RECONSTRUCTIONIST

West End Synagogue, 190 Amsterdam Ave. (at 69th St.), ☎ 212-579-0777.

KOSHER DINING

❖ Plenty of kosher-*style* fare can be found throughout the city. **Katz's Delicatessen** (205 E. Houston St., ☎ 212-254-2246), where Meg Ryan's memorable scene from *When Harry Met Sally* was filmed, has plenty of people asking for what she ordered. But New York City is one of the rare places where certified kosher dining is readily available. The supervisory organizations of these restaurants vary widely, but all places listed were under kosher certification at press time. Here's a listing of just a few of Manhattan's kosher dining choices.

Abigael's Grill, 9 East 37th St. (between Madison and Fifth Ave.), ☎ 212-725-0130. This restaurant advertises as the first-place winner in the James Beard Chili Cookoff. A meat menu features chicken, beef, fish, and pasta, and is open for lunch and dinner, including after Shabbat on Saturday.

All American Café & Health Bar, 24 E. 42nd St. (between Fifth and Madison), ☎ 212-370-4525. A wholesome menu of dairy and vegetarian dishes features salads, pastas, and pizza. Open for breakfast, lunch, and dinner.

American Café Health Bar & Pizza, 160 Broadway (Liberty and Maiden in Wall Street area), ☎ 212-732-1426. Open for breakfast, lunch, and dinner, this restaurant offers a number of Italian entrées on its dairy menu.

Bissaleh Classic Café, 1435 Second Ave., ☎ 212-717-2333. The restaurant serves a light dairy menu, but dessert-lovers will be drawn to cakes and cappuccino. Open for breakfast, lunch, and dinner.

Café 18, 8 E. 18th St., ☎ 212-620-4182. A dairy menu offers Mexican entrées, as well as sandwiches, pastas, and salads. Open for lunch and dinner.

China Shalom II, 686 Columbus Ave., ☎ 212-662-9676. Chinese favorites on the menu for lunch and dinner.

Colbeh, 43 W. 39th St., ☎ 212-354-8181. The meat menu showcases Persian cuisine for lunch and dinner.

Deli Casbah, 251 W. 85th St., ☎ 212-496-1500. Middle Eastern fare is featured at this meat restaurant. Open for lunch and dinner.

Diamond Dairy Restaurant, 4 W. 47th St. (Fifth Ave.), ☎ 212-719-2694. A great spot to watch the action in the diamond district. Stop for soup and dairy favorites such as blintzes for breakfast or lunch.

Dougie's Barbecue and Grill, 222 W. 72nd St. (West End), ☎ 212-724-2222. Ribs, chicken, burgers, and pasta dishes fill the menu for lunch and dinner.

Esti Hana Noodle Shop & Sushi Bar, 221 W. 79th St., ☎ 212-501-0393. It's a meat restaurant, but the star of the menu is the sushi. Open for lunch and dinner.

Fine and Schapiro, 138 W. 72nd St., ☎ 212-877-2721. Serving the neighborhood since 1927, the restaurant features a traditional menu, including chicken in a pot, matzah ball soup, and stuffed cabbage.

Galil, 1252 Lexington Ave., ☎ 212-439-9886. Israeli and Middle Eastern favorites draw crowds for lunch and dinner at this meat restaurant.

Glatt Dynasty, 1049 Second Ave., ☎ 212-888-9119. From sweet and sour to spicy Szechwan, the menu features traditional Chinese entrées for lunch and dinner.

Haikara, 1016 Second Ave., ☎ 212-355-7000. Japanese dishes from tempura to sushi are featured. Open for lunch and dinner.

Joseph's Café, 50 W. 72nd St., ☎ 212-595-5004. Pizza, pasta, and fish are standards on the café's dairy menu. Open for breakfast, lunch, and dinner.

Le Marais, 150 W. 46th St.(Sixth and Seventh avenues), ☎ 212-869-0900. A fine-dining French restaurant offers elegant ambiance. Open for dinner only.

Levana, 141 W. 69th St., ☎ 212-877-8457. The continental menu offers meat entrées for lunch and dinner.

Mendy's, 61 E. 34th St. (Park Ave.), ☎ 212-576-1010; **Mendy's West,** 208 W. 70th St., ☎ 212-877-6787. The first location serves lunch and dinner, the west dinner only. Both feature traditional cooking and meat menus.

My Most Favorite Dessert Co., 120 W. 45th St., ☎ 212-997-5130. Desserts are the highlight, but the restaurant offers an appealing range of Italian, dairy, and vegetarian dishes. Open for breakfast, lunch, and dinner.

Pongal, 110 Lexington Ave., ☎ 212-696-9453. An entirely pareve menu features Indian vegetarian cuisine for lunch and dinner.

Provi Provi, 228 W. 72nd St., ☎ 212-875-9020. An upscale atmosphere makes this restaurant, featuring northern Italian fare, a good choice for lunch or dinner. Dairy.

Ratner's Kosher Dairy Restaurant, 138 Delancey St. (between Norfolk and Suffolk Streets), ☎ 212-677-5588. Ratner's is more than a restaurant – it's an experience. Arrive at 6 am for a breakfast of blintzes, or have a late-night snack after Shabbat – it's open all day until 2 am. Also open is the Lansky Lounge, Ratner's cocktail bar with musical entertainment.

Rectangles, 159 W. Second Ave., ☎ 212-677-8410. Yemenite and Israeli meat dishes are offered for breakfast and lunch. The restaurant is open Friday and Saturday.

Second Avenue Deli, 156 Second Ave., ☎ 212-677-0606. It's decorated with artifacts that celebrate the Yiddish theater that flourished in the neighborhood. The restaurant is open on Shabbat.

Tevere 84, 155 E. 84th St. (Lexington Ave.), ☎ 212-744-0210. The meat menu features Italian fare for lunch, dinner, and brunch.

Vege Vege II, 544 Third Ave., ☎ 212-679-4710. Japanese and Chinese cuisine highlight a pareve menu for lunch and dinner.

The Vegetable Garden, 15 E. 40th St. (Fifth and Madison), ☎ 212-545-7444. Dairy-based soups, pasta, and sandwiches, in addition to fish draw customers for breakfast, lunch, and dinner.

Village Crown, 96 Third Ave, ☎ 212-674-2061. Middle Eastern meat and vegetarian dishes are on the menu for lunch and dinner. A second location next door offers a dairy menu and Italian specialties.

Yummi Restaurant, 63 Reade St. (Church and Broadway), ☎ 212-587-8204. Barbecue and grilled meats are highlights on this menu, open for lunch and dinner.

❖ BAGELS, KNISHES, PICKLES & RUGELACH

You can't really take away the flavor of Jewish New York without indulging in some street eating. On the Lower East Side, you'll savor the tastes that have been tempting locals for generations. Load up on knishes at **Yonah Schimmel's Knishes Bakery,** 137 E. Houston St. (Orchard St.), ☎ 212-477-2858. Born during pushcart days, this neighborhood enterprise continues to serve up potato, spinach, and kasha knishes. Don't pass up **Guss's Pickles,** 35 Essex St. (at Grand and Hester Streets), ☎ 212-254-4477. Choose your pickle from a briney barrel. Or ship some home. For baked goods – a glistening Sabbath challah or a dozen rugelach for starters – visit **Gertel's Bakery,** 53 Hester St. (at Essex), ☎ 212-982-3250, or **Kossar's Bialystoker Kuchen Bakery,** 367 Grand St., ☎ 212-473-4810. Throughout the city, you can find fresh-made bagels at dozens of locations. And, no matter what anyone says, New York bagels *are* better. Try **H&H Bagels,** 2239 Broadway, ☎ 212-692-2435. Order a dozen or so to take home.

JEWISH COMMUNITY CENTERS

A full-service facility is in the works on Amsterdam Ave., which will offer fitness, pool, classes, spa services, and more. But, alas, the new JCC won't be up and running until late 2001. In the meantime, the landmark 92nd Street Y offers reciprocal privileges to JCC members.

The 92nd Street Y, 1395 Lexington Ave., ☎ 212-996-1100. It's more than a community center – it's a virtual city within a city. A rich schedule of classes and activities keeps members and guests busy from 5 am when the fitness center opens until the lights go out on a musical concert, theater production, or lecture. A year-round program offers something for everyone. Lectures bring the biggest names in the world; a recent catalog pictured notables from every walk of life, from Jane Goodall to John Glenn, from Elie Wiesel to Carl Reiner. In addition to lectures, there are poetry readings, storytelling, and a schedule of classes that cover topics from Yiddish to chanting Torah, to creative writing and coping with divorce. There are plenty of single-session classes, so even if you're only in town for a few days, you have lots to choose from. The fitness center features more than 125 pieces of exercise equipment, a 25-yard indoor pool, whirlpool sauna and steam rooms, and more than 100 weekly exercise classes. The Y is also a great resource for Jewish-focused walking tours of the city (see the listing under *Heritage Tours*, page 145).

Shopping

Eichler's Judaica, 62 W. 45th St., ☎ 212-719-1918.

Jewish Museum Design Shop, 92nd St. and Fifth Ave., ☎ 212-423-3260.

Judaica Experience, 208 W. 72nd St., ☎ 212-724-2424, and **Judaica Experience Too,** 220 W. 72nd St., ☎ 212-769-4242

Michael Strauss Silversmiths, 164 E. 68th St., ☎ 212-744-8500.

West Side Judaica, 2412 Broadway, ☎ 212-362-7846.

Ziontalis, 29 W. 35th St., ☎ 212-643-8863. Emphasis on talitot, tefillin, and kippot.

Lodging

Midwood Suites, 1078 East 15th St., Brooklyn, ☎ 718-253-9535, www.midwoodsuites.com. If you'd like to stay in Brooklyn's observant Flatbush neighborhood, check out this comfortable kosher guest suite. Rooms are homelike, attractively decorated, and well-appointed with microwave and refrigerator. In lieu of the standard soap and shower cap complimentary kit, guests receive Shabbat candles, a hot water urn and other items to make Shabbat more homey. The place is within walking distance of Judaica shopping, kosher restaurants, and synagogues – as well as public transit to Manhattan. And at press time, rates were published at $89 to $169 per night for two.

EVENTS

American Jewish Theater, 307 W. 26th St. (Eighth and Ninth avenues), ☎ 212-633-9797.

Folksbiene Yiddish Theater, 45 East 33rd St., ☎ 212-213-2120. This theater has been featuring Yiddish classics for more than 80 years. Currently, one play per year, which runs for 10 to 12 weeks, is scheduled. Venues change from year to year; call for current information. Tickets run $30 to $35.

Jewish Repertory Theater, 92nd Street Y, 316 E. 91st St., ☎ 212-831-2000.

HERITAGE TOURS

Big Onion Walking Tours, ☎ 212-439-1090, www.bigonion. com. In 1998, Big Onion was recognized by *New York Magazine* for offering the best walking tours of the city. Among the more than two dozen tours are several with a Jewish focus, including a walk through the Lower East Side. Show-up tours are offered every weekend and holiday year-round. $10 adults, $8 students and seniors. Ellis Island is $16 adults, $14 students and seniors and includes the ferry ticket. The eating tours are $13 adults, $11 students and seniors, and includes the meals.

92nd Street Y, 1395 Lexington Ave., ☎ 212-415-5420. Several tours focus on neighborhoods such as the Lower East Side, but others point out Jewish traces in sights surprising to the visitor, such as Harlem and the East Village. Tours venture farther, taking in Jewish enclaves such as Crown Heights, Brighton Beach, Borough Park, Williamsburg in Brooklyn, and Riverdale in the Bronx. The Y also offers day excursions, weekend getaways, and tour themes as diverse as chocolate-lover's guide to New York and hardhat tours of current construction. You can also arrange for custom tours by calling ☎ 212-415-5628. Reservations are required, and costs range from $15 to $60, but most are around $20 to $30.

Hassidic Discovery Welcome Center, 305 Kingston Ave., Brooklyn, ☎ 718-953-5244, www.jewishtours.com. Show up at the New York Public Library in Manhattan (42nd St. and Fifth Ave.) by 9:30 Sunday morning, and you can be transported into Brooklyn by bus, for a tour of a world both mystical and observant. The half-day tour of one of Brooklyn's Chasidic neighborhoods includes a demonstration from a Torah scribe, and a peek into a world that for many remains mysterious. Oddly, the Web site emphasizes that the tours are led by *friendly* Chasidic Jews – perhaps an acknowledgment that most Jews are intimidated by the fervor and commitment of the Chasidim. The price of a half-day tour is $36 and includes lunch.

RESOURCES

UJA Federation of Jewish Philanthropies of New York, 130 E. 59th St., ☎ 212-980-1000.

The Jewish Week, 1501 N. Broadway, ☎ 212-921-7822, www. thejewishweek.com. The Federation's newspaper keeps locals up-to-date on area happenings. Also available through *Jewish Week* is *Directions,* a comprehensive guide to Jewish life in Manhattan. Separate editions are published for the other boroughs.

Jewish Historical Society of New York, Inc., 8 West 70th St., ☎ 212-415-5544.

Online, visit **www.kosherlink.com** for the scoop on the lengthy list of kosher restaurants and food purveyors in New York City.

New York City Convention and Visitors Bureau, ☎ 800-692-8474, 212-484-1200; www.nycvisit.com.

PHILADELPHIA

Not far from Independence Mall, where visitors marvel at the Liberty Bell and other symbols of America's beginnings, the curious explorer can go a little farther, dig a little deeper, and discover that Jews, too, played a role in the founding of the country. Center City has had a Jewish presence since pre-Revolutionary War times. In fact, records indicate that kosher food was served following the Grand Federal Procession celebrating ratification of the Constitution by Pennsylvania in 1787.

A wealth of Judaic sightseeing attractions are concentrated in a relatively small area here. Just a walk from the Philadelphia's historical heart, a fascinating museum housed in a Sephardic synagogue, and four more historic congregations (all still active) are found in the Society Hill neighborhood. An explorer with a keen eye (or a knowledgeable guide) will also pick out other structures with Jewish connections. Telltale cornerstones reveal Hebrew script, a small bronze plaque identifies another site.

The pattern of Jewish settlement in Philadelphia is similar to that of other East Coast cities. In its earliest years, Sephardic families settled, followed by communities from Germany in the late 1700s to mid-1800s. These Jews thrived. In fact, one historic source described the pre-1880 community of 15,000 as "a prosperous community with no poor." Interestingly, the Jews of the pre-immigrant period did not live in Society Hill, a wealthy area even before American independence.

❖ DID YOU KNOW?

Many an influential leader, writer, and artist paid tribute to Rebecca Gratz. The daughter of a prominent merchant family played hostess to the likes of Washington Irving and artist Thomas Sully. In fact, Gratz, who helped launch many charitable organizations, was reputed to be the inspiration for the character Rebecca in Sir Walter Scott's classic, *Ivanhoe*.

It was the poor Eastern European Jews flooding into the country between 1882 and 1924 who built their synagogues in decaying neighborhoods of mansions and grand homes. The Jewish Quarter flourished with peddlers, rag men, horseradish men, and others scrambling to make a living in the area that stretched from Spruce Street on the north to Christian Street south, and South 2nd on east and South 6th on west. The heart of the area was South Street.

A Jewish population remains in Society Hill, but most of the more than 200,000 Jews of Philadelphia are dispersed to other parts of the city and the suburbs and in Montgomery and Bucks County. Some of the larger clusters in or nearer the city are in Elkins Park, Lower Merion and other communities along the Main Line, and northeast Philly. Here, Jewish commerce supports Orthodox neighborhoods. JCC branches, agencies, and Jewish colleges (the Reconstructionist Rabbinical College and Gratz College) are found in these areas. Other libraries and archives, including the Jewish Archives Center, hold a treasure of historical documents, as well as genealogical information that attracts Jews who are interested in developing their family trees.

SIGHTSEEING HIGHLIGHTS

MUSEUMS & GALLERIES

National Museum of American Jewish History, 55 North Fifth St., ☎ 215-923-3811, www.nmajh.org. Just a few steps from the Liberty Bell and Independence Mall, this museum chronicles the American Jewish experience from its beginnings in 1654 to the present. Its exhibits recount historical moments and Jews of note – such as artist-adventurer-writer Solomon Nunes Carvalho, who painted both Jews and Indians of the West. But perhaps more compelling are the artifacts and stories of everyday life. The elaborate invitation to a 1951 Bar Mitzvah, with a collage of menu, guest list, and baby pictures on a tiny scroll. The artful postcards wishing a sweet new year or featuring local synagogues. The display recounting the story of an immigrant peddler making his way to a wilderness without Jews. Its permanent exhibit, "Creating American Jews," focuses on the experiences and circumstances that have shaped the Jewish identity in the United States. The museum is housed in the historic Temple Mikvah Israel. Hours: Monday-Thursday, 10-5; Friday, 10-3; Sunday, noon-5. Admission: $3 adults; $2 seniors and students.

Philadelphia Museum of Jewish Art, Congregation Rodeph Shalom, 615 North Broad St., ☎ 215-627-6747. The museum's permanent exhibit contains a collection of Judaica, including pieces ancient and modern. Changing exhibits focus on 20th-century Jewish art and photography. The synagogue is also noteworthy (see *Historic Sites*, page 151). Hours: Monday-Friday, 9-4; Saturday, open one hour before services, 9:45-10:45; Sunday, 10-1.

Rosenbach Museum and Library, 2010 Delancey Pl., ☎ 215-732-1600. The Rosenbach brothers bought art and rare books – including the original manuscript for Joyce's *Ulysses.* But their collection also features Judaica, such as the Portuguese Hebrew bible dated to 1491, and the first Haggadah printed in the United States. The museum also holds several letters and portraits of the Gratz family, including the famous 1831 portrait of Rebecca Gratz by Thomas Sully. Hours: Tuesday-Sunday, 11-4; closed August. Access to specific items and books is by appointment only.

Temple Judea Museum of Keneseth Israel, Old York Rd. and Township Line Rd., Elkins Park, ☎ 215-887-8700. A Torah commentary dating to 1574 and an early-American ketubah are just two of the 600-some pieces that represent the combined collections of two merged synagogues. Temporary exhibits of Judaica and Jewish art change three times a year. Hours: Monday-Wednesday, 1-4; Friday evening before and after services. Group tours by appointment.

Philadelphia Jewish Sports Hall of Fame and Museum, Gershman Y, 401 S. Broad St., ☎ 215-545-4400. Photos, biographies, and banks of lockers containing sports memorabilia commemorate the achievements of the 31 inductees. Particularly popular is the display about Bernie Lemonick, All-American for the University of Pennsylvania – visitors are fascinated by the 1950s uniform, which looks quite different from the football team's current uniform. A display about the Maccabee Games and a memorial to the Munich Eleven also draw interest. Hours: 9-5; closed Shabbat.

Fred Wolf, Jr. Gallery, Klein JCC, 10100 Jamison Ave., ☎ 215-698-7300. The art gallery located in the JCC offers a variety of exhibits, both secular and Jewish in theme. Call for hours.

Borowsky Gallery, Gershman Y, 401 S. Broad St., ☎ 215-545-4400. The small gallery is housed in a separate room, but its changing exhibits often spill out into the lobby. Themes are typically of special interest to the Jewish community. Call for hours.

HISTORIC SITES

B'nai Abraham, 527 Lombard St., ☎ 215-238-2100. An active Orthodox congregation, founded in 1882, has worshiped at this Society Hill site since 1885. The Byzantine structure that stands today, however, was constructed in 1910. During the city's immigrant period, B'nai Abraham served as a cornerstone of daily Jewish life, feeding the hungry and sheltering the homeless. Bernard Levinthal, rabbi from 1891 to 1952, helped to found New York's Yeshiva University. Of note are the rose windows with the Magen David patterns, Doric columns, and yarzeit boards made of Italian glass. Also of note is the fact that the synagogue was built exclusively by Jewish workmen. This building is the oldest continuously used synagogue structure in Philadelphia. Visitors are welcome for daily and Shabbat services.

Kesher Israel, 412 Lombard St., ☎ 215-922-7736. Another Society Hill institution, the structure that houses the still-active Traditional congregation has stood since 1796. It served as a Universalist Church originally, but was purchased and used as an Orthodox synagogue from 1887. Some restoration and expansion occurred in the late 1890s, with the addition of a Romanesque Revival entrance, separate doors for men and women, a Moorish minaret, stained glass, and more. In 1939, the congregation became Conservative. Recent restoration has added a new pressed-tin ceiling. The building's historic murals, towering stained-glass windows, walls, benches, and hardwood floors have all been restored. Visitors are welcome to attend services.

Vilna Shul, 509 Pine St., ☎ 215-592-9433. At one time, the Vilna Shul was among several row-house shuls in the neighborhood. Today it is the only one. The Orthodox congregation has been worshiping at this site since 1922. The building is tiny, compared to many grand, historic synagogues that stand today, but it is described as jewel-like. Two rows of vivid stained-glass windows dominate and reflect light in kaleidoscope patterns on its walls. Gilded lions top the Torah ark, and the women's balcony, no longer used, wraps around the gallery above. The synagogue is open to the public and visitors are welcome to attend services.

Society Hill Synagogue, 418 Spruce St., ☎ 215-922-6590. A Reform congregation has worshiped at this site since 1967. But once the imposing building, which has stood since 1829, served as the Spruce Street Baptist Church. It became a synagogue in 1911 – first as Beth Hamedrash Hagodol, later as the Roumanian Shul. Still inscribed in Yiddish above the massive entrance doors are the words, "The Great Roumanian Shul."

Congregation Rodeph Shalom, 615 North Broad St., ☎ 215-627-6747. Rodeph Shalom split from Congregation Mikvah Israel in 1801, becoming the first Ashkenazi congregation in the United States. The current synagogue, built in the 1920s, was modeled after the Great Synagogue of Florence, Italy. The grandeur of the sanctuary is accentuated with large, pink marble columns guarding an ornate Ark.

Beth Sholom Synagogue, 8231 Old York Rd. (at Foxcroft Rd.), Elkins Park, ☎ 215-887-1342. Frank Lloyd Wright designed this, his only synagogue, in 1954. Described as a Mt. Sinai in modern materials, the steel, concrete, aluminum, and glass structure glows with the light from the sanctuary at night. Wright incorporated biblical themes into the design, including a fountain symbolizing the purification before sacrifice and prayers, the menorah, and a six-sided shape visible from an aerial view. Call for information about guided tours.

Congregation Mikvah Israel, 44 North 4th St., ☎ 215-922-5446. The synagogue is home to the National Museum of American Jewish History, but the Spanish-Portuguese synagogue, founded in 1740, is visit-worthy on its own merits. First, it is home to the city's first Jewish congregation, also known as the "Synagogue of the Revolution." Secondly, its own collection holds some valuable art and archives, including letters from George Washington and Abraham Lincoln, as well as a Torah donated in 1782 by Haym Salomon, and an Italian megillah. Outside is a monument to Jonathan Netanyahu, the Israeli commander killed in the Entebbe raid on July 4, 1976.

The Frank Synagogue, Albert Einstein Medical Center, Old York and Tabor Roads, ☎ 215-456-6055. Modeled after first- and second-century synagogues discovered in the Galilee region of north central Israel, this small, historically certified synagogue on the grounds of a medical center was originally dedicated in 1901.

MONUMENTS, MARKERS & MEMORIALS

Mikvah Israel Cemetery, 8th and Spruce Streets, ☎ 215-922-5446. This is one of the oldest Jewish cemeteries in the United States (and today the oldest Jewish landmark in Philadelphia), with graves dating from 1740. Interred here are Haym Solomon, Rebecca Gratz, and 21 veterans of the American Revolution. The small graveyard in the heart of the city is enclosed by a high brick wall – where legend has it that British soldiers shot those suspected of treason.

Monument to the Six Million Jewish Martyrs, 16th St. and the Benjamin Franklin Pkwy., ☎ 215-832-0500. This memorial sculpture was the first public Holocaust monument in North America. The bronze sculpture stands at a busy street corner.

NEIGHBORHOODS

Society Hill. This area just a block south of Independence Mall was settled even before the Revolution and encompasses the largest collection of pre-Revolutionary homes in the country. This is also the neighborhood that thrived during the immigration period from 1880 through the 1920s. A strong Jewish presence remains, with four active synagogues of historic interest. Consider a guided tour – the neighborhood's Jewish legacy is rich, but many sites will go unnoticed unless you know what to look for. For example, you may miss the edifice at 603-05 S. 3rd Street – once the **Rosenbaum Bank**, serving the immigrant community from 1907 to 1933 (a plaque identifies it today), or the condo at 312 Catharine

Street, once the **Hebrew Literature Society**, or the former offices of the *Jewish Daily Forward*, at 508 S. 5th Street. (Look for the word "Forward" inlaid in the stoop.) Look for cornerstones at 615-21 S. 6th Street (today an antique market, once **B'nai Reuben**), and at 314-320 Catharine Street (**Talmud Torah**).

COLLEGES & UNIVERSITIES

Gratz College, Mandell Education Campus, 7605 Old York Rd., Melrose Park, ☎ 215-635-7300. The historic college was established in 1895. Its library maintains extensive collections of prayer books, Holocaust literature, music, and some art. Of interest to the visitor are outdoor sculpture reminiscent of Jewish cemeteries of Europe.

Center for Judaic Studies, 420 Walnut St., ☎ 215-238-1290. Within view of Independence Hall, the Center for Judaic Studies houses a large collection of books related to Judaic and Near Eastern studies. Although most who explore its archives are scholars earning advanced degrees, the institution holds a delightful surprise for visitors who discover its rare-book room. In the small rosewood-paneled sanctuary, ancient artifacts from archaeological excavations are displayed as well as some 14th-century Hebrew books.

GENERAL-INTEREST SIGHTS WITH JEWISH CONNECTION

University of Pennsylvania Museum of Archaeology and Anthropology, 33rd and Spruce Streets, ☎ 215-898-4031, www.upenn.edu/museum. "Canaan and Ancient Israel" opened in 1998 as a major permanent exhibit. This exhibition claims to be the first ever to focus on the development of cultural identity in ancient Israel and neighboring lands. Artifacts include pottery, statuary, seals, and objects of gold, ivory, and semi-precious stones. Hours: Tuesday-Saturday, 10-4:30. Admission: $5 adults, $2.50 students and seniors.

The Library Company of Philadelphia, 1314 Locust St., ☎ 215-546-3181. Founded by Benjamin Franklin in 1731, the Library Company was once the country's largest public collection of books. Its rare-book holdings include a number of Jewish books

PHILADELPHIA

bequeathed by A. S. W. Rosenbach, such as the first Hebrew grammar book printed in America (1735), and what may be the first Jewish prayer book, published in 1760. These items are not always on display, but the institution is worth a visit. Hours: Monday-Friday, 9-4:45.

SYNAGOGUES

ORTHODOX

Mikveh Israel, 44 N. 4th St., ☎ 215-922-5446.

Aitz Chaim Synagogue Center, 7600 Summerdale Ave., ☎ 215-742-4870.

B'nai Abraham, 527 Lombard St., ☎ 215- 238-2100. A historic congregation (see *Historic Sites,* page 150).

Beth Hamedrosh of Overbrook Park, 7505 Brookhaven Rd., ☎ 215-473-1019.

Lower Merion Synagogue, 123 Old Lancaster Rd., Bala Cynwyd, ☎ 610-664-5626.

Lubavitch, 7622 Castor Ave., ☎ 215-725-2030

Vilna Congregation, 509 Pine St., ☎ 215-592-9433. Historic congregation (see *Historic Sites,* page 151).

Young Israel of Elkins Park, 7715 Montgomery Ave., Elkins Park, ☎ 215-635-3152.

CONSERVATIVE

Adath Israel, 250 N. Highland Ave., Merion Station (Main Line), ☎ 610-664-5150.

Adath Jeshurun, 7763 Old York Rd., Elkins Park, ☎ 215-635-6611.

Beth Sholom Congregation, 8231 Old York Rd., Elkins Park, ☎ 215-887-1342.

Beth Zion-Beth Israel, 300 S. 18th St., ☎ 215-735-5148.

Har Zion Temple, 1500 Hagys Ford Rd., Penn Valley, ☎ 610-667-5000.

Society Hill Synagogue, 418 Spruce St., ☎ 215-922-6590.

Congregation Beth T'fillah of Overbrook Park, 7630 Woodbine Ave., ☎ 215-477-2415. Conservative synagogue with a 10-foot-high replica of the Western Wall in its lobby.

TRADITIONAL

Kesher Israel, 412 Lombard St., ☎ 215-922-7736. Historic congregation, traditional (see *Historic Sites*, page 150).

REFORM

Keneseth Israel, 8339 Old York Rd., Elkins Park, ☎ 215-887-8700 (see *Museums & Galleries*, page 149).

Main Line Reform Temple, Beth Elohim, 410 Montgomery Ave., Wynnewood, ☎ 610-649-7800.

Old York Road Temple-Beth Am, 971 Old York Rd., Abington, ☎ 215-886-8000.

Rodeph Shalom, 615 N. Broad St., ☎ 215-627-6747. Also historical (see *Historic Sites*, page 151).

Temple Beth Torah, 608 Welsh Rd., ☎ 215-677-1555.

RECONSTRUCTIONIST

Leyv Ha-ir Center City, Gershman Y, 401 S. Broad St., ☎ 215-629-1995.

Beth Israel, 542 S. New Middletown Rd., Media, ☎ 610-566-4645 or 610-566-5619.

Congregation Kol Emet, 65 N. Main St., Yardley, ☎ 215-493-8522.

PHILADELPHIA

KOSHER DINING

❖ Several local rabbinical associations and individual rabbis provide kashrut supervision in the Greater Philadelphia area. Contact the **Board of Rabbis of Greater Philadelphia,** ☎ 215-985-1818, the **Rabbinical Assembly** (Conservative), ☎ 215-635-9701, or the **Vaad Hakashruth and Beth Din of Philadelphia,** ☎ 215-725-5181.

Cafeteria Tiberias, 8010 Castor Ave., ☎ 215-725-7444. Light meals, pizza, and pasta are highlights at this dairy establishment open for lunch and dinner.

Cherry Street Chinese Vegetarian, 1010 Cherry St., ☎ 215-923-3663. Vegetarian and dairy dishes feature Asian cuisine. Tofu dishes are recommended. The restaurant is open for lunch and dinner.

Dragon Inn, 7628 Castor Ave., ☎ 215-742-2575. Filling entrées feature Chinese meat favorites that can be spiced to taste. Come for lunch, dinner, or carry-out.

Genya Snack Bar, 10100 Jamison Ave., ☎ 215-677-0280. This quick stop at the Klein JCC is open for breakfast, lunch, and dinner, and offers sandwiches, soups, and hot dogs.

Hatikva, 7638 Castor Ave., ☎ 215-725-4400. Israeli and Middle Eastern specialties are on the menu at this meat restaurant. Portions are ample – reservations are advised.

Hillel Dining Room, University of Pennsylvania, 202 S. 36th St., ☎ 215-898-7391. All-you-can-eat lunches (dairy) and dinners (meat) are offered at student-friendly rates. Shabbat dinners are available, but you must arrange in advance.

Linietsky's Traditions Restaurant, 9550 Bustleton Ave., ☎ 215-677-2221. Described as "glatt gourmet," the restaurant has an upscale ambiance and fine food. Downstairs is **Kosher Kaos,** a fast-food version of kosher cuisine. Open for dinner.

Maccabeam, 128 S. 12th St., ☎ 215-922-5922. This meat menu features Israeli and Middle Eastern dishes for lunch and dinner. The bean soup comes highly praised.

17th Street Felafel, 17th and Market St., ☎ 215-879-6956. A place to pick up a fast, vegetarian lunch, the restaurant features felafel and fixings.

Rajbhog, 738 Adams Ave., ☎ 215-537-1937. The dairy restaurant features a vegetarian Indian menu. A great stop for health-conscious diners who want to select from low-fat and low-oil items. You can also control the spice factor. Closed on Monday, open for lunch and dinner.

Singapore Kosher Vegetarian, 1029 Race St., ☎ 215-922-3288. A range of Asian specialties, including Chinese and Thai. Open for lunch and dinner.

Time Out Felafel Kingdom, 9846 Bustleton Ave., ☎ 215-969-7545. Popular are the steak sandwiches and generous shwarma platters. Prices are pleasing, whether for lunch or dinner.

❖ DID YOU KNOW?

Stooge Larry Fine (the one with the curly hair) started out in Philadelphia. Even at the tender age of 3, Louis Feinberg was getting his share of "nyuk-nyuk-nyuks" in his South Street neighborhood of Society Hill.

JEWISH COMMUNITY CENTERS

Kaiserman JCC, 45 Haverford Rd., Wynnewood, ☎ 610-896-7770. This JCC branch offers a full range of fitness facilities and programs. Indoor and outdoor pools, a track, an extensive cardio-vascular center, sauna, steam, and whirlpool draw members of all ages.

Klein JCC, 10100 Jamison Ave., ☎ 215-698-7300. Athletic facilities include indoor pools, jogging track, basketball, racquetball, and tennis courts, complete cardio center, as well as sauna, steam room, and whirlpool. The Klein Branch also houses the Fred Wolf Jr. Gallery.

Gershman Y, 401 S. Broad St., ☎ 215-545-4400. The place to go for arts and culture, the Gershman Y is home to two film festivals,

PHILADELPHIA

the Philadelphia Jewish Sports Hall of Fame, the Borowsky Gallery, and Israel programs.

SHOPPING

Bala Judaica Center, 222 Bala Ave., Bala Cynwyd, ☎ 610-664-1303.

Dahlia-Treasures from the Holy Land, 2003 Walnut St., ☎ 215-568-6878.

Jerusalem Israeli Gift Shop, 7818 Castor Ave., ☎ 215-342-1452.

JCC Shoppe, Klein Branch, 10100 Jamison Ave., ☎ 215-698-7300.

Mazel Stuff, 44 Antler Dr., Holland, ☎ 2215-860-7744.

National Museum of American Jewish History, 55 North 5th St., ☎ 215-923-3811.

Rosenberg Hebrew Book Store, 409 Old York Rd., Jenkintown, ☎ 215-884-1728, and 6408 Castor Ave., ☎ 215-744-5205.

EVENTS

Film Festivals, Gershman Y, 401 S. Broad St., ☎ 215-545-4400. Two events bring films of special interest. The **Israeli Film Festival,** co-sponsored by the Israeli Consulate, is scheduled annually in the spring; the **Jewish Film Festival** kicks off in the fall for a lengthy season of films focusing on Jewish themes. Both bring classics and cutting-edge works to the attention of Philadelphia and attendees from all over the world. The Jewish Film Festival runs one weekend (Saturday, Sunday, and Monday) a month from October through April.

❖ DID YOU KNOW?

Actor Eddie Fisher (Debbie's, Liz's, and Connie's husband, Carrie's and Joely's dad) grew up in South Philadelphia before he left for Hollywood fame in the 1940s.

Jewish Book Festival, Gershman Y, 401 S. Broad St., ☎ 215-545-4400. Philadelphia celebrates the nationwide Jewish Book Month each November, and activities are planned at JCC branches throughout the Greater Philadelphia area.

Jewish Festival, in Bucks County at Middletown Grange Fairgrounds, ☎ 215-579-9300. Held the first weekend in June, the annual event features food, music, art, crafts, activities for children, hayrides, Jewish vendors, and a full day of activity. There is no admission fee.

HERITAGE TOURS

National Museum of American Jewish History, 55 North 5th St., Independence Mall East, ☎ 215-665-2300. Call the museum to arrange wallking tours of historic Jewish Philadelphia.

Walking Tour of Jewish Historic Society Hill, Harry D. Boonin, ☎ 215-934-7184, www.boonin.com. Author and historian Harry D. Boonin leads tours of the Society Hill area on Tuesdays and Thursday mornings, April through Thanksgiving. Tours are $10; children under 18 are free. Call in advance.

RESOURCES

Jewish Federation of Greater Philadelphia, Jewish Community Building, 2100 Arch St., ☎ 215-832-0500, www.phljnet.org. The Web site lists museums, exhibits, synagogues, restaurants, events, and more.

Jewish Information and Referral Service, Jewish Community Building, 2100 Arch St., ☎ 215-832-0500.

PHILADELPHIA

Jewish Genealogical Society of Philadelphia, 1279 June Rd., Huntingdon Valley, ☎ 215-947-7374.

Philadelphia Jewish Archives Center, 18 South Seventh St., ☎ 215-925-8090. A great resource for those researching genealogy or other aspects of Jewish history. It contains complete and indexed passenger ship records from 1884-1921. Housed in the same building as the **Balch Institute for Ethnic Studies.** Hours: Tuesday, Thursday, Saturday, 10-4.

Jewish Exponent, Jewish Publishing Group, Jewish Community Building, 2100 Arch St., ☎ 215-893-5700. Weekly newspaper covering world news of Jewish interest and detailed information on local activities.

Inside Magazine, Jewish Publishing Group, Jewish Community Building, 2100 Arch St., ☎ 215-893-5797. Quarterly magazine of Jewish life and style. Sold at newsstands. Also publishes an annual *Guide to Everything Jewish in Greater Philadelphia.*

The Jewish Quarter of Philadelphia, by Harry D. Boonin (Jewish Walking Tours of Philadelphia, Inc., 1999). The comprehensive detail of history of the neighborhood around South Street. What makes it different from many local Jewish histories is that the author describes these historic sites as they once were and as they are today, and tells how you can see them.

WNWR 1540AM, ☎ 610-664-6780 Throughout the week, talk shows and topics of Jewish interest are scheduled on this station. Including Keneseth Israel Sabbath Services, on Saturdays, 11 am until noon.

Philadelphia Convention and Visitors Bureau, 1515 Market St., ☎ 800-321-9563 or 215-636-1666.

SAN FRANCISCO

As Jewish pioneers made their way across the Rocky Mountains – or around South America's Cape Horn – to reach San Francisco, it seems they left behind much of the anti-Semitism that often plagued other burgeoning communities farther east. While Jews elsewhere often maintained segregated communities until well into the 20th century, San Francisco Jews enjoyed involvement from the earliest days. From the time of the city's gold rush roots in the 1840s, Jews served as mayors, congressmen, senators, and leaders.

Thus, the contribution made by Jews is quite evident throughout the city. Take Golden Gate Park, for example. There's the De-Young Museum, the Steinhardt Aquarium, Sigmund Stern Grove, the Fleishhacker Zoo – all names of prominent Jewish families in San Francisco. Jews were instrumental in the development of BART (Bay Area Regional Transit), the Golden Gate Bridge, hospitals, and higher learning institutions such as Berkeley and Stanford.

In addition to an overall visibility of Jewish names and contributions, there are many sites in San Francisco that attest to a communal commitment as well. Sadly, little evidence of the pre-1906 Jewish community remains. Its synagogues, shops, and neighborhoods were destroyed, as was everything else in the devastating earthquake that sparked a citywide conflagration. Still, visitors will discover some wonderfully preserved synagogues, one of the top Jewish museums in the country, and an exciting new Jewish Museum in the making in the city's arts district.

❖ DID YOU KNOW?

The "San Francisco" chapter of a "who's who" in Jewish America would be a big one, including modern politicians (Dianne Feinstein, Barbara Boxer, and Harvey Milk), musical masters (Isaac Stern and Yehudi Menuhin), and literary legends (Gertrude Stein and Alice B. Toklas).

Unlike many other cities where the Jewish population has moved out, there remains a sizeable Jewish community in San Francisco proper – Pacific Heights, Nob Hill, and Sea Cliff, in particular. Thus a Jewish infrastructure remains, with active synagogues and services within a walk or a short drive from many tourist areas.

SIGHTSEEING HIGHLIGHTS

MUSEUMS & GALLERIES

The Jewish Museum of San Francisco, 121 Steuart St., ☎ 415-788-9990, www.jewishmuseumsf.org. Excitement is building as the museum readies for its move in 2003 to a magnificent new location – 90,000 square feet of exhibit and programming space in the Yerba Buena arts district. Plans are to create a flourishing Jewish "neighborhood" with café, bookstore, and lobby where people will gather. In addition to permanent and changing exhibits, the museum will feature a 299-seat theater offering cinema, concerts, performance art, comedy, puppet theater, and storytelling – as well as lectures, discussions, and readings. In the meantime, ongoing programming and limited exhibitions are scheduled at the current JCC location on Steuart St., experimenting with the kinds of programming to be featured in the new location.

Judah L. Magnes Museum, 2911 Russell St., Berkeley, ☎ 510-849-2710, www.magnesmuseum.org. In a rambling, renovated Victorian mansion, a wealth of art, artifacts, ritual objects, photographs, textiles, and archive materials testifies to Jewish life worldwide. Highlights are silver ceremonial pieces, a Sephardic Torah, and an Ark from Cochin, India. A large poster collection offers a walk through modern Jewish history. And works from Marc

Chagall, among other well-known Jewish artists, are represented. Families are attracted by an abundance of programming, not to mention the pleasant grounds, perfect for picnicking, and taking in a breathtaking view of the Golden Gate Bridge. The fourth-floor archives harbor historic documentation of the Jewish westward movement, including diaries from pioneers who came west on wagon trains. The museum is named for Judah Magnes, the first rabbi born west of the Mississippi. Docent tours are scheduled Sundays and Wednesdays, or by special arrangement. Hours: Sunday-Thursday, 10-4. No admission fee, although a $3 donation is suggested.

Elizabeth S. Fine Museum, Congregation Emanu-El, 2 Lake St., ☎ 415-751-2535, www.emanuelsf.org. The small museum in the landmark synagogue features rotating exhibits of Jewish content and Jewish artists, particularly those from the Bay area. Several display cases throughout the building showcase ceramics, jewelry, and ritual objects. Open Monday-Friday, 1-3 p.m. and by appointment.

HISTORIC SITES

Congregation Emanu-El, 2 Lake St., ☎ 415-751-2535, www.emanuelsf.org. Ask anyone in the San Francisco community to identify one of the top sights of Jewish interest and they'll tell you Congregation Emanu-El. Its grand Moorish architecture and massive dome, modeled after Istanbul's Hagia Sofia, has won it architectural recognition since its dedication in 1926. The building was the third home to San Francisco's oldest congregation, established in 1850. Highlights are the 150-foot dome, a grand organ, and the nine-foot-high Ark, a glittering jewel box. Its roster of guests (Golda Meir, Dr. Martin Luther King, Jr., Maya Angelou, Elie Weisel) and congregants (Dianne Feinstein) makes up a "who's who" of international celebrities. Monday-Friday, 1-3, docent-led tours.

Congregation Sherith Israel, 2266 California St., ☎ 415-346-1720. Fortunately for the court system, this historic structure withstood the earthquake and fire of 1906. Its expansive sanctuary was the only place in San Francisco large enough to serve as a site for court cases after government buildings were destroyed. (The original UN charter was ratified here.) Like its neighbor Congregation Emanu-El, Sherith Israel exhibits Moorish influences.

Its dome, however, was inspired by Yosemite's famed Half Dome peak. Rich reds – in tapestries, upholstery, carpets, and cushions – warm the large and well-lit spaces, as do the ruby-dominant stained-glass windows that depict Moses on Mt. Sinai. The historical Ark was built in 1854.

Haas-Lilienthal House, 2007 Franklin St., ☎ 415-441-3000, www.sfheritage.org. A grand turret, welcoming bay windows, and generous gingerbread trim give this stately structure a fairy-tale feel. Inside, the rooms are warm with rich woods and deep-colored upholstery. One of the few Queen Anne Victorian structures that survived fire and earthquake, the Haas-Lilienthal home reigns supreme in the Pacific Heights neighborhood. Built by German-born grocery merchant William Haas in 1886, the mansion remained in the family for nearly a century. (His daughter Alice Lilienthal lived in it until she died in 1972.) The Haas family was active in the Jewish community and as members of Congregation Emanu-El. The only fully furnished Queen Anne Victorian house museum open to the public is now owned by the San Francisco Architectural Heritage Foundation. One-hour scheduled tours are offered as well as private tours. Hours: Wednesday, noon-3 pm; Sunday, 11-4. Admission: $5 adults, $3 seniors and children under 12.

Temple Ohabai Shalome, 1881 Bush St. at Laguna, no telephone. Built in 1895, this landmark structure is the only known redwood synagogue in existence, and one of the oldest redwood buildings in San Francisco. Currently the building is owned by the San Francisco Redevelopment Agency and is slated to become an assisted-living facility. There are some efforts within the Jewish community to gain control of the building and turn it into a cultural center.

Zen Center, 300 Page St. at Laguna, ☎ 415-863-3136. The former Temple Emanu-El Sisterhood House offered a home to young Jewish girls who came to San Francisco in the 1930s. In its well-appointed parlors, they entertained gentlemen callers under the watchful eyes of house mothers. The building was designed by architect Julia Morgan, who is most famous for her work on San Simeon.

MONUMENTS, MARKERS & MEMORIALS

Holocaust Memorial, Lincoln Park, Legion of Honor Dr., entrance at Clement and 34th Ave., ☎ 415-751-6040. The bronze sculpture commands attention on an incline overlooking the Golden Gate Bridge in Lincoln Park. A life-sized male figure peers out from behind a barbed-wire fence at a tragic scene before him. Fresh flowers, wreaths and yarzeit candles are often found at the base of the statue. The memorial, installed in 1984, was created by sculptor George Segal. The original plaster cast is on exhibit at the Jewish Museum in New York City. The gentle landscaping, offering a note of peace, was done by a Japanese-American artist who'd been interned in an American camp during World War II. Open daily.

Hills of Eternity Memorial Park, Congregation Sherith Israel, 1301 El Camino Real, Colma, ☎ 650-756-3633. This historic cemetery is the final resting place of Josephine Marcus and her famous gun-slinging husband, Wyatt Earp.

> ## ❖ DID YOU KNOW?
>
> Famed Western lawman Wyatt Earp wasn't Jewish, but his wife was. As a teenager, Josephine Marcus ran away from her prosperous San Francisco parents to become an actress. She met Earp in Tombstone, Arizona, and even witnessed the famed gunfight at the O.K. Corral. The two are buried in the Hills of Eternity Jewish cemetery in nearby Colma.

Site of first Jewish worship service, corner of Montgomery and Washington streets, in the financial district. A small plaque on the east side of the old Transamerica building marks the site where a second-floor room in a store drew 40 pioneers to worship for Yom Kippur on September 26, 1849.

GENERAL-INTEREST SIGHTS WITH JEWISH CONNECTION

Levi Strauss & Co., Valencia Street Plant, 250 Valencia St., ☎ 415-565-9100. Part of the tour through this operating factory is the history of denim blue jeans, attributed to company founder Levi Strauss and tailor Jacob Davis, both Jews. The tour includes the story of Levi Strauss, a 10-minute video and a walk through the plant – and ends up in the on-site store. Tours are scheduled Tuesdays and Wednesdays, at 9, 11, and 1:30. Reservations are required. The site is closed the first two weeks in July, and the last two weeks of December. No admission fee.

❖ DID YOU KNOW?

San Francisco is the birthplace of blue jeans as we know them – and the fathers of the famed riveted denim pants are two Jews: Levi Strauss, a dry goods merchant, and Jacob Davis, a tailor from Latvia. The two got together and patented their invention in 1873.

Golden Gate Bridge, southeast of the bridge entrance, no telephone. A visitor center, gift shop, and café stand at the base of the most photographed bridge in the world. Also a part of this plaza is a bronze statue of Joseph Strauss, Viennese-born Jew and chief engineer of the Golden Gate Bridge.

Sutro Heights Park, 48th Ave. and Point Lobos, no telephone. Adolph Sutro arrived in San Francisco in 1840, a young immigrant from Prussia who eventually came to own one-twelfth of the city and become its mayor in 1894. Sutro Heights Park is the site of his former estate. On it he built the Sutro Baths in 1881, an opulent three-acre swim park with seven massive swimming pools. The ruins provoke awe at the scope of the pool system, which held more than 1.6 million gallons of sea water, and the former grandeur of the park, which included Greek-columned portals, trapezes, slides, and high dives. Also in the park is Cliff House, a restaurant offering some of the most dramatic views of the bay found anywhere.

SYNAGOGUES

ORTHODOX

Adath Israel, 1851 Noriega St., ☎ 415-564-5665.

Chabad of SF Downtown Center and Offices, 468 Bush St., Fourth Floor, ☎ 415-362-6355. Check in for home hospitality.

Congregation Keneseth Israel, 655 Sutter St., #203, ☎ 415-771-3420. The synagogue offers Shabbat meals for travelers.

Young Israel of San Francisco, 1806 A Noriega St., ☎ 415-387-1774.

CONSERVATIVE

Beth Israel-Judea, 625 Brotherhood Way, ☎ 415-586-8833.

Congregation Beth Sholom, 1301 Clement St., ☎ 415-221-8736.

Congregation B'nai Emunah, 3595 Taraval St., ☎ 415-664-7373, www.uscj.org/ncalif/sanfranbe.

Congregation Ner Tamid, 1250 Quintara St., ☎ 415-661-9041.

REFORM

Congregation Emanu-El, 2 Lake St., ☎ 415-751-2535, www.emanuelsf.org. This historic building is also listed under *Historic Sites*, page 163.

Congregation Sha'ar Zahav, 290 Dolores St., ☎ 415-861-6932, www.shaarzahav.org. Progressive congregation with special outreach to gay/lesbian Jews.

Congregation Sherith Israel, 2266 California St., ☎ 415-346-1720. Another landmark structure (see *Historic Sites*, page 163).

KOSHER DINING

❖ For restaurants with strictest observance, check with the **Vaad HaKashrus of Northern California,** ☎ 559-432-2770. While all the restaurants listed were certified kosher at press time, not all may be certified by Vaad HaKashrus.

Café Olam, Berkeley Hillel, 2736 Bancroft Way, Berkeley, ☎ 510-665-1818. Middle Eastern fare and standard kosher dishes, as well as college favorites such as pizza and a coffee menu, draw students and visitors to the Hillel for breakfast and lunch.

Jerusalem Restaurant, 420 Geary St., ☎ 415-776-2683. Middle Eastern fare such as shwarma, felafel, and fresh-baked pita are featured at this eat-in/carry-out establishment.

New Lotus Garden, 532 Grant Ave., ☎ 415-397-0707. A fun fusion of Asian vegetarian cuisine.

Sabra Grill Restaurant, 419 Grant Ave. at Bush, ☎ 415-982-3656. For a plentiful menu of Israeli Middle Eastern cuisine, a family atmosphere, and entrées that don't exceed $15, Sabra Grill is the place to go. The restaurant is open from noon until 9.

Noah's Bagels, Laurel Heights, 3519 California St., ☎ 415-387-3974. Light meals – featuring bagels, of course – are offered at this dairy, sit-down restaurant. (There are several other locations in the Bay area.)

Tel Aviv Strictly Kosher Market, 2495 Irving St. at 26th, ☎ 415-661-7588. A meat menu features barbecued chicken, knishes, piroshkis, and more. Sit-down or carry-out.

This Is It Grill and Restaurant, 430 Geary St., ☎ 415-749-0201. More Middle Eastern! A glatt kosher selection of meats, salads, and fish – and featuring home-baked pita.

JEWISH COMMUNITY CENTERS

JCC of San Francisco, 3200 California St., ☎ 415-346-6040. At this center, reciprocal privileges do not apply to the fitness center, which is run by a private company. Out-of-town members can, however, participate in non-fitness programs, such as yoga classes and ballet. Or pay $15 a day for fitness guest passes. Other than certain programs, there's not much else to draw in visitors.

SHOPPING

Afikomen Jewish Books, Gifts & Arts, 3042 Claremont Ave., Berkeley, ☎ 510-655-1977, www.afikomen.com.

Judah L. Magnes Museum Shop, 2911 Russell St., Berkeley, ☎ 510-549-6950, www.magnesmuseum.org. Handmade Judaica, crafts, books, cards, jewelry, textiles, and gifts are available at the Magnes Shop. Hours: Sunday-Thursday, 10-4; Friday, 10-noon.

Mazel Tov Gifts and Books, 5138 Geary Blvd. at 16th Ave., ☎ 415-668-7876.

EVENTS

San Francisco Jewish Film Festival, 346 Ninth St., ☎ 415-621-0556. Director Janis Plotkin describes it as the "godmother" of all Jewish film festivals. It is, after all, the world's first, largest, and oldest – setting the standard for the 57 other Jewish film festivals around the country. Held in mid-July each year, the festivities are kicked off at the Castro Theatre. Throughout the two-week period, 35 to 40 independent feature films, documentaries, and shorts are introduced to audiences in four locations throughout the Bay Area. Don't expect to see a series of "Fiddlers on the Roof." The objective is to expose new and unknown works by Jewish artists and with Jewish content. Recent festival opening night tickets sold for $20; call for current prices. Tickets go on sale a few weeks in advance.

Jewish Food Festival, 1414 Walnut St., Berkeley, ☎ 510-848-0237. International Jewish cuisine and culture from every continent is the star attraction at this annual celebration, scheduled in November. Local caterers, chefs, and restaurants show off their signature dishes. An authentic Turkish market, live music, and food demonstrations entertain attendees when they're not eating.

HERITAGE TOURS

San Francisco Jewish Landmarks Tours, 2865 Green St., ☎ 415-921-0461. Felix and Sue Warburg started their tour operation – which now includes Jewish-focused trips to New Mexico, Charleston, Savannah, and France – in San Francisco. The half-day and full-day city excursions are designed for groups of 20 or more, and must be scheduled 60 days in advance. Per person rates range from $30 to $45 and often include lunch.

SIDE TRIPS

Hagafen Cellars, 4160 Silverado Trail, Napa, ☎ 888-424-2336, and 707-252-0781, www.hagafen.com. Its wineries have lured Bay Area visitors for day-trip and weekend wine tours since the first grape vines took root in the sun-blessed hills of Napa Valley. But soon, oenophiles will have the opportunity to tour an award-winning *kosher* winery. Hagafen Cellars, a small family enterprise, produces Napa varietals that have won several gold medals, and silver and bronze medals too numerous to count. Owners Ernie and Erit Weir broke ground in 1999 for a winery that will offer tours by appointment, as well as special events linked to Jewish holidays.

RESOURCES

Jewish Community Federation of San Francisco, the Peninsula, Marin and Sonoma Counties, 121 Steuart St., ☎ 415-777-0411, www.sfjcf.org.

Jewish Bulletin **of Northern California,** 225 Bush St., Ste. 1480, ☎ 415-263-7200, www.jewishsf.com. The weekly publication features local happenings as well as national and international news of interest to the Jewish community.

❖ DID YOU KNOW?

Phil Bronstein, editor of the *San Francisco Examiner* (and, incidently, married to actress Sharon Stone) was once the editor of San Francisco's *Jewish Bulletin*.

Jewish Community Information & Referral, 121 Steuart St., ☎ 415-777-4545. Whether you want to seek out the nearest synagogue, check into community events, or request home hospitality, knowledgeable staff at the JCI&R are helpful.

San Francisco Bay Area Jewish Genealogical Society, ☎ 415-666-0188, www.jewishgen.org/SFBAJGS.

Our City: The Jews of San Francisco, **Irena Narrell** (Howell North Publishers, Inc., 1981).

San Francisco Visitor Information Line, ☎ 800-965-2531.

ST. LOUIS

Some standout sights of Jewish interest command attention in St. Louis, not the least of which is a small but not-to-be-missed Holocaust Museum. But what's most fascinating is how much the city's Jewish sights are interwoven with the general history of St. Louis. Three key tourist attractions – Gateway Arch, St. Louis Union Station, and Forest Park – are scattered with sites, most unmarked, that tell the story of Jewish contributions. For example, a visitor can spend the day at the Gateway Arch area, take the tram to the top of the renowned manmade rainbow, visit the Museum of Westward Expansion – *and* peer up at the Old Cathedral and discover Hebrew letters on the Catholic basilica. Or stand at the spot where the first Jewish worhip service west of the Mississippi was held. Or visit the courthouse where Justice Louis Brandeis was admitted to the Bar in 1878, then cross the street to the site of his first law office.

Part of the reason for this interwovenness is that Jews have been in St. Louis since its earliest days – the first Jew, Joseph Philipson, arrived in 1807. And from department store founders such as David May (Famous-Barr), to giants of justice such as Louis Brandeis, Jews have played an active role in the city's development for nearly 200 years. A stroll along the St. Louis Walk of Fame identifies prominent Jewish actors, writers, scientists, public officials, and explorers who've been connected to St. Louis.

Bob Cohn, editor of the city's community paper, *Jewish Light*, describes the St. Louis Jewish community as dynamic, with some two dozen synagogues, and 60,000 people. The population has dispersed west of the city core in a wide geographic arc, now established in such neighborhoods as Chesterfield, Creve Coeur, Wildwood, and Olivette. But the heart of the historic Jewish community can be found in University City, where a sizeable Orthodox community remains. The majority of the Jews of St. Louis (90%) are Conservative or Reform.

SIGHTSEEING HIGHLIGHTS

MUSEUMS & GALLERIES

Holocaust Museum and Learning Center, 12 Millstone Campus Dr., ☎ 314-432-0020. This small museum is considered one of the top Holocaust museums in the country. What's unique is that an active survivor community participates and contributes to its state-of-the-art educational exhibits. Many of the recorded interviews and displays are from the perspective of survivors who live or lived in St. Louis. Allow at least an hour and a half for a visit through its seven exhibit areas that walk you through Jewish life before, during, and after the Holocaust. The Center supports a monthly film series and a small book store. Call in advance for guided tours (tours book up fast during the school year). Hours: Monday-Thursday, 9:30-4:30; Friday, 9:30-4 (3 in winter); Sunday, 10-4:30. No admission charged.

JCC Art Gallery, 2 Millstone Campus Dr., Creve Coeur, ☎ 314-432-5700. Changing exhibits every four to eight weeks feature works by Jewish artists or with Jewish themes. Ceramics, glass works, sculpture, fabrics, and Judaica are available for purchase. Call ahead for hours.

HISTORIC SITES

Gateway Arch Jefferson National Expansion Memorial, St. Louis Riverfront, ☎ 314-982-1410. A small group of Jews gathered in Max's Grocery Store on the St. Louis levee on September 12, 1836. It was Rosh Hashana, and the first time that Jews worshiped on soil west of the Mississippi. Today, this spot is marked by a fountain in the main lobby of the Gateway Arch, St. Louis's signature landmark and site of a national park that includes museums, shops, historical exhibits, and more. No plaque or sign indicates the spot.

Missouri Historical Society, 225 S. Skinker Blvd., ☎ 314-746-4508, www.mohistory.org. The Society's Library and Collections Center is housed here, but the structure was built in 1927 as the United Hebrew Synagogue, and served the congregation until 1982. The grand sanctuary has been restored and is in use as the main reading room. Painstaking renovations and modifications resulted in rich dark wood paneling, chandeliers that matched the originals, the use of rich colors of blue and burgundy and renovating the ornate Greco-Byzantine dome. The building is listed on the National Register of Historic Places. Open Tuesday-Saturday, 10-5.

Tercentenary Monument, Corner of Kingshighway and Lindell. Nearly 1,000 miles from the original colony of New Amsterdam (New York City), St. Louis is the site of a sculpture that commemorates the 300th anniversary of the first Jews who landed on America's shores in 1654. Why? In 1954 (the tercentenary anniversary), Jewish communities throughout the country were invited to help celebrate, so St. Louis erected a monument and flagpole in Forest Park, site of the 1904 World's Fair. The monument is shaped like a wave and on it is a bas relief of the *St. Catherine*, which brought the 23 Jews from Recife, Brazil, to New Amsterdam.

MONUMENTS, MARKERS & MEMORIALS

Ohave Shalom Cemetery, 7400 Olive Rd., no telephone. At 88 by 91 feet, it's the smallest active Jewish cemetery west of the Mississippi. But the tranquil space hedged from the outside world offers final refuge for Holocaust survivors, and a 17,000-pound granite monument flanked by red granite urns commemorates those lost. The city's German Jewish community established the cemetery in 1938. The only people buried there are those who survived the Holocaust.

New Mt. Sinai Cemetery, 8430 Gravois, ☎ 314-353-2540. The land for the cemetery was purchased in 1847, during a cholera epidemic that gave birth to this historic cemetery. The visitor familiar with St. Louis Jewish history will discover many notable family names on the headstones.

COLLEGES & UNIVERSITIES

Washington University, 1 Brookings Dr., ☎ 314-935-5000. In addition to a large Jewish student body, major campus structures named for notable Jewish philanthropists create a Jewish presence. The Edison Theater and the Wohl Recreation Center are named for two shoe-manufacturing families. The Olin Library contains a large Yiddish collection and about 200 books and manuscripts of the Third Reich.

GENERAL-INTEREST SIGHTS WITH JEWISH CONNECTION

Old Courthouse, 11 N. 4th St., ☎ 314-655-1600, www.nps.gov/jeff/arch-home. A bust of United States Supreme Court Justice Louis (no, the city's *not* named for him) D. Brandeis stands in the second-floor courtroom of the city's historical Old Courthouse. Brandeis was admitted to the bar and had his first law office in St. Louis. While you may be able to peek through a door to see the bust, you won't be able to enter the courtroom without prior okay from park rangers – the building is part of the Jefferson National Expansion Memorial National Park. Hours: 8-4:30. Free admission.

The Old Cathedral, 209 Walnut St., ☎ 314-231-3250. The oldest cathedral west of the Mississippi was built in 1834, and is one of only two buildings to survive a great fire in 1849 that destroyed 27 blocks in the heart of the city (the Old Courthouse was the other). Atop the Old Cathedral, in one-foot-high bronze letters is the Hebrew word for God. Why Hebrew on a Catholic church? No one knows for sure. But what any student of the Alef-Bet will notice is that the word is misspelled.

> ### ❖ DID YOU KNOW?
>
> The St. Louis Walk of Fame includes 90 city natives who've achieved fame; take this walk in University City loop (6504 Delmar, ☎ 314-727-7827) and discover 10 who are Jewish. Shelley Winters is one.

Aloe Plaza and Kiener Plaza, downtown St. Louis. A mile-long, grassy causeway connects two historic parts of the downtown area – and at each location stands a monument with a Jewish connection. The historic Carl Milles Fountain stands outside Union Station in Aloe Plaza. The fountain, which commemorates the confluence of three rivers – the Mississippi, Missouri, and Illinois – was built in memory of Louis P. Aloe, a celebrated Jewish denizen who served as acting mayor between 1917 and 1919. At the other end, Kiener Plaza, named for Russian-born sculptor Harry J. Kiener, features the artist's work celebrating the 1904 Olympics, which were held in St. Louis during the World's Fair. The legend – which was *not* corroborated by anyone from the St. Louis Jewish community – is that the model for the statue of a runner was actually a young rabbinical student.

SYNAGOGUES

Most of the Orthodox synagogues in the St. Louis area are clustered in University City. Nearly two dozen congregations serve the community, with all movements represented. A mikvah is located on the Millstone campus, maintained by the Va'ad Hoeir of St. Louis.

ORTHODOX

Bais Abraham, 6910 Delmar Blvd., ☎ 314-721-3030.

Nusach Hari B'nai Zion, 8630 Olive Blvd., ☎ 314-991-2100.

Sha'arei Chesed Shul, 700 North and South Rd., ☎ 314-863-7485.

Young Israel, 8101 Delmar Blvd., ☎ 314-727-1880. Shabbat and Yom Tov mikvah maintained here.

CONSERVATIVE

B'nai Amoona, 325 South Mason Rd., ☎ 314-576-9990. The large, historic congregation founded in 1881, is spiritual home to 1,000 families. The 33-acre campus includes gift shop, campgrounds, nature trail, and Solomon Schechter day school.

Brith Sholom Kneseth Israel, 1107 Linden, ☎ 314-725-6230. Gift shop.

Shaare Zedek Synagogue, 829 North Hanley Rd., ☎ 314-727-1747. Gift shop.

REFORM

Congregation Temple Israel, #1 Rabbi Alvan D. Rubin Dr. (at Ladue Rd. and Spoede), ☎ 314-432-8050, www.shamash.org/re-form/uahc/congs/mom/mo002. An active congregation and one of few with its own retreat center (Troy, Missouri). Frequently scheduled family Shabbat dinners. Gift shop.

Shaare Emeth Congregation, 11645 Ladue Rd., ☎ 314-569-0010. One of the largest Reform congregations in the country. Gift shop.

Temple Emanuel, 12166 Conway Rd., ☎ 314-432-5877.

United Hebrew Congregation, 13788 Conway Rd., ☎ 314-469-0700. Gift shop.

❖ DID YOU KNOW?

St. Louis is the only US city presided over by a chief rabbi. The Beth Din Zedeck of Greater St. Louis (☎ 314-863-5511 or 569-2770) is headed by Rabbi Sholom Rivkin of the Va'ad Hoeir United Orthodox Jewish Community of St. Louis. Rabbi Rivkin, chief rabbi since 1982, serves on the national Bet Din.

KOSHER DINING

❖ The offerings are currently limited in St. Louis. While plenty of kosher bakeries, meat markets, and carry-out services meet the needs of the community, there are only a handful of places where you can grab a seat and have a meal. Check with the **Va'ad Hoeir,** ☎ 314-569-2770, for the latest updates.

Diamant's Kosher Meat Market, 618 North & South, ☎ 314-721-9624. Primarily a butcher and carry-out service, Diamant's offers a couple of tables for lunchtime clients to enjoy a sandwich or cup of soup.

JCafé, 2 Millstone Campus Dr., ☎ 314-432-5700. Currently the café offers dairy meals, including pasta dishes that change each week, salads, soups, and sandwiches. A meat menu is available, although meat items are prepared in a different kitchen. The café is open most days from 10 until 7, closing early on Friday and Sunday.

Simon Kohn's Kosher Meat & Deli, 10405 Old Olive, ☎ 314-569-0727. Specials change daily at the sit-down counter – ranging from felafel to barbecued ribs to wraps – and two soups every day. Convenient to the JCC and Federation campus, the place is open for lunch, for dinner one night a week (Thursday), and brunch on Sunday.

Adams Mark, 4th and Chestnut, ☎ 314-241-7400. While the kitchen does not offer a standard kosher menu, guests who observe kashrut may be able to arrange in advance for kosher meals. The chef requests a week's notice.

Sheraton Clayton Plaza Hotel, 7730 Bonhomme Ave., Clayton, ☎ 314-863-0400 or 800-325-3535; **Radisson Hotel Clayton,** 7750 Carondelet Ave., ☎ 314-726-5400 or 800-870-6556; **Hilton St. Louis Frontenac,** 1335 S. Lindbergh Blvd., ☎ 314-993-1100 or 800-325-7800. Each of these hotels schedules a full-course kosher dinner one Sunday a month on a rotating basis – so the kosher connoisseur is guaranteed at least three meals out a month. The hotels will also prepare kosher meals for guests with at least three days advance notice.

JEWISH COMMUNITY CENTERS

Jewish Community Centers Association, 2 Millstone Campus Dr., Creve Coeur, ☎ 314-432-5700. A 108-acre campus, with full-service fitness facilities, indoor and outdoor pools, health club, tennis, fitness classes, and therapy pool offers many services to visiting JCC members. The campus also includes the Holocaust Center. Stop at the Saul Brodsky Jewish Community Library – for its children's section, community archives, and Russian and Hebrew newspapers.

JCC Marilyn Fox Building, 16801 Baxter Rd., Chesterfield, ☎ 314-432-5700. The new satellite branch offers all the recreational amenities featured at the main campus – and *then* some! A new outdoor pool attracts families with two flume slides, water shooters, lazy river, and beach entry. In addition, an on-site Treadwall (a recreational climbing wall) is the first of its kind in St. Louis. Those interested in modern Israeli artists will want to see the Agam sculpture at the main entrance.

Shopping

Several of the area's synagogues offer gift shops, including **Kol Am** at 14455 Clayton Rd., ☎ 314-227-7574.

Midwest Jewish Book & Gift Center, 8318 Olive St. Rd., ☎ 314-993-6300.

The Source Unlimited, 11044 Olive Blvd., ☎ 314-567-1115.

Small Indulgences, 1045 S. Big Bend Blvd., ☎ 314-644-4667.

Events

Jewish Book Festival, Jewish Community Center, 2 Millstone Campus Dr., ☎ 314-432-5700, Ext. 3299. Each fall, the Jewish Community Center brings in more than two dozen authors to speak, sign, and share their experiences as authors and Jews. This 10-day event also, of course, offers plenty of opportunities to buy books. Call for dates and schedule of events.

Jewish Film Festival, Jewish Community Center, 2 Millstone Campus Dr., ☎ 314-432-5700, Ext. 3299. Five days and nights of film entertainment at various venues has drawn increasing crowds each year to this relatively new event in St. Louis. The annual film series is scheduled for late June. Films shown range from early Yiddish classics to recent works from Israel, and everything in between. Tickets range from $6 to $10. Call for schedule.

Chanuka at the Missouri Botanical Gardens, 4344 Shaw, ☎ 314-432-5700, Ext. 3169. The community's annual Chanuka candle-lighting service is held at the Missouri Botanical Gardens and includes crafts for children, musical performances, folk dancing, and food. Admission is currently $3 for adults, $1.50 for seniors, and free for children 12 and younger. Call for exact times.

New Jewish Theatre, Sarah and Abraham Wolfson Studio Theater, JCC, ☎ 314-432-5700, ext. 3175. The New Jewish Theater is indeed new to St. Louis, opening for its first season in 1997. Currently, the season runs from fall to spring and features three to four plays that run two weekends each, Thursday through Sunday (no Friday evening performance). Tickets range from $9 to $12. A special spring event features a production performed by and for youth.

HERITAGE TOURS

St. Louis Jewish Legacy Tours, ☎ 314-527-7926. Linda Meckfessel is intimately familiar with St. Louis, having served as a tour operator and guide in the area for a number of years. She's developed a tour with a Jewish focus, unearthing for visitors and residents alike the city's best-kept Jewish sites of interest. Included in her five-hour, fully narrated tour are stops at the Arch, Old Courthouse, Missouri Historical Society, Forest Park sites, University City Loop, and Ohave Shalom Cemetery. Meckfessel charges $120 per group, regardless of size (she can take up to 45 people at a time). Cost of a van or bus, if necessary, is additional. Schedule as early as possible – certain dates are booked months in advance.

RESOURCES

The Jewish Federation of St. Louis, 12 Millstone Campus Dr., ☎ 314-432-0020, www.jewishinstlouis.org.

Jewish Genealogical Society of St. Louis, 13788 Conway Rd., ☎ 314-469-0700. Affiliated with United Hebrew Congregation.

Jewish Information Service, 12 Millstone Campus Dr., ☎ 314-991-2299.

ST. LOUIS

St. Louis Jewish Archives, Saul Brodsky Jewish Community Library, 12 Millstone Campus Dr., ☎ 314-432-0020.

St. Louis Jewish Light, 12 Millstone Campus Dr., ☎ 314-432-3353.

Zion in the Valley, by Dr. Walter Erlich, 1997. A book about St. Louis Jewish history.

St. Louis Convention and Visitor's Commission, One Metropolitan Sq., Ste. 1100, ☎ 314-421-1023.

TORONTO

For the traveler, discovering Jewish Toronto is surprisingly easy. Former synagogues, museums, galleries, and lively neighborhoods are concentrated in easy-to-reach places. A good public transit system gets visitors easily and quickly to centers of modern Jewish life as well as to the historic neighborhoods and sites.

Although most of the post-immigrant-era synagogues that once populated the Kensington Market area are now razed or converted to churches, the area, which is now absorbed into the city's Chinatown, is still an intriguing walk. Two structures, the Kiever Congregation and Anshei Minsk, still stand as synagogues. It's important to imagine how vibrant this area once was as a Jewish market, just after World War I.

A Jewish presence here began much earlier, however; the first Jews to settle permanently began arriving in 1838 – from England, the United States, and Canada's eastern regions. In 1856, the first Rosh Hashanah worship services were held in a room above Coombs Drugstore at the corner of Richmond and Yonge streets. That same year, the first synagogue, Toronto Hebrew Congregation, was built nearby at the corner of Victoria and Richmond streets. The congregation still exists as the Holy Blossom Temple – Canada's largest Reform synagogue. It was in this fashionable neighborhood just east of Yonge that the city's prosperous English Jewish families settled, and nearby another former Holy Blossom synagogue stands at Bond Street, near Dundas.

With the influx of Eastern European Jews, several new congregations formed. Today's largest congregation in Canada, Beth Tzedec, is the byproduct of mergers of two: Goel Tzedec and Beth Hamedrash Hagadol Chevra Thillim. By World War I, the community had moved to the Kensington area, creating a vibrant neighborhood and renowned marketplace that thrived until the 1950s, when Jews began moving north, clustering in neighborhoods along the Bathurst corridor.

The Bathurst Jewish Community Centre is a massive complex that includes the Koffler Gallery and Holocaust Centre. The surrounding neighborhoods are filled with kosher restaurants, Judaica shops, butchers, groceries, and synagogues.

Toronto enjoys a thriving and diverse Jewish life, and a high level of affiliation. There's even a Jewish motorcycle club that promotes charity efforts (**Yidden on Wheels, ☎** 905-881-9822) and a **Jewish Vegetarian Society** (☎ 416-785-9091). With a directory full of organizations and a calendar liberally sprinkled with activities, visitors will find Toronto a worthwhile stop on their Jewish travel itinerary.

SIGHTSEEING HIGHLIGHTS

MUSEUMS & GALLERIES

Reuben and Helene Dennis Museum, at Beth Tzedec, 1700 Bathurst St., ☎ 416-781-3511. An impressive Cecil Roth collection resides in this gallery in Canada's largest synagogue, Beth Tzedec. One of the highlights of the collection is a medieval megillah from a Chinese Jewish community, which disappeared by the 19th century. Other items of interest are circumcision kits, some 100 ketubot – some dating to the 1600s, and a collection of disturbing anti-Semitic cartoons. Hours: Monday, Wednesday, Thursday, 11-1, 2-5.

Holocaust Education and Memorial Centre, Lipa Green Building, 4600 Bathurst St., ☎ 416-631-5689. Ghetto money, prison uniforms, rescued Torah scrolls, photos of Canadian soldiers liberating the camps. These are some of the objects in the Centre's small museum. It's located on the fourth floor of the Lipa Green Building, and brings in students and groups to view its audiovisual presentation and hear testimony from Holocaust survivors. Victims are remembered in the Hall of Memories, where their names are inscribed on the walls. Hours: Tuesday, 1-4:30; Thursday, 1-4:30, 7-9; Sunday, 11-4:30.

Judaica Gallery, Royal Ontario Museum, 100 Queen's Park, ☎ 416-586-5549, www.rom.on.ca. The Judaica Gallery opened in 1989, displaying more than 60 works that date from the 1500s to 1980. Ancient Hebrew scrolls are among the artifacts that include ritual objects. In addition the gallery features changing temporary exhibits. Themes are feasts and festivals, and life cycle. Hours: Wednesday, Friday, Saturday, and Sunday 10-6; Tuesday and Thursday, 10-8.

My Jewish Discovery Place, Bathurst Jewish Centre, 4588 Bathurst St., ☎ 416-636-1880, Ext. 456, www.bjc.on.ca. A satellite facility of the Los Angeles museum, this branch, too, offers hands-on fun for kids two to eight. It's Purim year-round here, where young visitors dress up as their favorite Jewish heroes, role-play, make crafts, and play games to help teach Jewish values and history. Hours: Monday-Thursday, 10-5; Sunday, 11-4. Admission: $2 adults and children.

Koffler Gallery, Bathurst JCC, 4588 Bathurst St., ☎ 416-636-1880. Works by several Jewish Canadian artists decorate the lobby area of the Bathurst JCC. Changing exhibits feature mostly contemporary art, but often Judaica artifacts are displayed as well.

Silverman Heritage Museum, Baycrest Geriatric Center, 3560 Bathurst St., ☎ 416-789-2500 Ext. 2802, www.Baycrest.org. Artifacts from the geriatric center's permanent collection (more than 600 objects) are showcased along with temporary exhibits with Jewish themes, or by Jewish artists. Historic ketubot and mysterious-looking amulets catch the eye. Hours: Sunday-Thursday, 9-9; Friday, 9-6.

HISTORIC SITES

Kiever Congregation, 25 Bellevue Ave., ☎ 416-593-9702. The Kensington Market area, now the home to the city's Portuguese community and its Chinatown, was once the epicenter of Jewish immigrant life. The Kiever Congregation, built in 1927, was at its heart and served the Congregation Rodfei Shalom-Anshei Kiev. The congregation is still active. Although there is not a daily minyan, Shabbat and holiday services are held. The architecture is Byzantine Romanesque, with twin towers and a bimah in the center of the sanctuary. The upstairs gallery for women is still used in this Modern Orthodox congregation. A gallery of photos recounts the history of the Kiever Congregation. The province has designated the structure as a historic landmark. Call in advance to schedule a tour.

Anshei Minsk, 10-12 St. Andrew St., ☎ 416-595-5723, www. theminsk.com. Despite the fact that the Jewish community no longer lives in the Kensington Market area as it once did, this synagogue, opened in 1930, is experiencing a rejuvenation of membership and activity. A changing population – with young Jewish professionals migrating back to the downtown area – is injecting some new life into the community. Services are held daily, and visitors are welcome to Shabbat dinners after services Friday evening.

St. George's Greek Orthodox Church, 115 Bond St., north of Dundas, no telephone. Today, the graceful structure serves as a church. But it was built in 1897 by the Holy Blossom congregation, which evolved from an Orthodox to a Reform congregation over the period of 1880 to 1920. The structure was home to the Holy Blossom Synagogue until 1938, when the congregation moved to its current building. Two striking domed towers and tall, arched windows and entries identify the building as Moorish Revival. There is nothing, however, that identifies it as a synagogue today.

Holy Blossom Temple, 1950 Bathurst St., ☎ 416-789-3291. The Holy Blossom congregation dedicated its current home in 1938. A distinction that few modern observers will appreciate is that the structure was the first in Canada with a continuously poured concrete foundation. More interesting to the visitor will be the synagogue's sanctuary – designed to resemble the sanctuary of Temple Emanu-El in New York City. The congregation boasts a large historical archive and a fair amount of art displayed throughout the building. The building is a designated national resource. Call in advance to arrange a tour.

MONUMENTS, MARKERS & MEMORIALS

Jewish Cemetery, east side of Pape Ave., south of Dundas, no telephone. This burial ground is no longer active – it's been closed since the 1930s – but the small space makes an interesting stop for those curious about Toronto history. The cemetery, Toronto's first Jewish burial ground, was established in 1849 and acquired by the Holy Blossom congregation in 1858. The tiny patch is well-maintained. Visitors will notice a scruffy vacant area – this is where infants younger than three months were buried, according to custom, without markers. Those who wish to visit are advised to knock on the caretaker's door to be let in.

Historical site of first Jewish worship services, Richmond St., southeast corner of Yonge. Posted on the modern office building is a small plaque that identifies this spot as the site of Toronto's first Jewish worship services, held in 1856. The plaque also indicates that the city's first synagogue was just a block away, at 2529 Richmond Street. The building no longer exists.

> ### ❖ DID YOU KNOW?
>
> In 1950, as workers were digging a hole in which to place a gasoline tank for a gas station, they discovered a large, concrete vault buried deep in the ground. Inside were years of synagogue records of the Holy Blossom Congregation dating back to 1856, buried at the spot for safekeeping some time in the late 1800s. The members of Holy Blossom were thrilled with the discovery, and the records are now included in the congregation's archives.

Biblical Garden, Temple Emmanu-El, 120 Old Colony Rd., Willowdale, ☎ 416-449-3880. In the Bayview-York Mills area of the new city of Toronto, Temple Emmanu-El harbors a small garden in its courtyard that features all the plants mentioned in the Bible.

NEIGHBORHOODS

Bathurst Corridor. Currently the Jewish population is concentrated north, especially along the Bathurst corridor, stretching all the way to North York, now part of the Mega-City of Toronto. The communities are diverse, ranging from Chasidim to secular Jews, representing Israeli, Russian, and North African origins. From Eglinton Avenue and north, you'll find concentrations of Jewish commerce, communities, synagogues, and restaurants in suburbs such as Thornhill, Markham, and Vaughan. The Number 7 Bathurst bus travels north, from either the Bloor/Danforth subway, or from the Saint Clair West station on the Spadina subway line. The subways are easily accessible from downtown hotel locations.

SYNAGOGUES

ORTHODOX

Anshei Minsk, 10&12 St. Andrew St., ☎ 416-595-5723 It's listed as a "small" synagogue, but the spirit is mighty at the only downtown Orthodox congregation with daily services. The historic shul (see *Historic Sites*, page 186) welcomes visitors to Shabbat dinner Friday after services. (Call ahead.)

Kiever Congregation, 25 Bellevue Ave., ☎ 416-593-9702. or 416-593-9956. No daily minyan at this historic downtown congregation, but there are services on Shabbat and holidays.

Beth Avraham Yoseph of Toronto, 613 Clark Ave. West, Thornhill, ☎ 905-886-3810, http://bayt.org. A large congregation with a mikvah.

B'nai Torah Congregation, 465 Patricia Ave., Willowdale, ☎ 416-226-3700, www.bnaitorah.net. Mikvah.

Shaarei Shomayim, 470 Glencairn Ave., ☎ 416-789-3213, www.shomayim.org.

Shaarei Tefillah, 3600 Bathurst St., ☎ 416-787-1631.

Sephardic Kehila Center, 7026 Bathurst St., Thornhill, ☎ 905-669-7600. The young congregation worships in a magnificent structure built of Jerusalem stone; the interior is reminiscent of Moroccan synagogues, with pillars, a central dome, and Moorish influences.

CONSERVATIVE

Beth Tzedec Synagogue, 1700 Bathurst Street, ☎ 416-781-3511. Canada's largest synagogue, with 2,700 families, features a 60-foot mosaic wall. A gift shop is available (by appointment only).

Beth Emeth Bais Yehuda, 100 Elder St., Downsview, ☎ 416-633-2828.

Beth Sholom Synagogue, 1445 Eglinton Ave. West, ☎ 416-783-6103. Its 18 stained-glass windows depict biblical scenes. Gift shop.

Adath Israel, 37 Southbourne Ave., Downsview, ☎ 416-635-5340. Gift shop.

Beth Tikvah Synagogue, 3080 Bayview Avenue, ☎ 416-221-3434. The antique, hand-carved Ark is impressive. Gift shop.

REFORM

Holy Blossom Temple, 1950 Bathurst St., ☎ 789-3291. It's the largest Reform synagogue in Canada. A gift shop is on-site.

Temple Emmanu-El, 120 Old Colony Road, ☎ 416-449-3880. Park-like surroundings in a wooded area with ponds is a tranquil setting for services – Friday evening and Shabbat morning. There's a biblical garden in the courtyard.

Temple Sinai, 210 Wilson Ave., ☎ 416-487-4161.

Temple Kol Ami, 36 Atkinson Ave., Thornill, ☎ 905-709-2620.

KOSHER DINING

❖ Call the **Kashruth Council of Toronto,** ☎ 416-635-9550, for the most current information about kosher establishments.

Milk Street Café, 441 Clark Ave., West Thornhill, ☎ 905-886-7450. This dairy café serves light meals; open for breakfast, lunch, and dinner.

Chicken Nest, 3038 Bathurst St., ☎ 416-787-6378. Mainly chicken dishes are served at this sit-down lunch and dinner restaurant. Carry-out is available, too.

Tovli Pizza and Falafel, 5982 Bathurst St., ☎ 416-650-9800. Locals claim this is one of the best spots for felafel in the city. The dairy establishment is open for lunch and dinner.

Rachel's Café, Bathurst Jewish Centre, 4588 Bathurst St., ☎ 416-636-1880 or 633-4660. The kosher cafeteria is dairy and open during the day and early evening for light meals and carry-out.

Milk 'n Honey, 3457 Bathurst St., ☎ 416-789-7651. A full-service dairy restaurant serves pastas and other favorites for lunch and dinner.

My Zaidy's Pizza, 441 Clark Ave., Thornhill, ☎ 905-731-3029; **My Zaidy's Café,** 7241 Bathurst St., Thornhill, ☎ 905-731-3831. Pizza and felafel are featured at the quick-stop dairy restaurant on Clark; the Café showcases additional dairy dishes.

Miami Grill, 441 Clark Ave. W., Thornhill, ☎ 905-709-0096. Open for lunch and dinner, the restaurant serves up Chinese, Israeli, chicken, or ribs. Carry-out available, too.

A Taste of Tikvah, 770 Bathurst St., Promenade Village Plaza (corner of Bathurst and Centre), ☎ 905-771-0699. Shwarma, felafel, and other Middle Eastern quick meals are on the menu.

Yehudaleh's, Chabad Gate Plaza (corner of Chabad Gate and Bathurst), ☎ 416-667-8999. Another popular pizza and felafel place, open for lunch and dinner.

Oasis, 2 First Canadian Pl., Main Exchange Tower, ☎ 416-368-8805. The only kosher restaurant downtown! Healthy dairy selections are the hallmark for breakfast and lunch.

Orly Café, 3464 Bathurst St., Downsview, ☎ 416-256-9537. Light bites at the dairy café, sit-down or carry-out.

Samy's, Plaza (one block west of Bathurst and Steeles), ☎ 416-736-7227. The steak house features steaks, shwarma, burgers, and grilled meats.

Marky's Glatt Kosher Delicatessen & Restaurant, 280 Wilson Ave., Downsview, ☎ 416-638-1081. Deli and sit-down. Another location at 6233 Bathurst St., ☎ 416-227-0707.

Bloor Jewish Community Centre Cafeteria, 750 Spadina Avenue, ☎ 416-924-6214.

King Solomon's Table, 3705 Chesswood Dr., Downsview, ☎ 416-630-0303. Kosher meat restaurant across the street from the Montecassino Hotel.

Le Chinoix, 7117 Bathurst St., Thornhill, ☎ 905-709-8211. A very upscale Chinese kosher restaurant, open for dinner.

JEWISH COMMUNITY CENTERS

Bathurst Jewish Centre, 4588 Bathurst St., Willowdale, ☎ 416-636-1880, www.bjc.on.ca. The Bathurst JCC offers a lot for the JCC member seeking reciprocal privileges. A fitness center and swimming pool allow travelers to stick to their fitness routines. In addition, a schedule of activities that includes theatrical performances (the Leah Posluns Theatre is on-site) and concerts keeps everyone entertained. A kosher café is available, too. The Koffler Gallery in the lobby presents art exhibits.

Bloor Jewish Community Centre, 750 Spadina Ave., ☎ 416-924-6211, www.lglobal.com/JCC or www.bloorjcc.on.ca. Like the Bathurst Centre, the Bloor JCC also offers a well-rounded recreational and entertainment facility, including workout areas, pool, kosher café, and a range of programs and events. It is located near downtown and the historic Jewish neighborhoods.

TORONTO

SHOPPING

Israel's Judaica Centre, 897 Eglinton Ave. W., ☎ 416-256-1010, and 441 Clark Ave. W., Thornhill, ☎ 905-881-1010, www. israels-judaica.com. Both locations offer a full assortment of Jewish books and religious objects.

Artfully Chosen, 484 Rushton Rd., ☎ 416-656-5650. Hand-crafted Judaica, including jewelry, ceramics, and glassware.

Aleph Bet Judaica, 3453 Bathurst Street, ☎ 416-781-2133.

Barak Jewellery Shalom Judaica, 294 Wilson Ave., North York, ☎ 416-633-6311.

Miriam's, 3007 Bathurst, ☎ 416-781-8261.

Negev Book Store and Gift Shop, 3509 Bathurst Street, ☎ 416-781-9356.

Matana Judaica, 248 Steeles Ave. West., #6, Thornhill, ☎ 905-731-6543.

Yaffa's Judaica, 750 Spadina Ave., ☎ 416-921-6996.

LODGING

Montecassino Place Suites Hotel, 3710 Chesswood Dr., Downsview, ☎ 416-630-8100. In the Sheppard area of North York (west of Bathurst), the hotel is within a 45-minute walk of several congregations (including both Orthodox and Conservative) and offers a kosher restaurant, King Solomon's Table, in the hotel. Kosher room service may be ordered by calling in advance.

Holiday Inn, 3450 Sufferin St., ☎ 416-789-5161. It's a long walk to the nearest synagogues on Bathurst, but the hotel offers kosher meals; however, they must be ordered in advance. Call at least two days ahead of your stay.

❖ DID YOU KNOW?

Toronto elected three Jewish mayors in the last half of the 20th century. The first, Nathan Phillips, elected in the late 1950s, is the namesake of Nathan Phillips Square, which is part of the City Hall. The current mayor is Mel Lastman, re-elected for a second term in 2000.

EVENTS

Toronto Jewish Film Festival, 33 Prince Arthur Ave., 2nd floor, ☎ 416-324-8226 for tickets and information, or 416-324-8668. The festival outgrew its previous location at the Bloor JCC, and moved to the two-screen Hyland Cinemas at Yonge and St. Clair in 1999. And what with more than 60 films scheduled, two screens comes in handy. The week-long event is held in April or May each year. In 1999, Keiko Ibi's *The Personals* was already in the lineup even before it was nominated (and won) the Oscar for Best Short Documentary. The TJFF prides itself on diversity, with films on the Holocaust, feel-good comedies, gay/lesbian themes, and documentaries. Festival passes are available (for around $100), as well as single tickets (in 1999, $8; $5 for students and seniors).

Ashkenaz: A Festival of New Yiddish Culture, 642 King St., Ste. 100, ☎ 416-703-6892, www.ashkenaz.org. This relatively new biennial event (begun in 1995) has been attracting increasingly larger crowds at its Harbourfront Centre festival site. Eight days of performances and exhibitions feature klezmer bands, poets, storytellers, painters, dancers, and other artists celebrating the culture of Yiddish and Eastern European Jewry. Most of the more than 100 events are free, and many are geared for children. The festival usually falls at the end of August or the beginning of September.

Jewish Book Fair, Bathurst JCC, 4588 Bathurst St., Willowdale, and Bloor JCC, 750 Spadina Ave., ☎ 416-636-1880, Ext. 281. The annual November celebration of Jewish books, and features readings, signings, children's events, and books for sale. All events are held at the Bathurst JCC.

Jewish Music Toronto, Bathurst JCC, 4588 Bathurst St., Willowdale, ☎ 416-636-1880, Ext. 228. The JCC sponsors concerts throughout the year, as well as a choral festival once a year.

Leah Posluns Theatre, Bathurst JCC, 4588 Bathurst St., Willowdale, ☎ 416-636-1880, Ext. 231. A modern 450-seat theater in a park-like setting features year-round theatrical performances.

HERITAGE TOURS

Jewish Federation of Greater Toronto, 4600 Bathurst St., ☎ 416-635-2883. Dr. Stephen Speisman, archivist for the Federation, is a valued resource in the Toronto Jewish community. While there aren't any formal tours offered on a regular basis, it is possible to contact Speisman through the Federation. He will arrange tours to accommodate all interests and group sizes.

RESOURCES

Jewish Federation of Greater Toronto, 4600 Bathurst St., ☎ 416-635-2883. www.feduja.org. The Web site is particularly helpful in tracking down information about Jewish Toronto.

Jewish Information Service, 4588 Bathurst St., Ste. 214, ☎ 416-635-5600.

Toronto Jewish Historical Society, 7 Austin Crescent, ☎ 416-533-6304.

Jewish Genealogical Society of Toronto, ☎ 416-638-3280.

Canadian Jewish News, 1500 Don Mills Rd., North York, ☎ 416-391-1836, www.cjnews.com. Canada's weekly Jewish newspaper features the latest on Canadian Jewish issues. The paper can be found in large bookstores downtown or at one of the Jewish businesses along Bathurst.

Jewish Standard, 77 Mowat Avenue, ☎ 416-537-2696.

Chabad Lubavitch Community Centre, 770 Chabad Gate, Thornhill, ☎ 905-731-7000. Call for Shabbat home hospitality.

Metropolitan Toronto Convention and Visitors Association, 207 Queens Key West, ☎ 416-203-2500, www.torontotourism.com.

WASHINGTON DC

The nation's capital is not a place to find much in the way of historic Jewish neighborhoods or other legacies of the immigrant era – although Jews have been represented here since 1795. Nor is it a spot where you'll find enclaves of modern Jewish life, with clusters of kosher restaurants, synagogues, and other institutions. The majority of the Jewish population live in outlying suburbs of Virginia and Maryland. But the District of Columbia contains vast collections of international significance. And represented in those collections are world-class Jewish museums, archives, libraries, and monuments.

The first Jews settled here in 1795. Isaac Polock, a merchant from Savannah, built several large homes on Pennsylvania Avenue, which through time have been occupied by noted leaders, including then-Secretary of State James Madison and wife Dolly. The last remaining structure was torn down in the 1980s.

Throughout most of the 1800s, the Jewish population grew slowly, with families from Germany and Hungary trickling in. Even in those early days, a few Jews held offices in national government. In the 1840s, David Levy Yulee of Florida became the first Jew elected to Congress.

The District's first congregation, Washington Hebrew Congregation, was organized in 1852. In 1857, the 34th Congress granted Jewish congregations full equality with Christian congregations – but Jews couldn't keep their stores open on Sundays.

The Civil War attracted many in search of government jobs and economic opportunities. The growing Jewish population resulted in the establishment of new congregations, such as Adas Israel

Synagogue. The Washington Hebrew Congregation expanded and moved to increasingly larger accommodations, eventually building a grand, Moorish structure in 1897. The stature of the Jewish community was strong; President Grant attended the dedication of the Adas Israel Synagogue in 1878, and President McKinley was present at the 1897 dedication of the new Washington Hebrew Congregation building.

❖ DID YOU KNOW?

One of the first Eastern European Jews to arrive in Washington DC was a man named Yoelson, a shohet and mohel. The father of Al Jolson arrived around 1882.

The impact of Eastern Europe immigration waves didn't hit DC until after the turn of the century. The population jumped from approximately 2,500 in 1900 to 8,000 in 1917. Just four years later, it had exceeded 13,000. By the end of World War II, there were 25,000 Jews.

In the 1950s, the Jewish community grew as the general community did – northward toward Rockville and Baltimore. Synagogues, agencies, and services moved, too. The District's two oldest congregations, Washing Hebrew Congregation and Adas Israel, had enough stature to remain in the city and retain congregants.

In DC proper, while the remaining structures of historic Jewish significance are rare, rich collections of Jewish art and artifacts are found everywhere. From the Smithsonian to the Library of Congress to the National Archives, the contributions of Jews, among others, are commemorated.

SIGHTSEEING HIGHLIGHTS

MUSEUMS & GALLERIES

United States Holocaust Memorial Museum, 100 Raoul Wallenberg Place, S.W., ☎ 202-488-0400.www.ushmm.org. Its space brightened by a skylight, the six-sided Hall of Remembrance is a welcoming place to return after exploring the exhibits, both permanent and temporary, that recount the Holocaust. The museum does not so much focus on showing artifacts, but rather in provoking thought, contemplation, and hope. The museum does display artifacts – uniforms, collections of shoes, glasses, and personal effects of victims, two bricks from the remaining section of the Warsaw Ghetto, and camp barracks. The main exhibition spans three floors and is presented chronologically, beginning with life in Europe in the early 1930s. The Wexner Learning Center allows visitors to learn about specific aspects of the Holocaust using touch-screen computers. The Benjamin and Vladka Meed Registry of Jewish Holocaust Survivors, on the fifth floor, permits visitors to access a database via touch-screen monitors. The Children's Wall is created of tiles by American schoolchildren. Hours: Daily 10-5:30; 10-8 Memorial Day-Labor Day. No admission charged. Same-day passes are distributed beginning at 10 am at the 14th street entrance. Timed at 15-minute intervals. Advance passes are available by calling ☎ 800-400-9373.

❖ DID YOU KNOW?

The Jewish population in DC boomed after World War II, as young men poured in to do governmental work. What resulted was a rare occurrence in the Jewish community – a shortage of young Jewish women. It's been estimated that men outnumbered women four to one.

B'nai B'rith Klutznick National Jewish Museum, 1640 Rhode Island Ave., NW, ☎ 202-857-6583. Its objects range from the ornate – an elaborate 19th-century clock with Hebrew letters on its face and a gracefully scribed megillah from 18th-century Italy – to the starkly spare – an inscribed circumcision knife and a modern chanukiah glazed and shaped to look ancient. Its collections span the sweep of Jewish existence, from ancient artifacts to colonial documents such as the correspondence between George Washington and the Touro Synagogue. Additional highlights are the oldest Torah scroll in America, an Italian Torah binder marking the marriage uniting the Finzi-Contini family in 1556, and a pair of Sabbath candlesticks from 1685 that survived the Holocaust. The museum added the popular **Jewish American Sports Hall of Fame** in the early 1990s, celebrating Jewish involvement in the world of sports and recognizing greats such as Sandy Koufax,

WASHINGTON DC

Hank Greenberg, and Red Auerbach as "Stars of David." The Museum Shop displays handmade ceremonial objects, among other items (see *Shopping*, page 206). Hours: Sunday-Friday, 10-5. No admission charged; donations appreciated.

National Museum of American Jewish Military History, 1811 R St., NW, ☎ 202-265-6280, www.penfed.org/jwv/home.htm. Asser Levy arrived in New Amsterdam in 1654 and had to fight for the right to serve in the militia. Jacob Beser rode in the *Enola Gay* as Radar Countermeasures Observer, when the plane dropped the bomb on Hiroshima. Their stories are recounted, along with those of countless Jews who've served in the American military. Exhibits change and illustrate such pages in history as women in the military. A poignant display recounts the personal stories of Jewish Americans who worked with survivors of the Holocaust in Displaced Persons Camps. An exhibit slated for 2002 will highlight the role of Jews during the Civil War. Hours: Monday-Friday, 9-5; Sunday 1-5. No admission charged; donations appreciated.

Goldman Art Gallery, JCC of Greater Washington, 6125 Montrose Rd., Rockville, MD, ☎ 301-230-3711. This gallery hosts the country's largest annual exhibition of contemporary Jewish ceremonial art in December. Hours: Sunday-Thursday, 11-5; Friday, 11-4; Tuesday and Thursday evenings, 7-9.

Ann Loeb Bronfman Gallery, District of Columbia JCC, 1529 16th St., NW, ☎ 202-518-9400, Ext. 208. Changing exhibits showcase Jewish themes and Jewish artists. Programs expand on exhibit themes through tours, discussions, lectures, workshops, films, poetry readings, and hands-on children's activities. Monday-Thursday 10-10; Friday, 10-4; Sunday 10-8.

JCC of Northern Virginia Fine Arts Gallery, 8900 Little River Tpke., Fairfax, VA, ☎ 703-323-0880, www.jccnv.org. or www.nicom.com-jccnv/. Frequently changing exhibits of Jewish artists or themed works are scheduled at this small gallery in the Fairfax JCC.

Washington Hebrew Congregation, 3935 Macomb St., NW, ☎ 202-362-7100. An art gallery holds works by Jewish artists and some dealing with Biblical themes, including Jim Dine's *Creation* and Alcalay's *The Burning Bush.* Also on display in the lobby is the synagogue's original charter, issued by the 34th Congress in 1857 and signed by President Franklin Pierce. The synagogue also houses a Judaica collection in Ring Hall.

Dennis and Phillip Ratner Museum, 10001 Old Georgetown Rd., Bethesda, MD, ☎ 301-897-1518, www.ratnermuseum.com. Artist Phillip Ratner's works are showcased in a museum in Safed, at the Statue of Liberty and Ellis Island, and in DC's B'nai B'rith Klutznick Museum. Now, another museum, established by Ratner and his family to "foster a love of the Bible through paintings, sculpture, and graphic arts," features his work, and serves as a walk-through history of the Bible. A brand-new facility offers self-guided tours of the art. A special children's gallery also has a project area. A 100-year-old farmhouse serves as a library, housing hundreds of rare, illustrated Bibles. Visits are arranged by appointment only. No admission charged.

HISTORIC SITES

Lillian and Albert Small Jewish Museum, Jewish Historical Society of Greater Washington, 701 Third St., NW, ☎ 202-789-0900. A Civil War-era ketubah documenting the marriage of a Confederate bride and Union groom. An exhibit featuring Jewish-owned "mom and pop" groceries. Photos commemorating families, weddings, births, and business launchings. These are some of the artifacts to be discovered in the collection. But most interesting is the structure housing the museum. The historic **Adas Israel Synagogue** is the District's oldest synagogue building, constructed in 1876; at the dedication was President Ulysses Grant. The congregation outgrew the graceful Federal-style structure in 1908. The site was used by several churches and eventually a barbecue restaurant marked by a giant neon pig. An Act of Congress resulted in the leasing of the building to the Jewish Historical Society in the 1960s. Since then it has been lovingly restored – with the original Ark and women's balcony salvaged – and today it houses the museum and the Jewish Historical Society. Exhibits cover social, cultural, and religious history in the greater Washington area. Hours: Sunday-Thursday, noon-4. No admission charged; donations appreciated.

Three neighborhood synagogues. At one time, the five-block area bounded by Massachusetts Avenue on the north and Pennsylvania Avenue on the south, and between Third and Eighth streets was considered the spiritual, cultural, and social center of Jewish life. During the late 1800s and into the 20th century, imposing synagogues were built and dedications were attended by the na-

WASHINGTON DC

tion's presidents. Today, there is no remnant Jewish community living within the area that edges on Chinatown. But it is an appealing walking tour. From the former Adas Israel synagogue (see preceding listing), three other former synagogues are within walking distance, representing the diversity of the immigrant community that populated the neighborhood at one time. At the **Greater New Hope Baptist Church,** 816 8th St. NW (8th and H streets, NW), the Magen David can still be seen in the window frames of this Moorish-style structure. The Washington Hebrew Congregation's second significant structure was built in 1897, and used until 1954. President McKinley attended the laying of the cornerstone. At 500 I St., NW (5th and I streets, NW), the **Corinthian Baptist Church** served as the Orthodox congregation Ohev Shalom between 1905 and 1958. And another former Adas Israel structure (1906-1951) at 600 I St. NW (6th and I streets, NW) is now the **Turner Memorial A.M.E. Church.**

MONUMENTS, MARKERS & MEMORIALS

Samuel Gompers Memorial Park, 10th and Massachusetts Ave., no telephone. Born in England, Samuel Gompers came to the United States as a teenager and earned a living as a cigar-maker. It wasn't long, however, before he emerged as a leader in the labor union movement, becoming the first president of the AFL. A monument of bronze and marble depicts Gompers. Another Gompers sight is the **AFL-CIO Building** at 815 16th St., NW, where Gompers' likeness appears in a wood sculpture and a portrait.

Oscar S. Straus Memorial, Commerce Department Bldg., 14th St. between Pennsylvania and Constitution, NW. Allegorical figures set on pedestals guard the fountain that honors Oscar Straus, of the family instrumental in the founding of Macy's Department Store, and the first Jew to serve in a President's cabinet.

Bernard M. Baruch Bench, in Lafayette Park, facing the White House. A granite monument holds a bronze plaque that identifies the bench next to it as the one on which Baruch, advisor to presidents, often sat.

GENERAL-INTEREST SIGHTS WITH JEWISH CONNECTION

Smithsonian Institution, 1000 Jefferson Dr., SW, ☎ 202-357-2700. The collection is unimaginably large – focusing on a theme is always helpful to narrow explorations or give structure to a visit. In that respect, there are plenty of Jewish-focused exhibits in its several museums: art by Jewish artists or portraits of Jewish subjects (The **National Portrait Gallery** at 8th St. at F and G St., NW, displays portraits of Albert Einstein, George Gershwin, and Golda Meir, among many others); contributions in history, science, communication, and other areas. The following are some highlights:

❖ **National Museum of American History,** 14th St. and Constitution Ave. NW, ☎ 202-357-3129. A new permanent exhibit opened in 1999 – "Communities in a Changing Nation: The Promise of 19th-Century America." Among the three communities in focus are the early Jewish immigrants of Cincinnati, Jews who arrived from Central Europe between 1820 and 1880. Displays trace the experiences of such settlers as Sophia Heller from Bohemia and Philip Goldsmith of Prague, who met, married, and struggled for success – which eventually came through the manufacture of dolls and baseballs. The exhibit also identifies Cincinnati as the birthplace of the Reform movement.

❖ **Hirshhorn Museum and Sculpture Garden,** Independence Avenue at Eighth St., SW, ☎ 202-357-3091. It is said that Joseph H. Hirshhorn was so poor as a boy that he never owned a toy. The immigrant from Latvia who went to work at age 12 amassed a fortune as a young man, and eventually built a collection of modern and contemporary art. He donated his collection to the public in 1974. The Hirshhorn Museum, designed by Jewish architect George Bunshaft, is considered art in itself. The sunken outdoor sculpture garden opens to views of the Washington Monument and Lincoln Memorial. Some Jewish artists are represented, as well as Jewish themes – *In a Jewish Café,* by Raphael Soyer, and *Needle Tower* by J. Snelson.

WASHINGTON DC

❖ **John F. Kennedy Center for the Performing Arts,** 2700 F St., ☎ 202-467-4600. An art-filled lounge that serves as a reception area for the Concert Hall was a gift from Israel when the Center opened. The room interior itself was by an Israeli architect, and all the art follows the theme of biblical-inspired music. Wood panels depict the 43 musical instruments referred to in the Bible. Fabric wall hangings tell the story of Israel; a dramatic ceiling mural by Shraga Weill illustrates great musical events from the Bible. Tours of the facility include a stop in the Israeli Lounge. No admission charged.

Synagogues

Nearly 100 congregations in the Greater Washington, DC area offer regularly scheduled Shabbat and holiday services. The **Jewish Chapel Downtown,** Rm. 621, New York Ave., NW, holds daily worship services and a place to say Kaddish.

Orthodox

Kesher Israel, 2801 N St., NW, ☎ 202-333-2337/4808, www.Kesher.org. Check for Shabbat hospitality.

Ohev Sholom Talmud Torah Congregation, 1600 Jonquil St., NW, ☎ 202-882-7225.

Congregation Ahavat Israel, 3939 Prince William Dr., Fairfax, VA, ☎ 703-426-1980

Young Israel Shomrai Emunah Congregation, 1132 Arcola Ave., Silver Spring, MD, ☎ 301-593-4465.

Conservative

Adas Israel, 2850 Quebec St., NW, ☎ 202-362-4433. Mikvah.

Tifereth Israel, 7701 16th St., NW, ☎ 202-882-1605.

Ohr Kodesh Congregation, 8402 Freyman Dr., Chevy Chase, MD, ☎ 301-589-3880. Gift shop.

Tikvat Israel, 2200 Baltimore Rd., Rockville, MD, ☎ 301-424-4396. Judaica shop.

Agudas Achim Congregation, 2908 Valley Dr., Alexandria, VA, ☎ 703-998-6460, www.uscj.org/seabd/agudasachim.

REFORM

Temple Micah, 2829 Wisconsin Ave., NW, ☎ 202-342-9175.

Washington Hebrew Congregation, 3935 Macomb St., NW, ☎ 202-362-7100. Gallery and gift shop.

Temple Sinai, 3100 Military Rd., NW, ☎ 202-363-6394.

Temple Emanuel, 10101 Connecticut Ave., Kensington, MD, ☎ 301-942-2000.

Congregation Beth Sholom, 515 Charlotte St., Fredericksburg, VA ☎ 540-373-4834.

RECONSTRUCTIONIST

Oseh Shalom Congregation, 7515 Olive Branch Way, Laurel, MD, ☎ 301-498-5151.

KOSHER DINING

❖ The **Va'ad Harabanim of Greater Washington** supervises kashrut in the area. Call ☎ 202-291-6052 for updates.

Center City Café Express, DCJCC, Q Street lobby. ☎ 202-387-3246. "Interesting, creative and upscale; first-class dining. It's too good to pass up." says the *Washington Jewish Week*. Serving a Mediterranean-inspired, strictly dairy menu. Open for breakfast, lunch, and dinner. Reservations are recommended.

Royal Dragon, 4832 Boiling Brook Pkwy., Rockville, MD, ☎ 301-468-1922. Chinese and American cuisine includes fish and pareve dishes, not to mention Persian fare, as well. The restaurant is open for lunch and dinner; in winter it opens after Shabbat.

Café Katz, 4860 Boiling Brook Pkwy., Rockville, MD, ☎ 301-468-0400. A sit-down section at Katz Kosher Supermarket offers a range of deli sandwiches, entrées, soups, and side dishes for lunch or dinner.

Kosher Express Restaurant and Catering, 5065 Nicholson Ln., Rockville, MD, ☎ 301-770-1919. Pizza, felafel, and other fast-food favorites are available, as well as other dairy and pareve entrées. Open for lunch and dinner.

Max's Kosher Café and Market Place, 2319 University Blvd., W., Silver Spring, MD, ☎ 301-949-6297. Deli sandwiches, steaks, chicken, kebabs, soups, salads, and more offer a menu with variety. Pareve desserts, including soft-serve ice cream, top off the meal. Open for lunch and dinner.

Nuthouse, 11419 Georgia Ave., Wheaton, MD, ☎ 301-942-5900. Dairy favorites include pizza, felafel, fries, and salads for lunch and dinner.

Roz's Place at the University of Maryland Hillel, 7612 Mowatt Ln., College Park, MD, ☎ 301-422-7929. During the school year, travelers wishing to eat kosher for lunch or dinner can take advantage of this Hillel, buffet-style restaurant. The proprietors describe it as "a nosh above the rest," and indeed the offerings are not your typical school-cafeteria fare. Mexican, Italian, or Greek entrées are often available among a selection of two or three entrées, including a vegetarian choice. Fixed price allows for second helpings. The buffet is also open for Sunday brunch. Shabbat meals may be arranged in advance.

Jewish Community Centers

District of Columbia JCC, 1529 16th St., NW, ☎ 202-518-9400, Ext. 229. The JCC is a full-service facility with swimming pool, racquetball, squash, sauna, and steam room. The indoor pool schedules separate hours for women-only and men-only swims as a courtesy to the Orthodox community. (Call for reservations.) The Center City Café offers kosher dining daily for breakfast, lunch, or dinner. Also on-site are a Judaica gift and book store, and a well-stocked library that includes a Jewish Heritage Video collection. A full schedule of classes, lectures, and activities are of interest to visitors. The historic structure was built in 1927 and served the Jewish community until 1967, when it was closed during riots. The site remained abandoned until the JCC bought it back in 1989; renovations were completed in 1996. The exterior and the lobby of the Henry S. Reich Health & Fitness Center are restored to their original state.

JCC of Greater Washington, 6125 Montrose Rd., Rockville, MD, ☎ 301-881-0100. The Maryland JCC houses a full fitness center and health club, including indoor and outdoor swimming pools. A busy arts calendar features dance, music, and theater performances. On-site is the first Jewish museum in the Washington suburban area, the Goldman Art Gallery (see *Museums & Galleries,* page 198). The Jerusalem Café offers take-out food only.

JCC of Northern Virginia, 8900 Little River Tpke., ☎ 703-323-0880, www.jccnv.org. or www.nicom.com-jccnv/. This full-service facility offers a fitness center with aerobics classes, indoor pool, full-court gym, as well as dance, music, and theater performances. The small gallery and gift shop features a wide selection of traditional and contemporary Judaica, and the center also holds a Jewish video collection of some 200 films.

SHOPPING

Gallery L'Chaim, 11503-C Rockville Pike, Rockville, MD, ☎ 301-468-1948.

Abramson Foundation Judaica Gift & Bookstore, District of Columbia JCC, 1529 16th St., NW, ☎ 202-518-9400, Ext. 209. In addition to gifts and books, Shabbat challas are available Thursdays and Fridays.

Israeli Accents, 4838 Boiling Brook Pkwy., Rockville, MD, ☎ 301-231-7999.

Lisbon's Hebrew Books & Gifts, 2305 University Blvd., W., Wheaton, MD, ☎ 301-933-7466.

Washington Jewish Bookstore, 11252 Georgia Ave., Wheaton, MD, ☎ 301-942-2237.

The Museum Shop, B'nai B'rith Klutznick National Jewish Museum, 1640 Rhode Island Ave., NW, ☎ 202-857-6583. Handcrafted ceremonial objects are featured at the Klutznick (see *Museums & Galleries*, page 197), in addition to jewelry, children's toys, cards, books, prints, gifts – not to mention Sports Hall of Fame T-shirts.

EVENTS

Washington Jewish Film Festival, 1529 16th St., NW, ☎ 202-518-9400, Ext. 248, www.wjff.org. The 10-day event scheduled each December is packed with classics and the latest films from around the world. Also scheduled are discussion groups, speakers, and festivities. Tickets range from $5.50 for matinees to $12 for opening night films.

Theater J, DC JCC, 1529 16th St., NW, ☎ 202-518-9418. The year-round Jewish theater performs plays by Jewish playwrights, and works with Jewish themes. On Sundays, discussions, readings, and acting classes are scheduled.

Theatrical performances are also held at the two other area JCCs – **The Center Company Professional Theater** of the JCCNV, and the **Washingotn Jewish Theatre** at the Greater JCC.

HERITAGE TOURS

The Jewish Historical Society of Greater Washington, 701 Third St., ☎ 202-789-0900. Although the society does not currently schedule regular tours for visitors, it is a great resource for individuals to call for advice and direction. The society will, however, arrange guided walking tours for larger groups. Plans are in the works to develop more structured self-walks as well as guided tours in conjunction with the Heritage Coalition of Washington DC. So call for updates.

RESOURCES

UJA Federation of Greater Washington, 6101 Montrose Rd., Rockville, MD, ☎ 301-230-7200, www.ujafwash.org.

The Jewish Historical Society of Greater Washington, 701 Third St., ☎ 202-789-0900.

Jewish Genealogy Society of Greater Washington, no address, ☎ 301-654-5524, www.jewishgen.org/jgsgw.

Jewish Information and Referral Service, ☎ 301-770-4848, www.ujafwash.org.

Washington Jewish Week, 12300 Twinbrook Pkwy., Ste. 250, Rockville, ☎ 301-230-2222. The weekly tabloid newspaper is packed with world and national Jewish news, as well as a calendar of events and activities in the DC area, including Virginia and Maryland communities. The paper also lists daily minyanim. The cover price is $1.

Washington, DC Convention and Visitors Association, 1212 New York Ave., NW, ☎ 202-789-7000, Web site www.washington.org.

ADDITIONAL SIGHTS

ARIZONA

TOMBSTONE

Check out **Boothill Cemetery** – some searching will reveal a marker with a menorah and stars of David. At the turn of the century, Tombstone's Jewish population was significant.

PHOENIX

The Phoenix area Jewish population is estimated at 80,000 and growing. Its history reaches back to the days of westward expansion, and Jews were settling there soon after the town was founded in 1870. One of its earliest residents was Michael Goldwasser, the grandfather of **Barry Goldwater**, now-deceased presidential candidate of the 1960s. (Barry's father, Baron, married a Christian and Barry was raised Episcopalian.)

A tuberculosis epidemic sent Jews from the East to seek out the healing dry air of the desert. In the past several decades, Phoenix-Scottsdale has become a warm-weather haven for retirees, but has also attracted a growing Orthodox population. The area supports some 25 congregations, as well as a JCC, a Jewish newspaper, and a few outlets for kosher food. Call the Jewish Federation of Greater Phoenix (☎ 602-274-1800) for more information.

Sylvia Plotkin Judaica Museum of Greater Phoenix, Temple Beth Israel, 10460 N. 56th St., Scottsdale, ☎ 602-951-0323. The museum was founded in 1966 by Sylvia Plotkin, whose husband had been rabbi at Temple Beth Israel since the 1950s. Its permanent collection has received national and international recognition. Particularly intriguing is the Tunisian Synagogue Display, a recreation of an ancient synagogue. The museum also hosts traveling exhibits featuring photography, original art, and ceremonial items. Hours: Wednesday-Thursday, 10-3; Sunday, noon-3.

Arizona Jewish Historical Society, 4710 N. 16th St., #201, ☎ 602-264-9773. The organization exhibits artifacts connected to the life of Jews in the Southwest. A small display features Jewish pioneer women.

ARKANSAS

VAN BUREN

A small bronze plaque on the wall of a downtown building at 213 Main Street marks the spot where Dr. Cyrus Adler was born in 1863. The great Jewish leader who at one time headed the Jewish Theological Seminary, National Jewish Welfare Board, American Jewish Committee, and other national organizations, escaped with his family from Union-held Arkansas when he was an infant, and moved to Philadelphia. (Call the Van Buren Chamber of Commerce for directions, ☎ 501-474-2761.)

CALIFORNIA

BAKERSFIELD

Weill House, Pioneer Village of the Kern County Museum, 3801 Chester Ave., ☎ 661-852-5000. Bakersfield's first frame building was built in 1882 by Alphonse Weill, a Jewish merchant. Most of his original furnishings, as well a few Hebrew books, are on display. Hours: Monday-Friday, 8-5; Saturday, 10-5; Sunday, noon-5. Admission: $5 adults; $4 seniors; $3 children three-12.

LA JOLLA

The Salk Institute, 10010 N. Torrey Pines Rd., ☎ 858-453-4100. Dr. Jonas E. Salk, who developed the first vaccine against polio, opened the institute in 1963. He employed architect Louis I. Kahn to design the complex. It has large angular shapes, open areas with lots of light, and massive windows. The institute is a UNESCO site, one of the most remarkable monuments of the last 50 years. The Hammer Center for Research was funded by Armand Hammer.

POMONA

Phillips Mansion, 2640 W. Pomona Blvd., ☎ 909-595-5166. Louis Phillips acquired 12,000 acres of land in Pomona Valley in 1864 and built the first brick house in the area in 1875. The mansion still stands, having been restored by the Historical Society.

SAN DIEGO

Temple Beth Israel, Heritage Park, ☎ 619-694-3049. The old, wood-frame structure in San Diego's Old Town District was built in 1889, and was moved to this site in recent years. It is believed by some scholars to be the oldest existing synagogue structure in the west.

Rose Canyon, north of downtown San Diego on I-5. A small plaque on a boulder at the entrance to the canyon bears the name of Louis Rose, the first Jew to settle in San Diego, arriving in 1850.

JUST ACROSS THE BORDER IN TIJUANA

You might be surprised to learn that the border town of Tijuana, Mexico, has two synagogues. **Centro Social Israelita** (Avenida 16 de Septiembre, ☎ 011-526-686-26-92) is an Orthodox congregation. Call ahead to arrange a visit unless you are planning to attend Shabbat services. The other congregation is the **Congregacion Hebreo de Baja** (Amado Nerbo #207, ☎ 011-526-681-49-52). It is made up almost entirely of Catholic converts and is led by an unordained rabbi; it is not recognized by the Orthodox community. The congregation is said to be welcoming and enthusiastic. But because both congregations may be difficult to find, it's suggested that you visit as part of a tour. Both the **University of Judaism** (☎ 310-476-9777, Ext. 246) and **Jerry Freedman Habush Associates** (☎ 818-994-0213) leads two-day tours from Los Angeles to visit the two congregations.

CONNECTICUT

HARTFORD

Charter Oak Cultural Center, 21 Charter Oak Ave., Hartford, ☎ 860-249-1207. The first purpose-built synagogue in the state of Connecticut was built in 1876. The ornate structure reflected the wealth of the neighborhood and the German Jewish community of that time. Designed to resemble Germany's Glockengasse synagogue in Cologne, it features Moorish influences, earth-toned colors, and Islamic-inspired designs. Saved from demolition in the early 1980s, the building's been completely restored and serves as a multicultural arts and humanities center.

FLORIDA

BOCA RATON

Sally and Lester Entin Holocaust Pavilion, Jewish Federation of South Palm Beach County, 9901 Donna Klein Blvd., Boca Raton, ☎ 561-852-3100. An outdoor memorial offers a place for quiet reflection. The Albert and Pearl Ginsberg Wall of Remembrance tells the story of the Holocaust through photographs and text on enamel plaques.

ELLENTON

Gamble Plantation State Historic Site, 3708 Patten Ave., Ellenton, ☎ 941-723-4536. Judah P. Benjamin, who served the Confederacy under Jefferson Davis, escaped capture at the surrender of the South by heading to Florida. He found refuge at the Gamble Plantation, where he narrowly escaped capture. The plantation stands today, operated by the Florida Park Service. It was saved in 1926 from destruction, and given to the state in memory of Benjamin, who eventually rebuilt his life as a successful barrister in England. The building is the oldest in Manatee County, designated the Judah P. Benjamin Confederate Memorial.

FORT MYERS

The city is named after **Colonel Abraham Myers,** who served in the Florida Indian Wars during the 1830s and 40s.

KEY WEST

B'nai Zion Cemetery, Passover Lane and Angela St., Key West, ☎ 305-292-8177. The above-ground Key West Cemetery is a place to find curious epitaphs on gravestones, such as, "I told you I was sick," and "I won't be home for dinner." There's a separate Jewish section of the graveyard.

Curry Mansion Inn, 511 Caroline St., ☎ 305-294-5349 or ☎ 800-253-3466; http://currymansion.com. Built by Florida's first millionaire family, the house is now owned by Al and Edith Amsterdam, who are Jewish. They turned the Beaux-arts wedding-cake structure into a bed-and-breakfast. There's not a strong Jewish ambiance – although there is a mezuzah on the front door. But for a more haimische environment, you might request the Chanuka Room, filled with menorahs and other ceremonial objects.

ORLANDO AREA

If you're planning to spend time at Walt Disney World (and who goes to Orlando *without* spending time there?), you'll be pleased to know that Disney keeps kosher... well, at least in some cases. With 48 hours advance notice guests may request hot kosher meals in a table-service restaurant at any Disney park or hotel. Bear in mind, they're not "homemade," but rather frozen meals from an outside kosher catering outfit.

Holocaust Memorial Resource and Education Center of Central Florida, 851 N. Maitland Ave., Maitland, ☎ 407-628-0555. The Orlando-area center was founded in 1980. The exhibit recounts pre-war Jewish life in Europe, as it traces the rise of Nazism, and chronicles the events of the Holocaust. Multi-media exhibits include materials from Jerusalem's Yad Vashem. The Founders Wall is built from Jerusalem stone. A library of archival and documentary materials. Hours: Monday-Thursday, 9-4, Friday, 9-1, first and third Sunday 1-4.

ST. PETERSBURG

Florida Holocaust Museum, 55 Fifth Street South, ☎ 727-820-0100, www.tampabayholocaust.org. The fourth-largest Holocaust museum in the country, this center features one of only a few original railroad boxcars used to transport prisoners to Auschwitz. The museum is open daily. Hours: Monday-Friday, 10-5; Saturday-Sunday, noon-5. Admission: $6 adults; $5 seniors and college students; $2 children.

GEORGIA

ATLANTA

The William Breman Jewish Heritage Museum, 1440 Spring St. NW, ☎ 404-873-1661. The large facility interprets and explores Jewish heritage, with a special emphasis on the Atlanta Jewish experience, highlighted in one of its core permanent exhibits. Another core gallery focuses in the Holocaust. A Discovery Center is appealing to younger visitors, with hands-on activities and interactive displays. Programming includes theater, dance, films, workshops, and lectures. A library, a gift shop, and archives for genealogical research are also on site. Hours: Monday-Thursday 10-5; Friday, 10-3; Sunday 1-5. Admission: $5 adults; $3 seniors, students; children under six free.

Memorial to the Six Million, 1173 Cascade Ave., SW, in the Jewish section of the Greenwood Cemetery. A stone tombstone, topped by six large candlesticks, stands in memory of the victims of the Holocaust. A small casket with ashes of unknown martyrs from Auschwitz is interred at the foot of the monument.

The Temple, 1589 Peachtree Rd., NW, ☎ 404-873-1731. The city's oldest congregation was rebuilt after a dynamite blast destroyed it in 1956. The design for the sanctuary is based on that of the Tabernacle in King Solomon's Temple. The Helen Massell Chapel is designed in the shape of a tent.

The Historic Oakland Cemetery, 248 Oakland Ave., SE, ☎ 404-688-2107, www.mindspring.com/~oaklandcemetery. The historic cemetery serves as the final resting place for Confederate soldiers, former slaves, *Gone With the Wind* author Margaret Mitchell, and golf great Bobby Jones. It's also served the Jewish community from the mid-1800s, making it the second-oldest Jewish cemetery in the state. A well-structured, self-guided tour leads visitors to the Jewish section, pointing out the plots of noted families and contributors – such as Joe Jacobs, the pharmacist attributed with developing the Coca-Cola formula. Helpful brochures also assist with the interpretation of symbols on gravestones. Guided tours are available: $3 adults; $1 children.

SAVANNAH

Shortly after James Oglethorpe established Savannah in 1733, *The William and Sarah* sailed into the harbor from London with 42 Jews on board. The mostly Spanish and Portuguese Jews were not enthusiastically welcomed. But since a doctor, Samuel Nunes Ribiero, was on board and the colony was battling a yellow fever epidemic, the passengers were allowed to stay.

By 1738, the Jewish colonists founded a congregation, then established a cemetery and mikvah. It would be nearly a century before the congregation Mickveh Israel actually had its own synagogue. In the meantime the small community thrived and produced citizens who contributed to Savannah's history.

Congregation Mickve Israel, 20 East Gordon St., ☎ 912-233-1547, mickveisrael.org. The first congregation in Georgia was formed in 1733 by the first Jewish settlers in Savannah. The present building, an ornate Gothic Revival structure, was erected in 1878. A small room holds display cases filled with artifacts connected to the congregation's history, including the Torah that was carried on *The William and Sarah* in 1733. The Torah is still used on special occasions. In the congregation's archives is correspondence from George Washington.

Site of first synagogue, northeast corner of Liberty and Whitaker streets. A small wooden structure was built by Mickve Israel in 1820, but it burned to the ground in 1829. The Torahs, including the one carried by the original settlers, and the Ark were saved. To-day, a plaque is embedded in the sidewalk marking the site of the synagogue.

Old Jewish Cemetery, Cohen St., west of MLK Blvd., ☎ 912-233-1547. The historic landmark was established for a community burial ground in 1773, but was not used until 1850. The cemetery is hidden behind a wall and locked gate, but you can contact Congregation Mickve Israel to arrange for a tour.

Sheftall Burial Ground, corner of Cohen and Spruce Streets, no telephone. Just a few blocks from the Old Jewish Cemetery, the Sheftall family plot also was established in 1773.

Sheftall House, 321 East York St., ☎ 912-233-7787. The small frame structure in Savannah's Historic District was built in 1810 by the Sheftall family. The home was moved from its original site at 245 Jefferson Street. Today it houses the Historic Savannah Foundation. Hours: Monday-Friday, 9-5.

IDAHO

BOISE

Many are surprised to learn that the state is the home of the country's first Jewish governor, the oldest synagogue in continuous use west of the Mississippi, and two Jewish-owned departments stores that are National Historic Landmarks, not to mention a new human rights monument in memory of Anne Frank.

The Idaho Anne Frank Human Rights Memorial and Education Park, 801 S. Capitol Blvd., ☎ 208-345-0304. "At present there is no memorial to Anne Frank in the United States. It is both ironic and deeply fitting that the first will be built in Idaho." So reads the park brochhure. The foundations of the park began in 1995 when the international Anne Frank Exhibition came to Idaho. It was an enormous draw, attracting nearly 5% of the state's total population. The Memorial design features a wall of large granite slabs constantly washed with a thin sheet of water. Spanning the wall is a quote from Anne Frank's diary, "In spite of everything, I still believe people are truly good at heart." A bronze sculpture of Anne Frank stands in a window in the highest panel. The park, dedicated in 1999, features a children's area, footbridge, reading knoll, reflective chasm, and flower garden – components designed to encourage reflection.

Temple Beth Israel, 1102 State St., ☎ 208-342-7247. The oldest synagogue in continuous use west of the Mississippi River was built in 1895. The congregation's first president, Moses Alexander, was also the first elected Jewish governor in the United States. His house, at **304 State Street,** and retail store, **820 Main Street,** are listed as historic sites in the state registry.

INDIANA

INDIANAPOLIS

A Jewish presence here stretches back before the Civil War, but there are no standing institutions left to remind visitors of this: no plaques, no Moorish-inspired synagogues, no permanent museum or Judaica exhibits. But an author who didn't include her own community in a Jewish travel guide would have some difficulty facing her neighbors. So let it be noted that the small but energetic Jewish population of 10,000 offers five congregations, and a large **Jewish Community Center** (☎ 317-251-9467) on a wooded campus that shelters a small **Holocaust Memorial**. As we go to press, it's also reported that the **Center Café**, housed at the JCC, is the only glatt kosher restaurant in the state. And finally, Indianapolis has the distinction of being home to Jewish **astronaut David Wolf**, who wished Rosh Hashana greetings to his congregation **Beth El Zedeck** (☎ 317-253-3441) from the Mir Space Station in 1997, and has bestowed the congregation with a Torah pointer and a shofar that have orbited the world. These items are on display in the synagogue.

LIGONIER

No Jews remain in this small community in northeastern Indiana. But everyone in town knows about the Jewish legacy – in fact the sign that greets visitors driving into town reads, "Ligonier: A Historic Jewish Community." Jews from Germany began settling in this agricultural area, today surrounded by Amish communities, in the 1850s. Two were Frederick Strauss and Solomon Mier. The Jewish families prospered, providing the town with retail stores, a carriage and buggy company that eventually produced automobiles, and even one of the largest agricultural real estate companies in the region. Several of the large, Victorian homes were built by Jews. Some, such as the **Solomon Meir** home at 508 South Cavin St. (☎ 219-894-3668) have been turned into B&Bs. **Congregation Ahavas Shalom** established a cemetery, dating to 1865 and found today off SR 33. Here 179 Jews are buried – one a Civil War veteran. The synagogue, built in 1889 (Rabbi Isaac Mayer Wise attended the dedication of the new sanctuary this year), is listed on the National Register of Historic Places and is now the **Ligonier Historical Museum**, located at 503 Main Street (for information call the Ligonier Library at ☎ 219-894-4511). Hours: Tuesday, Saturday, Sunday, 1-4. No admission charged; donations appreciated. Another site, also on the National Register of Historic Places, is the **Jacob Straus House** at 210 South Main Street.

IOWA

POSTVILLE

Meat packers from an East Coast Lubavitch community bought a plant here nearly a decade ago. Prior to their arrival, there had never been a Jewish community in the tiny town of Postville, tucked into the northeastern corner of Iowa. But the location is ideal for producing and supplying kosher beef to Midwestern markets such as Chicago. Today, there are some 150 Jews, a synagogue, and a kosher store and restaurant. **Jacob's Market** (121 W. Green St., ☎ 319-864-7087) is a rare opportunity to enjoy a kosher pastrami in the rural Midwest.

DES MOINES

Caspe Jewish Heritage Gallery, Harmon Fine Arts Center, 25th St. and Carpenter, Drake University, Des Moines, ☎ 515-277-6321. The new gallery, supported by the Iowa Jewish Historical Society, houses a collection that reflects the history of Jews in Iowa. Some exhibits retell the story of the Holocaust – a cup made in the Schindler factory was donated by a survivor who lives in Des Moines. Call for hours and information. No admission charged.

Temple B'nai Jeshuran, 5101 Grand, Des Moines, ☎ 515-274-4679. The oldest synagogue in the city was built in 1931, an example of Byzantine architecture – rare in this part of the country.

KENTUCKY

The state capital of **Frankfort** is named for one Stephen Franks, a settler killed by Indians in 1780, believed to have been a Jew.

LEXINGTON

The city's **Gratz Park Historic District** was named for Benjamin Gratz, of the renowned Philadelphia Gratz family, who settled in Lexington in the early 1800s. In 1824, he moved into the home (built in 1806) located at 231 N. Mill Street. The family lived in the house until 1925. Today, it is privately owned and not open for tours, but an interesting walk-by all the same. The area bounded by 2nd Street, the Byway, 3rd Street, and Bark Alley is a National Historic District.

LOUISVILLE

Brandeis Law Library, corner 3rd and Eastern Pkwy., ☎ 502-852-6565. Native son Louis Brandeis left a sizeable amount of his estate to establish the law library at the University of Louisville. His ashes and those of his wife are buried under the School of Law Portico. There are stones that indicate the graves.

LOUISIANA

NEW ORLEANS

The Big Easy is another city in which Jews comfortably contributed and participated in community life – and evidence remains of the role played by New Orleans' Jewish citizenry. **Canal Street** was once named Touro Street for Judah Touro. The **New Orleans Museum of Art,** established by Isaac Delgado (and formerly known as the Delgado Art Museum), houses two collections funded by Jews – the Chapman H. Hyams Collection and the Isaac M. Cline Collection. The museum is at 1 Collins Diboll Circle, located in the middle of City Park, ☎ 504-488-2631. **Preservation Hall** jazz club, ☎ 504-523-8939, on St. Peter Street was founded in 1961 by Allan and Sandy Jaffe. And just outside of New Orleans, the town of **Reserve** was established by sugar baron Leon Godchaux in 1837.

Temple Sinai, 6227 St. Charles Ave., ☎ 504-861-3693. Built in 1870, Temple Sinai is today the city's largest congregation. But what's most unique about it is its treasure trove of great art. The sanctuary, for example, boasts Tiffany windows. The Heller Room houses a priceless collection of art works by Jewish and non-Jewish artists alike, a gift of art gallery owner Jacob Weintraub. But most are Jewish or Jewish themes. Look for works by Marc Chagall, Louise Nevelson, Picasso, and Joan Miro. Hours: Monday-Friday, 9-5, and during services Friday evening and Saturday morning. Call for times.

Longue Vue House and Gardens, 7 Bamboo Rd., New Orleans, in Old Metairie. ☎ 504-488-5488. The magnificent estate of philanthropists Edgar and Edith Stern is open to the public as a museum of decorative arts. The decor has been described as "a battle of chintz, patterns, and painted furniture." The mix of styles and boisterous tastes may not be to everyone's liking, but the tour is entertaining. The gardens reflect Edith's love of yellow – her favorite color. Not much in the house reveals that the Sterns were Jewish, other than the mezuzah on the front door – which is affixed to the wrong side. The Sterns are buried at nearby Metairie Cemetery. Hours: Tuesday-Saturday, 10-4:30; Sunday 1-5. Admission: $7 adults; $3 students and children; $6 seniors.

Metairie Cemetery, 5100 Pontchartrain Blvd., ☎ 504-486-6331. New Orleans is known for its "cities of the dead," crowded aboveground cemeteries filled with fascinating art, funerary sculpture and a certain amount of voodoo lore. Jews, too, are buried in the cemeteries that tourists love to visit. In Metairie are the mausoleums of some of the city's most prominent former Jewish citizens, including Edgar and Edith Stern, Chapman H. Hyams, and Isaac

Delgado, founder of the New Orleans Museum of Art. A life-sized angel weeps over his tomb. Hours: 8-5 daily. No admission charged.

The Presbytere, Jackson Square, ☎ 504-524-9118, 568-8788. The site, part of the Louisiana State Museum Complex, is situated in the heart of historic Jackson Square. Displayed are Judah P. Benjamin's roll-top desk as well as a portrait of the Confederate statesman. There are other Benjamin artifacts that are occasionally on exhibit. Hours: Tuesday-Sunday, 9-5.

Dispersed of Judah Cemetery, near Metairie Cemetery at top of Canal St. near City Park Ave., no telephone. The burial grounds were established by the Spanish and Portuguese community in 1845. A slab indicates that Judah Touro was buried here, before his remains were moved to the cemetery of Touro Synagogue in Newport, Rhode Island.

GARDEN DISTRICT & UPTOWN AREAS

Take a driving tour of these two historic areas and you'll pass by two of the city's most distinguished synagogues. **Anshe Sfard Congregation,** 2230 Carondelet St., was built in 1926. **Touro Synagogue,** 4238 St. Charles Ave., was home to the oldest congregation in the state, founded in 1828. The structure was built in 1881. Inside is a stained-glass piece by Ida Kohlmeyer.

SCULPTURE

A number of sites in some of the New Orleans' most popular tourist neighborhoods feature engaging sculpture by Jewish artists. At the **Aquarium Collonade** are several water-themed sculpture by Ida Kohlmayer. **Audubon Park** and **Audubon Zoo** feature many sculpture and structures that honor the city's prominent Jews – including Gumbel Fountain at entrance to park, named for Sophie Gumbel. The bandstand is named for Isidore Newman.

MASSACHUSETTS

AMHERST

National Yiddish Book Center, 1021 West St., Amherst, ☎ 413-256-4900. A revival in interest of Yiddish and its culture is reflected in a new location with public appeal. A bookstore, a theater, some exhibits, and creative programming make it worthwhile to stop at this center, which collects and distributes Yiddish books, literature, and materials to locations worldwide.

MISSISSIPPI

"Mississippi Jews & Blues Alley," Historical Cycling International, 31566 First Ave., Laguna Beach, Calif., ☎ 949-499-0342, www.historical-cycling.com. This bicycle tour company offers a unique spin on tours of the South. The focus is Jewish heritage and, in addition to a number of European packages, the company offers a terrific tour of Jewish sites and landmarks in Mississippi. The tour includes some close-up and insider tours of historic Natchez, as well as stops in Jackson, Vicksburg, and Port Gibson. Evenings are spent in charming lodgings, often B&B's that were once Jewish-owned homes, or plantations now run by Jewish proprietors. All tours are supported with two experienced guides, guest lecturers, support van, luxury hotels, continental breakfasts daily and regional dining nightly.

JACKSON

Temple Beth Israel, 5315 Old Canton Rd., ☎ 601-956-6215. Dedicated in 1967, the synagogue at Old Canton Rd., was bombed by the Ku Klux Klan that same year. The event served to galvanize the community against violence and discrimination. The congregation dates back to the Civil War. The first building was destroyed during that war.

NATCHEZ

Jewish Hill, on Cemetery Rd., ☎ 800-647-6724. Rosalie Beekman, a seven-year-old Jewish girl, was the only Civil War casualty in Natchez. She was hit by a shell from a Union gunboat when a crowd gathered to watch the fighting from this hill overlooking the Mississippi River. The child is buried at the rear of the Natchez City Cemetery (2 Cemetery Rd) in a walled section.

Temple B'nai Israel, 213 S. Commerce, ☎ 601-445-5407, www. msje.org. A neo-classic structure, the synagogue houses the oldest Jewish congregation in Mississippi (dating from 1843). The cornerstone of the building reads 1870, and was dedicated by Rabbi Isaac Mayer Wise, founder of Reform Judaism. The Ark is constructed of Italian marble. The organ, built more than a century ago, is listed on the National Register of Historic Organs. In addition to guided tours, there is a video and exhibits on Jewish life in Natchez. The basement serves as a satellite site for the Museum of the Southern Jewish Experience. Tours are scheduled Tuesday-Sunday, 1-4 pm, or by appointment.

Glen Auburn, 300 South Commerce St., ☎ 601-445-5407, www. msje.org. This privately owned home located across the street from the synagogue was once the residence of Simon Moses, a merchant who owned stores, cotton houses, a street car line, and other businesses. Built in 1875, the stately brick home with servants wings and Southern touches is undergoing restoration. Visitors may arrange tours through Temple B'nai Israel.

In Natchez, there are several B&Bs to stay in. Though none are "Jewish" in nature, they are in homes that were built and owned by the city's Jews. For example, **The Burn** (712 North Union St, ☎ 601-442-1344) was once the home of former mayor Sam Laub. The Greek-Revival mansion was built in 1836. The **Bailey House Bed and Breakfast,** (corner of Commerce and Orleans streets) was once owned by the Jacobs family.

PORT GIBSON

Temple Gemiluth Chassed, 708 Church St., ☎ 800-729-0240 or ☎ 601-437-4350. The Moorish-Byzantine synagogue, built in 1891, is the only known example of this architectural style in the state. Its keyhole-shaped entries and windows and dome make it a unique silhouette in this Southern city. The structure is listed on the National Register of Historic Places. Call to arrange a tour. A few blocks away is a Jewish cemetery on Marginal Street. Look for Leopold Levy's grave. For those who read Hebrew, discover that a stone-cutter, unfamiliar with Hebrew, carved the letters of Levy's Hebrew name from left to right.

UTICA

Museum of the Southern Jewish Experience, 3863 Old Morrison Rd., ☎ 601-362-6357, www.msjc.org. Since 1970, children from all over the South have been gathering to connect with their Jewish roots at the Henry S. Jacobs Camp for Living Judaism. Then, in 1989, the museum opened its doors to a collection of art, artifacts, ceremonial objects, decorative items, photographs and historic papers, and memorabilia gathered from razed synagogues and homes of the South's dwindling Jewish populations. The museum is also renowned for its active education and outreach to communities and often takes its collections and exhibits on the road. Hours: June-August, 10-5; September-May by appointment only. No admission charged; donations appreciated.

VICKSBURG

The Shlenker House, 2212 Cherry St., ☎ 601-636-7086 or 800-636-7086. The Prairie-style design of the house seems out of place in the heart of the South. It was built in 1907 by a prominent Jewish cotton factory owner and wholesale grocer. The house is on the National Register of Historic Places. A B&B is also on-site. Hours: Tuesday-Saturday, 1:30-4:30. House tours: $5; $2 children.

WOODVILLE

Once known as "Little Jerusalem," Woodville claimed a small Jewish population in the past. A small yellow, wooden house on Second South Street features an ornate star of David cut into the gable. The **Wilkinson County Museum** (corner of Bank St. and Depot St., ☎ 601-888-3998) holds a few Jewish artifacts. Nearby, just west of Woodville, is the **Pond Store,** (182 Fort Adams-Pond Rd., ☎ 601-888-4426) once owned by Jews and alleged to be haunted by Julius Lemkowitz, a Russian immigrant who managed the store in the 1920s.

MISSOURI

INDEPENDENCE

Harry S Truman Library and Museum, US 24 and Delaware St., ☎ 816-833-1225. In the museum collection is the Torah that Chaim Weizmann, Israel's first president, presented to President Truman in May 1948, after Israel was voted in as a state. Other artifacts to see are a bust of Weizmann, a painting of an Israeli village named for Truman, paintings, art, and ancient Israel artifacts. Quite a collection here.

KANSAS CITY

Temple B'nai Jehudah, 712 East 69th St., ☎ 816-363-1050. The Reform synagogue contains a collection of Judaica in its Rabbi Harry H. Mayer Memorial Museum. But the building itself is filled with art. Several stained-glass windows were designed by John La Farge, who preceded Louis Comfort Tiffany. The windows were designed in 1907 – 10 periods in Jewish history are represented. Located in the halls and rotunda are displays of art and ritual objects. Also on the grounds is the Eddie Jacobson Memorial Garden. Call for hours.

Museum Without Walls, 6811 West 63rd St., Ste. 302, Overland Park, ☎ 913-432-8080. First-class exhibits with a Jewish focus make their way to Kansas City via the Museum Without Walls and are displayed at various venues in the area. The schedule varies, and changes constantly, so if you're planning a visit to the Kansas City area, call to find out what's showing – and where.

LIBERTY

Goldman-Duckworth House, 214 E. Mississippi St. Manheim Goldman, the first permanent Jewish settler in the Kansas City area, arrived in Liberty in 1852 and opened a store. He was twice mayor of Liberty and one of the founding members of Temple

B'nai Jehuda. His home, built in the 1870s, is a Clay County Historic Landmark identified by a plaque in a neighborhood of grand Gothic homes. A young family now owns the home, and they're painstakingly restoring it to its original splendor. The blue wooden structure sports the original Gothic windows, siding, porch, columns, and servant quarters. The home is not open for tours. For information, call the Clay County Historical Society, ☎ 816-792-1849.

NEW MEXICO

The Jewish population in New Mexico is a scant 7,500 (6,000 in Albuquerque and 1,500 in Santa Fe). Yet this Southwestern state harbors some of the most unusual and mysterious Jewish legacies in the country. At least that's what the evidence from research by **Dr. Stanley Hordes** of Santa Fe indicates. Dr. Hordes' studies reveal that there are Catholic and Protestant Hispanic New Mexicans whose families observe unusual customs – such as lighting candles behind closed windows on Friday night, adhering to certain dietary restrictions, and following a tradition of male circumcision. While it's not possible to visit or observe such households, travelers can still go to Santa Fe and learn about the history of crypto-Jews from Dr. Hordes, and find some evidence of this phenomenon – in cemetery headstones, for example.

ALBUQUERQUE

Home to the largest concentration of Jews in the state, Albuquerque offers three synagogues, agencies, a historical society, gatherings, and even a kosher restaurant. **The New Mexico Jewish Link** (9600 Regal Ridge Dr., NE, ☎ 505-797-1094, www.swcp.com/~ thelink) keeps the community informed. An event that attracts some 2,000 attendees is the **Chanukah Festival,** held at the Albuquerque Convention Center. For more information about Jewish travel to Albuquerque, contact the **Jewish Federation of Greater Albuquerque,** 5520 Wyoming Blvd., NE, ☎ 505-821-3215, www. swcp.com/~thelink/JFGA. For those interested in kosher accommodations or home hospitality, check with **Chabad of New Mexico,** 4000 San Pedro Dr., NE, ☎ 505-880-1181.

SANTA FE

While the curious traveler will not have an opportunity to visit or observe such families or communities (you can't very easily sneak into someone's yard on a Friday night and peer into the window to see if they're lighting candles), there are organized trips to Santa Fe that include lectures and audio-visual presentations about the crypto-Jews. Additionally, the small Jewish community of Santa Fe is quite welcoming, even offering special home hospitality to Jews visiting during Indian Market each summer. A short tour of Jewish sites includes a visit to the **Staab House** (once a private home to a prominent Jewish pioneer family, now a hotel), and a tour of the art gallery – and possibly the first indoor bathroom in Santa Fe – owned by Willie and Flora Spiegelberg. Because it is the Spiegelberg's private collection, few have the opportunity to see the art. For those interested in learning about special home hospitality programs at **Temple Beth Shalom,** call ☎ 505-982-1376. To learn more about tours, here are two guides to consider:

> **Freedman Habush Associates,** 6200 Mammoth Ave., Van Nuys, CA 91401, ☎ 818-994-0213.

> **Felix and Sue Warburg,** San Francisco Jewish Landmarks Tours, 2865 Green St., San Francisco, CA 94123, ☎ 415-921-0461.

LAS VEGAS

It's a virtual ghost town these days, what with just a few thousand inhabitants. But at one time the dusty New Mexico town was the capital of Jewish commerce, society, and culture. An important stop along the Santa Fe Trail, Las Vegas attracted Jewish merchants from the 1880s until the 1920s when the Dust Bowl ravaged the area. Just 1½ hours from Santa Fe, the tiny town maintains its turn-of-the-century character. And although no Jews remain, a synagogue, cemetery, homes, and storefronts offer a fascinating walk into Old West history – Jewish-style. Some of the Santa Fe tours offer a side-trip to Las Vegas.

NEW YORK

ACCORD

Elat Chayyim, Center for Healing and Renewal, 99 Mill Hook Rd., Accord, ☎ 800-398-2630 or ☎ 914-626-0157, www.elat-chayyim.org. Its pastoral setting in the Catskills is reminiscent of summer camp. The 35-acre facility offers a year-round schedule of retreats, workshops, and Shabbat weekends for families, couples, and singles. Summer retreats, for example, are a week long, and based on themes such as healing and the arts. Intriguing classes such as "Sex, Death, Suffering, and Money" and "Thank You for Being Such a Pain: Mystical Strategies for Healing Conflict" are led by rabbis, cantors, artists, healers, teachers, and scholars. The meditative retreats require silence. Shabbatot are joyous. The center describes itself as a "transdenominational" place where people from all movements of Judaism come together to discover more personal meaning within Judaism. While the catalog of retreats and programs is geared to adults, there are accompanying programs for children and teenagers. And prices, which include classes, and room and board, are reasonable – typically less than $100 a day per person. The experience is a communal one, although accommodations are private (some shared baths). The dining room is strictly kosher and visitors are asked not to bring in food. The staff are very accommodating of dietary needs, however, if you notify them three weeks before arrival. Call for a current catalog of activities.

ALBANY

The **New York State Capitol,** Capitol Hill, ☎ 518-474-4116 and 800-225-5697. In the Hall of Governors hangs the portrait of Herbert H. Lehman, first and only Jewish governor of New York, elected in 1932. Also of note are a mezuzah, a memorial to Jews of Albany, and a brief history of Jews in the city.

The New York State Museum, Empire State Plaza, ☎ 518-474-5877. The museum, located across from the state capitol, contains many exhibits, but of Jewish interest is the "Bitter Hope" exhibit. It recounts the plight of the a ship of Holocaust refugees who arrived in the U.S. in 1944 and were detained in a camp in Oswego, New York, where they remained imprisoned until the fall of 1945. In addition to poignant photos, the chain-link fence that surrounded them is on display. Hours: Daily, 10-5. No admission charged; donations appreciated.

BUFFALO

Jewish Community Center of Greater Buffalo, 2640 N. Forest, ☎ 716-688-4033. An art gallery with a permanent collection of Jewish art including several works by Marc Chagall.

Benjamin and Dr. Edgar R. Cofeld Judaica Museum, 805 Delaware Ave., ☎ 716-886-7150. Within the Beth Zion synagogue is this collection, including the capital from a 10th-century Ark, spice boxes, shofars, and jewelry. The sanctuary has stained-glass windows designed by Ben Shahn. Hours: Monday-Friday, 9-5; Saturday, 11-12. No admission charged.

CATSKILLS

The resort area just an hour and a half from New York City brings to mind rambling grand hotels, glitzy, lounge-style entertainment, and strictly kosher dining. Although its popularity as an easy pastoral getaway for Jews in the city has waned some in recent decades, the Catskills and the resort communities of Sullivan County still draw weekend vacationers. In the 1800s, the area was the site of several failed agricultural communities, such as **Sholom** (a plaque in the Ellenville synagogue Ezrath Israel at 31 Center Street commemorates its existence). The oldest known Jewish gravestone in the Catskills (near the Mongaup River in Lumberland Township) marks the burial site of **Nathan Friesleben**, a peddler who was murdered in 1851. One struggling immigrant gave up trying to farm his rocky 50 acres near Ferndale. Instead, Selig Grossinger began taking in boarders. By the 1930s, his boarding house blossomed into one of the country's most famed hotels, attracting Jewish clientele with kosher menus and popular entertainment. The area known as the "Borscht Belt" was at its peak in the 1950s, with as many as 1,200 hotels and rooming houses. Hotels such as **Grossinger's** (which has its own post office), the **Concord, Kutsher's**, and the **Nevele** continue to fill up. In Monticello, the **Sullivan County Hall of Fame** features a number of local celebrities, including legendary Boston Celtics coach Red Auerbach, Jerry Lewis, Moss Hart, and Danny Kaye.

COOPERSTOWN

National Baseball Hall of Fame, Main Street between Fair and Pioneer, ☎ 607-547-7200. Two baseball legends were Bronx-born Jews: Hank Greenberg and Sandy Koufax. Both refused to play on Yom Kippur, a point not mentioned in the displays commemorating these players. But the information can be found in the Hall of Fame archives, for those interested in more detailed research. Hours: October 1-April 30, 9-5 daily; May-September, 9-9. Admission: $9.50 adults, $8 seniors, $4 children seven-12.

ELMIRA

Woodlawn National Cemetery, David Street, ☎ 607-732-5411. Among the nearly 3,000 Confederate graves of those who died in the Elmira prison are 24 Jewish burial sites. Also buried here are Ossip Gabrilowitsch, musician, composer, and conductor, and his celebrated father-in-law, Mark Twain. The two share the same plot and their gravestone shows reliefs of their heads.

GRAND ISLAND

This island community in the Niagara River contains a cornerstone inscribed with the "Shema" in its city hall. In 1825, one Mordecai Manuel Noah had a vision to create a refuge for Jews on this island, which he called Ararat. All that was ever developed of his dream was the cornerstone.

LAWRENCE

May Museum of Temple Israel, 140 Central Ave., ☎ 516-239-1140. Changing collections of art and Judaica are featured in this small synagogue museum. Call for hours.

MARLBORO

Gomez Mill House, 11 Mill House Rd., Marlboro, adjacent to Route 9W, 12 miles north of Newburgh in the Hudson Highlands, ☎ 914-236-3126, www.gomez.com. The oldest known standing Jewish home in the United States was built around 1720 by Luis Moses Gomez, from Spain. Known in the area as "Gomez the Jew," he traded furs, thus his house was part of a trading station where Indians and European-born traders conducted business. A family Bible dates back to the 16th century and indicates the family were Marranos (secret Jews) in Spain. Programs and events are scheduled throughout the year, so call ahead to find out what's happening. Hours: April 30-October 31, Wednesday-Sunday; November 1-Passover, Monday-Friday; by appointment only. Admission: $5; $3 children.

NEW ROCHELLE

Gladys and Murray Goldstein Cultural Center of Temple Israel, 1000 Pinebrook Blvd., ☎ 914-235-1800. In a suburb outside New York City, the synagogue's collection includes Judaica, as well as paintings, lithographs, drawings, and etchings by Jewish artists. Hours: Monday-Friday, 9-5; Sunday, 9-noon during summers. No admission charged.

NORTH CAROLINA

CHARLOTTE

Judah P. Benjamin Memorial, South Tryon St. Just south of the town square, a sidewalk marker serves as a memorial to Confederate statesman Judah P. Benjamin. The plaque also marks the site of the home of Abraham Weil, where Benjamin hid from the Union army as the guest of a local merchant.

DURHAM

The Museum of the Jewish Family and Rosenzweig Gallery, Judea Reform Congregation, 2115 Cornwallis Rd., ☎ 919-682-

5095. The exhibits focus on Jewish holidays, festivals, and events. The permanent collection showcases ceremonial objects and other artifacts relating to family observance. Also of interest are collections of jewelry and art. The museum sponsors off-site exhibits throughout the state, and frequently hosts events, showings, and children's workshops. Hours: Friday, 9 pm-10:15 pm; Sunday, 10-1, or by appointment. No admission charged.

RALEIGH

North Carolina Museum of Art, 2110 Blue Ridge Blvd., ☎ 919-839-6262. This general art museum with a permanent Judaica exhibit contains ritual objects, silver kiddush cups, ketubot, and seder plates both contemporary and antique. One silver piece depicting a scene of David dancing before the Ark dates from the late 1600s. Hours: Tuesday-Saturday, 9-5; Friday, 9-9; Sunday, noon-5. No admission charged.

OHIO

CINCINNATI

Hillel Jewish Student Center, University of Cincinnati, Rose Warner House, 2615 Clifton Ave., ☎ 513-221-6728. The Hillel House contains an unusual but intriguing collection of remnants, bits of architecture, stained-glass, and furnishings salvaged from former synagogues in the Midwest. Most of the artifacts were pulled from attics or saved before final building demolition. Two gold-painted lions with red glass eyes once guarded the entrance to a synagogue in Kentucky. Hours: Monday-Friday, 9-5.

Plum Street Temple, Isaac M. Wise Temple, Plum and 8th streets, ☎ 513-793-2556, www.wisetemple.org. Although the Isaac M. Wise Temple has a large, modern facility nearby, the historic Plum Street Temple is still considered the main sanctuary, and the preferred place to host weddings and simchas. The dramatic Moorish structure dedicated in 1866 was the pulpit of Rabbi Isaac Mayer Wise and the birthplace of the American Reform movement. Today it is home to one of the largest Jewish congregations in the Midwest.

Skirball Museum, Hebrew Union College, Jewish Institute of Religion, 3101 Clifton Ave., ☎ 513-221-1875. Skirball headquarters are in Los Angeles, but the Cincinnati site houses part of its collection, including mizrachim, ketubot, and chanukiot among other ceremonial objects. Of note are the sculpture *Israel*, created in 1873 by Moses Jacob Ezekiel, and the 1955 cornerstone of Procter & Gamble – its plaque features the first line from *Genesis* in 43 languages. A special gallery features works of Jewish artists, a Torah section, an exhibit of American Jewish history, and an interactive center for children. The building was the original seminary for the Reform movement, which emerged in the 1800s. Hours: Monday-Friday, 11-4; Sunday, 2-4.

Rockdale Temple, 538 Broadway, ☎ 513-891-9900, www.uahc. org/oh/rockdale-temple. This National Historic Landmark has served K. K. Bene Israel since 1852, although the city's oldest congregation has been in existence since 1824. Call to schedule a tour. Its current building, at 8501 Ridge Rd., has a Holocaust Memorial on site and a 17-acre Biblical Garden.

OKLAHOMA

TULSA

Gershon & Rebecca Fenster Museum of Jewish Art, 1223 East 17th Pl., ☎ 918-294-1366. Located in the B'nai Emunah synagogue is a collection of ritual objects, as well as costumes and historical, archaeological, and Holocaust artifacts. Of note are a festive wedding headdress worn by traditional Yemenite brides and a brass cabinet designed by the father of Jerusalem's Bezalel School of Arts and Crafts, Boris Schatz. Hours: Tuesday-Friday, 10-4; Sunday, 1-4. Call in advance.

The Garden Center, 2435 South Peoria Ave., ☎ 918-746-5125. David Travis (formerly Rabinowitz) built a mansion in 1921 that included a mikvah in the basement and a special cupboard to hold Torahs, as the community was not large enough to support a synagogue. Today the house serves as a not-for-profit enterprise that sponsors gardening events and horticultural programs. The house shares a driveway with the home next door, built by David's brother Samuel. It is owned by the Tulsa Historical Society and is being developed as a museum. Hours: Monday-Friday, 9-4.

OREGON

PORTLAND

The Oregon Jewish Museum, 2701 NW Bond St., ☎ 503-226-3600. Among the art and artifacts of Jewish culture, the permanent collection includes more than 100 pieces of centuries-old ceremonial objects, a bequest from Gustav and Mira Berger of New York City, internationally respected art historians and collectors. Hours: Tuesday-Friday, 11-2. No admission charged; donations appreciated.

PENNSYLVANIA

PITTSBURGH

Some 45,000 Jews live in Pittsburgh. A heavily Orthodox neighborhood is Squirrel Hill, where synagogues, kosher enterprises, and day schools are concentrated. Pulitzer prize-winning playwright George S. Kaufman was from Pittsburgh, as was composer and musician Oscar Levant. Contact the **Jewish Federation**, 1700 City Line St., ☎ 412-921-2766, for further information on synagogues and community agencies. For a listing of kosher restaurants and home hospitality (geared to the Orthodox population), check out the Web site www.jewishpittsburgh.org.

Beth Hamedrash Hagadol, 1230 Colwell St., ☎ 412-471-4443, or 412-281-1965. The synagogue is fairly modern, built in 1964. But before the congregation's 1873 structure was torn down, the hand-carved wooden Ark was salvaged and moved to the new building. Plenty of artwork decorates the walls. Today, the synagogue is the only one downtown.

Rodef Shalom, 4905 Fifth Ave., ☎ 412-621-6566. The large structure resembles a jewel box, its mosque-like dome commanding the neighborhood skyline. The synagogue was built in 1906 by

Pittsburgh's oldest congregation and has been designated a National Historic Landmark. The synagogue's interior is equally impressive, with a historic turn-of-the-century Kimball organ.

Holocaust Center of Pittsburgh, 5738 Darlington Rd., Robinson Bldg., ☎ 412-421-1500. This educational resource center provides materials and information, sponsors activities, and exhibits some artifacts of the Holocaust, including a model of the Warsaw Ghetto. Monday-Thursday, 9-5; Friday, 9-4.

Fallingwater, Kaufmann Conservation and Bear Run, PA381, Connellsville, ☎ 724-329-8501. One of the most famous architectural wonders of the 20th century, Frank Lloyd Wright's cantilevered structure incorporating a natural waterfall was commissioned by Pittsburgh department store tycoon Edgar Kaufmann, and built in 1936. Kaufmann deeded the house and the surrounding property, 1,700 acres of wildlife, to the Western Pennsylvania Conservancy in the 1960s.

RHODE ISLAND

NEWPORT

Touro Synagogue, 85 Touro St., Newport, RI, ☎ 401-847-4794, www.tourosynagogue.org. The magnificent mansions of America's royalty overlook dramatic bluffs and ocean vistas in Newport. But a few blocks away, on a quiet side street stands a modest-sized structure commanding in its simplicity, dramatic in its stateliness. The Touro Synagogue, a National Historic Site, is perhaps the best-known Jewish structure in the United States. It is the country's oldest synagogue, and the only one surviving from the colonial period. Completed in 1763, the structure served as house of worship to a congregation comprised primarily of Sephardic Jews. The simple building reflects the popularity of Georgian architecture in its symmetry and classical elements. But there is definitely a Sephardic feel to it. The fact that the building sits diagonally on its plot allows for worshipers standing in prayer to face east toward Jerusalem. Five elaborate brass candelabra, gifts from Jews of the original congregation, hang from the ceiling, highlighted by a dome. The interior is welcoming and filled with beautiful architectural touches, decorative arts, and period pieces.

But there are hints of the fear that congregants still harbored; the children of Sephardim who'd escaped persecution in Spain and Portugal built a trapdoor on the bimah for a quick escape. While the synagogue's history has often been uncertain, as the building was abandoned and left for disrepair, today it houses an active congregation that gathers for services. Just a short walk away is the burial ground, consecrated in 1677. The plot inspired Longfellow's poem, *The Jewish Cemetery at Newport*, and it holds many of the congregation's early supporters, including Judah Touro. Tours are offered every half-hour when the synagogue is open: July 1-September 7, Sunday-Friday, 10-5; September 8-October 31 and May 1-June 30, Sunday, 11-3; Monday-Friday, 1-3; November 1-April 30, Sunday, 11-3; Monday-Friday, one tour at 1.

PROVIDENCE

Temple Emanu-El, 99 Taft Ave., ☎ 401-331-1616. A small museum room houses an eclectic collection of artifacts including menorahs ancient and modern, and an elaborate wedding dress from the 19th century. Call for hours.

Temple Beth-El, 70 Orchard Ave., ☎ 401-331-6070. A modern structure that was featured in a *LIFE* magazine article on the world's major religions in 1955. In wall cases, artifacts reflect the daily routines of congregants and Jews in the 20th century. The collection includes a USO kit of religious materials for a Jewish service man, as well as holiday cards.

SOUTH CAROLINA

CHARLESTON

That religious, political, and civil freedoms were granted as early as 1665 played an important role in attracting Jews to this South Carolina port colony. Throughout the colonial period and well into the 1800s, Charleston's Jewish community thrived as one of the most prosperous in the new nation. Thus, the historic sites visited today are some of the oldest to be found.

Kahal Kadosh Beth Elohim Museum, 86 Hasell St., ☎ 803-723-1090. The Congregation Beth Elohim dates back to 1749; its first synagogue, built in 1792, was destroyed in 1838 by a fire. The subsequent structure still stands. The white-columned Greek Revival building dating to 1841 is a National Historic Landmark. The museum contains art and ceremonial objects as well as historic documents, including the Grant of Arms to Francis Salvador, the first Jew killed in the Revolutionary War. Some of the archives document the struggles within the early congregation, that eventually fed into the Reform movement. Of note is a painting by Solomon Nunes Carvalho. Although the original synagogue had been destroyed, he painted it from memory. Be sure to tour the synagogue's sanctuary – it's the oldest in continuous use in America. Hours: Monday-Friday, 9-3.

Hebrew Orphan Society, 88 Broad St., no telephone. The structure, which dates from the American Revolution, is an office building today. But it has served the Jewish community since 1833. For nearly 100 years, it functioned as an orphanage, a temporary synagogue, a relief center during an epidemic, and a Jewish school. In fact, Confederate Secretary of War Judah Benjamin attended classes here.

Holocaust Memorial, JCC, 1645 Raoul Wallenberg Blvd., ☎ 803-571-6565. A peaceful garden and a plaque stand in memory to the six million who died in the Holocaust, on the grounds of the Jewish Community Center.

Francis Salvador Marker, City Hall Park. Near the monument to General Beauregard stands a granite pedestal bearing a bronze plaque. The memorial is a tribute to the 29-year-old Salvador who was noted as the first Jew to die in the Revolution. He was scalped in 1776 by Cherokees fighting for the British.

Beth Haim Cemetery, 189 Coming St., no telephone. The oldest Jewish burial ground existing in the South was established in 1762 by Congregation Beth Elohim. The plot of land surrounded by a red brick wall is final resting place to soldiers of the Revolution, War of 1812, and Civil War. The oldest tombstone tops the grave of Moses Cohen, Beth Elohim's first rabbi who died in 1762. Also buried here is Hartwig Cohen, great-grandfather of Bernard Baruch. The observant will note something curious – there are no stars of David to be found on any gravestone or monument.

TENNESSEE

CHATTANOOGA

Congregation Mizpah, 923 McCallie Ave., ☎ 423-267-9771. Funded by Adolph S. Ochs in honor of his parents, the synagogue, built in 1923, is also referred to as the Julius and Bertha Ochs Memorial Temple.

MEMPHIS

Herta and Justin Adler Collection, at Temple Israel, 1376 East Massey Rd., ☎ 901-761-3130. In the upstairs hallway of the synagogue, Judaica and ceremonial artifacts are displayed.

NASHVILLE

Congregation Ohabai Sholom, 5015 Harding Rd., ☎ 615-352-7620. Ben Shahn's mosaic, *The Call of the Shofar,* features a man blowing a shofar, above five heads representing different peoples. The synagogue, dedicated in 1955, also houses stained-glass windows illustrating Jewish holidays, and lots of art and sculpture inside and out. Call to schedule a tour.

TEXAS

AUSTIN

Hirschfeld/Moore House, 814 Lavaca St., ☎ 512-479-0895. The interiors of the mansion, cottage, and carriage house located in downtown Austin are no longer open to tours. But the site, a National Historic Landmark, is worth a walk-by. Henry Hirschfeld was a prominent Austin banker and businessman, and active in the Jewish community. The structures were built around the turn of the century. State markers and plaques identify the buildings.

DALLAS

The Dallas Memorial Center for Holocaust Studies, 7900 Northaven Rd., ☎ 214-750-4654. Permanent and changing exhibits chronicle the horrors of the Holocaust at this center, established by a group of survivors. The Memorial Room is entered through the cast-iron Gates of Fire. Twelve marble pillars represent the camps where Dallas survivors were imprisoned. A boxcar that was once used to transport people to death camps is displayed. Hours: Sunday-Friday, 10-4 all year; Thursday, 10-9, September through May.

HOUSTON

Holocaust Museum Houston, 5401 Caroline St., ☎ 713-942-8000, www.hmh.org. Through photographs, film, text, and displays, the museum recounts the process through which Jews were dehumanized and unimaginable atrocities became reality. The museum houses a permanent collection, as well as a memorial, theater, library, archives, and changing exhibits.

Judaica Museum of Houston, Congregation Beth Yeshuran, 4525 Beechnut Blvd., ☎ 713-666-1881. A few paintings and prints are displayed, but most of the exhibits are dedicated to ritual objects such as a silver etrog container, spice boxes, and unusual marriage belts. A Nathan Rappaport sculpture, "The Last March," commemorates the Holocaust. Hours by appointment, Monday-Friday.

Robert I. Kahn Gallery, Congregation Emanu-El, 1500 Sunset Blvd., ☎ 713-529-5771. This permanent collection with some 300 works includes items Jewish and non-Jewish, featuring artists such as John Singer Sargent, Andy Warhol, Salvador Dali, Jim Dine, and Ben Shahn. Subjects are tied to ethical issues. Warhol's *Ten Jews of the 20th Century* is a series of silkscreens – and includes the Marx Brothers and Einstein. Hours by appointment.

Rothko Chapel, Institute of Religion and Human Development, Barnard and Yupon St., ☎ 713-524-9839. The chapel is recently renovated, and the paintings of Mark Rothko are newly restored at this unusual interfaith chapel. Call for hours.

Mollie and Louis Kaplan Judaica Museum, Congregation Beth Yeshuran, 4525 Beechnut Blvd., Houston, ☎ 713-666-1881. A collection of art and Judaica, and a Holocaust memorial.

JEFFERSON

Jefferson Playhouse, corner of Henderson and Market, ☎ 903-665-2513. Two adjoining buildings have historic Jewish resonance in this community in the northeast corner of Texas. What stands today as the Excelsior House Hotel is an 1860 structure that once served as the home of a rabbi. In 1876, the Hebrew Sinai Congregation was built next door. Today it serves as the Jefferson Playhouse. Both buildings are owned and maintained by the local Garden Club. The historically attuned community celebrates a pilgrimage each May with special events – including the presentation of "The Diamond Bessie Murder Trial," the tale of a scandalous murder involving a Jewish man and his wife. Call ☎ 888-467-3529 for tickets.

VIRGINIA

NORFOLK

Moses Myers House, 323 East Freemason St., ☎ 804-620-1211. The stately Federal brick home sits on the corner of downtown Norfolk in an area undergoing revitalization. Inside, visitors will discover the world of Moses and Eliza Myers, a Jewish couple who came to the city to start an export business in 1792. Much of the furnishings are original – the home had stayed in the family for five generations before being sold to the City of Norfolk. The large, open front hall leads to a small glass display case featuring a few items of Jewish interest. The kitchen – detached from the house as was the style of the times – is particularly fascinating, with typical foods of the day displayed. There is, however, no indication whether the Myerses kept kosher, and the tour guides don't seem to know. Hours: Tuesday-Saturday, 10-5; Sunday, noon-5. Admission: $3.

RICHMOND

Beth Ahabah Museum and Archives Trust, 1109 West Franklin St., ☎ 804-353-2668, www.jewishculture.org/jewishmuseums/ahabah.htm. A 500-pound stone salvaged from a German synagogue destroyed during Kristallnacht is one of the highlights of this small museum housed in the synagogue of a historic congregation. Many of the museum's exhibits recount Jewish life in Richmond. Be sure to ask to see the synagogue's sanctuary, where a signed Tiffany window representing Mt. Sinai is displayed. Hours: Sunday-Thursday, 10-3. Suggested admission: $3 adults; $2 seniors and students.

WASHINGTON

SEATTLE

From pioneer peddlers who outfitted the gold-seekers heading for the Klondike to fishmongers and fruit vendors conducting commerce at what is now the Pike Place Market, Jews from cultures as diverse as Germany and Turkey were drawn to Seattle as early as the 1860s. Today, a detailed guidebook leads the curious on a city tour that follows a Jewish trail of history. *Historic Seattle: A Tour Guide,* by Jane Avner and Meta Buttnick, is a self-guided tour of popular neighborhoods including Pioneer Square, Pike Place Market, and Seward Park. The sights are varied. Historic **Schwabacher Hardware Building** and **Schwabacher Wharf** in the Pioneer Square area were built by the successful Schwabacher brothers from Bavaria—subsequent to the devastating city fire of 1889. In Pike Place, the guide identifies places where Jewish businesses once flourished as well as a couple of fish markets still owned and operated by Jews. Followers of the guide will also discover the Jewish connections to **Starbucks** and **Harry and David.** Contact the Washington State Historical Society to order a copy of the guidebook; ☎ 253-238-4373, www.wshs.org.

WISCONSIN

MADISON

Shaarei Shamayim, James Madison Park, ☎ 608-245-3775. The limestone-and-brick structure is an eclectic mix of architectural designs – a little Spanish mission, a little Victorian. Built in 1863, it is the oldest synagogue in Wisconsin, and is a designated National Historic Landmark. The building, which is still used for events, was moved from its original location to the James Madison Park. The lower level is named Klauber Hall, in commemoration of the first Jewish settler, Samuel Klauber, who arrived in the late 1840s.

Jastrow House, 237 Langdon St., ☎ 608-264-6470 (State Historical Society of Wisconsin). This three-story stucco residence in the heart of the Langdon Street Historic District was once the home of noted psychologist Dr. Joseph Jastrow, who lived here from the 1890s until 1927.

MILWAUKEE

Joseph Baron Museum, Congregation Emanuel B'ne Jeshuran, 2419 East Kenwood Blvd., ☎ 414-964-4100. The museum devotes its displays primarily to ritual objects, with some 350 pieces. Also exhibited, however, are paintings, prints, and sculpture. The synagogue, built in 1923, houses the oldest congregation in Wisconsin. Call for museum hours.

Golda Meir Elementary School, 1555 N. Martin Luther King Jr. Dr., ☎ 414-271-6840. In her autobiography, Golda Meir described her Milwaukee grade school as "fortress-like." The National Historic Landmark remains much as it was when the late prime minister of Israel attended from 1906 to 1909. High ceilings, original light fixtures, and elegant wainscoting distinguish the public school from its more modern counterparts. A conference room and lounge are maintained exactly as they were during the early 1900s. Visitors are welcome to call for a tour – when school is in session.

CANADA

BRITISH COLUMBIA

Vancouver Holocaust Education Centre, Jewish Community Centre, 50-950 West 41st, Vancouver, ☎ 604-264-0499. Art is the vehicle that teaches tolerance and combats racism here: a triptych photo of Lithuanian children who died in concentration camps, rubbings of gravestones from Europe's Jewish cemeteries, and anti-Semitic cartoons tell the story of hatred and destruction during the Holocaust and even modern times. Hours: Monday, Wednesday, and Sunday, 9-5; Tuesday and Thursday, 9-9; Friday, 9-3.

Congregation Beth Israel, 4350 Oak St., ☎ 604-731-4161, Vancouver, ww3.bc.sympatico.ca/bethisrael/. A small museum features both ceremonial objects as well as historical artifacts and art. Hours: Open for Shabbat, from Friday 3 pm through Saturday, or by appointment.

VICTORIA

Temple Emanu-el, 1461 Blanshard St., Victoria, ☎ 250-382-0615. On Vancouver Island, in British Columbia's capital city, the oldest synagogue in the province – and the oldest synagogue in continuous use in Canada – still reigns. In 1863, the cornerstone was laid for the structure that would inspire great pride from the community. The Romanesque Revival building reflects the grand synagogues of Europe. The structure was completely restored in the 1980s and the cornerstone re-dedicated. There is also a cemetery.

MANITOBA

Marion and Ed Vickar Jewish Museum of Western Canada, C116-123 Doncaster St., Winnipeg, ☎ 204-477-7460, www.jhcwc. mb.ca. Part of the campus of the Jewish Heritage Centre of Western Canada, the museum showcases major changing exhibitions, such as the internationally acclaimed "Anne Frank in the World." Its permanent exhibits emphasize local and Canadian Jewish history. Also on-site are the Freeman Family Foundation Holocaust Education Centre, an educational resource, as well as historical archives and genealogical resources. Hours: Sunday-Tuesday and Thursday-Friday, noon-4; Wednesday, noon-8. No admission charged; donations appreciated.

Winnipeg Jewish Theatre, 123 Doncaster St., Winnipeg, ☎ 204-477-7515. The theatre prides itself in providing performances of high artistic quality that showcase new Canadian plays with Jewish content.

NEW BRUNSWICK

SAINT JOHN

Saint John Jewish Cultural Museum, 29 Wellington Row, Saint John, ☎ 506-633-1833. The Jewish population of Saint John is small, but the community strives to capture and preserve local Jewish history and culture in this museum located at the same location as the Shaarei Zedek synagogue. The exhibits tell the stories of Jewish life in northeastern Canada, and celebrate notables who've achieved fame beyond its borders, such as Louis B. Mayer of MGM renown. "From the Cradle to the Grave" is a permanent exhibit that features Jewish customs, traditions, and ceremonies. The museum offers scheduled hours from late May through September, but will open by appointment at other times. Hours: Monday-Friday, 10-4; Sunday (July and August only), 1-4. This museum offers quite a bit of local focus, with an art gallery featuring Jewish artists from the area.

RESOURCES

HELPFUL ORGANIZATIONS

United Jewish Communities, 111 Eighth Ave., Ste. 11E, New York, NY 10011, ☎ 212-284-6500, www.jon.cjfny.org. The result of the merger of the Council of Jewish Federations and United Jewish Appeal. Call to get listings of local Federations – frequently a great source of information about the local Jewish scene.

Jewish Community Centers Association of North America, 15 East 26 St., New York City, NY 10010, ☎ 212-532-4949, www. jcca.org. Check here to find out whether there's a JCC in the location you're traveling to.

International Association of Jewish Genealogical Societies. 104 Franklin Ave., Yonkers, NY 10705-2808, ☎ 914-963-1059, www. jewishgen.org. Call for details about more than 70 Jewish Genealogical Societies worldwide – organizations that offer help to individuals researching family history.

Association of Jewish Libraries, 15 East 26th St., Rm. 1034, New York City, NY 10010, ☎ 212-725-5359, aleph.lib.ohio-state.edu/ www/organization.html. Find out about locations of Jewish libraries nationwide.

American Jewish Historical Society, 15 West 16th St., New York City, NY, 10011, ☎ 212-294-6160, www.ajhs.org. A source for genealogical information and resources.

Council of American Jewish Museums, 330 Seventh Ave., 21st Floor, New York City, NY ☎ 212-629-0500. Administered by the National Foundation for Jewish Culture, the Council makes available a list of member museums throughout the country.

www.shamash.org. This Web site is helpful for tracking down a number of Jewish resources, including lists of kosher restaurants by location.

www.kosherdelight.com. A site for finding kosher restaurants, recipes, and religious guidelines.

RELIGIOUS ORGANIZATIONS

The following umbrella organizations for various religious movements offer directories of or information about affiliated congregations in locations throughout the United States and, in some cases, beyond.

ORTHODOX

National Council of Young Israel, 3 W. 16th St., New York, NY 10011, ☎ 212-929-1525.

Union of Orthodox Jewish Congregations, 333 Seventh Ave., New York, NY 10001, ☎ 212-563-4000.

CONSERVATIVE

United Synagogue of Conservative Judaism, 155 Fifth Ave., New York City, NY ☎ 212-563-4000, www.uscj.org.

REFORM

Union of American Hebrew Congregations, 633 Third Ave., New York, NY 10017-6778, ☎ 212-650-4169.

RECONSTRUCTIONIST

Jewish Reconstructionist Federation, 7804 Montgomery Ave., Ste. 9, Elkins Park, PA 19027-2649, ☎ 215-782-8500.

JEWISH TRAVEL

Historical Cycling International, PO Box 1267, Beverly Hills, CA 90213, ☎ 877-733-2518, www.historical-cycling.com. This bicycle touring company specializes in Jewish cultural, historic, and art discoveries in locations from the Mississippi Delta to the hills of Tuscany.

Historic Landmark Tours, 2865 Green St., San Francisco, CA ☎ 415-921-0461. Based in San Francisco, and offering city tours, the organization features Jewish-focused trips to New Mexico, Charleston, Savannah, and France.

Freedman Habush Associates Jewish Tours, 6200 Mammoth Ave., Van Nuys, CA 91401, ☎ 818-994-0213. Themed tours of Los Angeles, including "Hollywood and the Jews." The firm also takes groups to Tijuana, Santa Fe, and other destinations.

JTEN Tours, 3731 N. Country Club Dr., Ste. 1728, Aventura, FL 33180-1721, ☎ 305-931-1782. South Florida is the focus of Milton Heller's JTEN Tours, but he also leads trips to Savannah, Charleston, and other East Coast cities with Jewish history.

92nd Street Y, 1395 Lexington Ave., New York City, NY 10128, ☎ 212-415-5420. New York City neighborhood tours are a highlight of the 92nd Street Y travel program, but the catalog also advertises trips to destinations throughout the United States as well as abroad.

Mosaic Outdoor Clubs of America, 262 S. Coconut Ln., Miami Beach, FL 33139, ☎ 888-MOSAICS, www.mosaics.org. This network of nonprofit organizations puts together outdoor, active, or environmentally oriented outings for Jewish adults. Currently, there are 20-some clubs in the United States, Canada, and Israel.

Endangered Spirit, PO Box 13316, Chicago, IL 60613, ☎ 888-202-2930, www.endangeredspirit.com. All trips, ranging from weekend getaways to 21-day excursions, include elements of outdoor wilderness training and Jewish ecological education. Trips are strictly kosher and observe Shabbat.

Global Explorers, ☎ 800-923-2645, www.globalexplorers.com. Global explorers is an adventure travel operator that *also* offers trips targeted to the Jewish adventurer. Destinations range from exotic spots such as China, Southeast Asia, and Morocco, to domestic locales, including ski trips in Colorado, rafting trips in Utah, and dude ranch trips to Wyoming. Glatt kosher meals are served, no tours are planned for Shabbat, and davening is scheduled.

Kosherica Enterprises, Inc., PO Box 2729, Boca Raton, FL 33427, ☎ 877-724-4467 or 305-935-4412, www.kosherica.com. Kosher cruises are this operator's specialty. Trips feature kosher meals, Jewish entertainment, and luxurious cruises to the world's most popular ports.

www.jewishtravel.com. This Web site has resources for finding synagogues, kosher restaurants, candlelighting times, plus news and features about special places with Jewish resonance.

GLOSSARY

Ashkenazi. The culture of Jews originating from Central and Eastern Europe, distinguished by ritual, liturgy, customs, and pronunciation of Hebrew.

Bar/Bat Mitzvah. The status of a boy or girl upon reaching the age of 13 (in traditional communites, the age is 12 for girls), when he or she is recognized as an adult who must meet religious obligations. The Hebrew term for "Son/Daughter of the Commandments."

Besamim. The Hebrew name for the spice box used in the Havdalah service at the end of Shabbat.

Bimah. The raised area of the synagogue from which services are conducted and the Torah is read.

Brit. Covenant, often referring to the Brit Milah, the covenant of circumcision.

Cantor. The musical leader of synagogue services.

Chanukiah. A candelabra or menorah with nine branches, specifically used in celebration of the festival of Chanuka.

Chasidim. Members of a Jewish movement founded in 18th-century Poland, and emphasizing strict ritual observance and elements of mysticism.

Conservative. A religious movement that evolved in the United States as a response to the development of Reform Judaism.

Haggadah. The book that contains the liturgy for the Passover seder.

Havdalah. The ceremony that marks the end of the Sabbath, occurring Saturday evening. The word means "separation" in Hebrew.

Hazzan. The Hebrew word for Cantor.

Holocaust. Referring to the systematic mass slaughter of Jews led by Nazi Germany during World War II.

Kaddish. The Aramaic prayer glorifying God, recited during daily services and by mourners.

Kashrut. The religious dietary laws that govern what Jews may eat and how food is prepared.

Ketubah. A marriage contract; ketubot, in plural form.

Kiddush. Sanctification; most frequently referring to the blessing said over wine, and invoked on the Sabbath and holidays.

Kippah. Head covering also referred to as "yarmulke"; kippot in plural form.

Kol Nidre. The "All Vows" prayer that opens the evening service for Yom Kippur, the Day of Atonement.

Kosher. Adhering to the religious dietary laws of Judaism; fit to be eaten.

Matzah. Unleavened bread eaten during Passover; matzot in plural form.

Mazel Tov. Used as a congratulatory greeting; "good luck," in Hebrew.

Megillah. The scroll containing the Book of Esther, read from on the holiday of Purim.

Menorah. A candelabra used in the Temple, and often found in modern synagogues. It typically has seven branches; a menorah used for Chanuka has nine branches.

Mezuzah. The small container that holds the "Shema" written on parchment, and affixed to the doorposts of Jewish homes; "doorposts," in Hebrew.

Mikvah. Ritual bath.

Minyan. A quorum of 10 Jews, required for prayer. (Orthodox and some Conservative and Traditional congregations require 10 men.)

Mitzvah. The Hebrew word for an action commanded by Torah; often understood as a "good deed."

Orthodox. A movement of Judaism that adheres to a strict interpretation of Torah and Jewish Law, and believing that the Torah is divine word.

Pareve. Regarding kashrut, refers to foods that can be eaten with either dairy or meat products.

Passover. The Jewish holiday celebrating the exodus from Egypt; "Pesach," in Hebrew.

Reconstruction. A movement in Judaism that developed in the 20th century; adherents view Judaism as an evolving religious-based civilization.

Reform. A movement in Judaism that developed in the 19th century in the United States, originating as an attempt to reconcile tradition with the modern world.

Rosh Hashanah. The holiday that marks the beginning of the Jewish year; "Head of the Year," in Hebrew.

Seder. The structured, festive meal that celebrates the story of the exodus during Passover; the word means "order" in Hebrew.

Sephardic, The culture of Jews originating from Spain and Portugal, but reaching communities of the Mediterranean as well as the Caribbean and Central and South America; distinguished by ritual, liturgy, customs, and pronunciation of Hebrew.

Shabbat. The Sabbath.

Shalom. Hebrew for "peace." Also used as a greeting, for "hello" or "good-bye."

Shema. A passage from the Torah (Deut. 6:4) that acclaims God's oneness; recited at daily, Shabbat, and holiday services.

Shofar. A ram's horn typically blown on Rosh Hashana; shofarot in plural form.

Shtetl. A Yiddish word for village, typically referring to the small Jewish communities in Eastern Europe.

Shul. A Yiddish word for synagogue.

Tallit. Prayer shawl; tallitot in plural form.

Talmud. The collection of rabbinic thought on Jewish law and tradition, consisting of the Mishna and Gemara; compiled between 200 to 600 CE.

Torah. The first five books of the Bible, read from a scroll in weekly segments; also may refer to the entire body of Jewish law as contained in the Bible and Talmud.

Tzedakah. Commonly understood to mean "charity"; based on the Hebrew word for justice or righteousness.

Yarmulke. Head covering, also referred to as "kippah."

Yarzeit. The anniversary of a death, observed by lighting a special candle.

Yiddish. A dialect language, originating from Eastern Europe and spoken by Ashkenazi Jews; a mix of German and Hebrew.

Yom Kippur. The Day of Atonement, falling during the High Holy Days and involving fasting, repentance, and intense prayer.

INDEX

leans, 220, 221; Newport, Rhode Island, 235-236; New Rochelle, New York, 231; New York City, 138-140; Philadelphia, 154-155; Pittsburgh, 234-235; Port Gibson, Mississippi, 223-224; Providence, 236; St. Louis, 177-178; San Diego, 211; San Francisco, 167; Savannah, 215-216; Tijuana, Mexico, 211-212; Toronto, 188-189; Vancouver, 243; Victoria, British Columbia, 243; Washington, DC, 202-203

T

T'filat Haderekh, 9
Tijuana, Mexico, 211-212
Tombstone, Arizona, 209
Toronto, 183-194; events, 192-193; heritage tours, 193; historic sites, 185-187; Jewish community centers, 191; kosher dining, 189-191; lodging, 192; museums and galleries, 184-185; neighborhoods, 187-188; resources, 193-194; shopping, 191-192; sightseeing highlights, 184-188; synagogues, 188-189
Travel resources, 247-248
Trivia, 8
Tulsa, Oklahoma, 233-234

U

Utica, Mississippi, 224

V

Van Buren, Arkansas, 210
Vancouver, British Columbia, 242-243
Vicksburg, Mississippi, 224
Victoria, British Columbia, 243

W

Washington, DC, 195-207; events, 206; heritage tours, 206; historic sites, 199-200; Jewish community centers, 204-205; Jewish connection, 201-202; kosher dining, 203-204; museums and galleries, 196-199; resources, 206-207; shopping, 205-206; sightseeing highlights, 196-202; synagogues, 202-203
Wayfarer's Prayer, 9
Winery, San Francisco, 170
Winnipeg, Manitoba, 243
Woodville, Mississippi, 224-225